Collecting and the Internet

Collecting and the Internet

Essays on the Pursuit of Old Passions Through New Technologies

Edited by
Susan Koppelman *and*
Alison Franks

McFarland & Company, Inc., Publishers
Jefferson, North Carolina, and London

LIBRARY OF CONGRESS CATALOGUING-IN-PUBLICATION DATA

Collecting and the Internet : essays on the pursuit of old passions through new technologies / edited by Susan Koppelman and Alison Franks.
p. cm.
Includes bibliographical references and index.

ISBN 978-0-7864-3845-7

softcover : 50# alkaline paper ♾

1. Collectors and collecting — Computer network resources. 2. Collectors and collecting — Social aspects. 3. Collectibles — Computer network resources. 4. Selling — Collectibles — Computer network resources. 5. Internet auctions. 6. Electronic commerce. 7. Computer networks — Social aspects. I. Koppelman, Susan. II. Franks, Alison, 1944–
AM215.C65 2008
790.1'3202854678 — dc22 2008033621

British Library cataloguing data are available

The cover (design concept by Brenda Oelbaum): *top row, left to right*— Menorah (Susan Koppelman photo); Watch (Dennis Mills photo); Kelly doll (Brenda Oelbaum photo; not affiliated with Mattel); *middle row, left to right* — Harold Smith painting *Sunday Morning* (Jeffrey Kessler photo); "La Vie en Rose" album (Brenda Oelbaum photo); "Don't Eat" photo installation ©2008 Brenda Oelbaum (Daphne Doer photo); *bottom row, left to right* — Susan Koppelman's bone china (Jeffrey Kessler photo); Harold Smith painting *Shotgun Houses* (Harold Smith photo); Stangl fruit pattern teapot, designed by Kay Hackett (Dennis Mills photo)

Manufactured in the United States of America

McFarland & Company, Inc., Publishers
Box 611, Jefferson, North Carolina 28640
www.mcfarlandpub.com

To my granddaughters,
Jasmine Grace Cornillon, collector of stuffed animals,
especially dogs, and Webkinz,
and
Sarah Jade Cornillon, collector of blankets and stuffed animals.
— Susan Koppelman

To Larry and Annelise for making this possible
and
to those resourceful and patient good sports,
our contributing essayists.
— Alison Franks

Acknowledgments

It's always fun to thank people who were responsible for triggering a train of thought that enriched our work.

One of the literary accomplishments of feminism is that we changed, enriched, and expanded the acknowledgments section of books. We recognized the reality of the web that is all our lives. We began to include many more names in acknowledgments than had ever been included before. And then we began to detail why we were acknowledging those people. And we acknowledged our animal companions. Not that here and there those things hadn't, one or another, been done, but feminists made these things almost *de riguer.* Pioneers in the field of popular culture studies supported this change as well.

And those increasingly long and complex acknowledgments began to become a rich literary form of their own rather than the curt professional template that had been the norm before we came along and raised our voices. And so we would like to acknowledge the women's liberation movement writers and writer-scholars and writer-activists who pioneered in this humanizing project.

Also, we want to salute the Popular Culture Association — American Culture Association (PCA/ACA) and all its regional subsidiaries, with thanks to J. Brian Wagaman, webmaster for PCAACA.org, their website, for all the postings of calls for the conferences and calls for essays for this book. Most especially we want to honor the Southwest-Texas PCA/ACA, certainly the beginning source for our book, *Collecting and the Internet.* During our heyday following Susan's founding of the Collecting, Collectibles, Collectors, Collections Area of panels (2001–2004), various heroes of the organization were at work (and some are to this day) to make the annual meeting happen and function miraculously.

Organization founder Peter Rollins, then-secretary/treasurer Mike Schoeneke, president and later executive director Phil Heldrich, and now-secretary/treasurer Ken Dvorak rolled up their sleeves and staffed tables, handled fees, rolled AV equipment carts, fielded questions— at the meeting and online beforehand—and somehow seemed to know everyone, despite there being approximately 900 attendees, many of them presenting. Susan Rollins, who hitched her wagon to Southwest-Texas PCA/ACA when she married Peter in 1992, handled details of registration, hotel arrangements, speakers, luncheon planning, registration payments, nametags, program design and printing—a generous gift to us all. In those years Leslie Fife conducted the orchestration of the schedule—as Sally Sanchez has done more recently seemingly with magic wand rather than baton—and somehow got us all into assigned rooms, giving our talks. To all of them we curtsy. In this heady environment did *Collecting and the Internet* begin.

Susan Koppelman:

I want first to acknowledge my co-editor, my book partner, my teacher of so much in both this project, in my long dream of happy collaboration, and in my life, Alison Franks. Working on this project with her has been all I hoped it would be and more.

And next I want to acknowledge Martin Daniel Richardson, Jr., Emily Toth, Alan Goldberg, Ph.D., Esq., Mary and Tom Hanson, and, of course, as always, Dennis Mills for providing me with genuine life support during this difficult time in my life.

Thanks to Angela Soliz who arrived at the perfect moment to do wonderful work.

There are handbooks with instructions for preparing acknowledgments and other book parts. The most influential one has been the MLA Handbook. Years ago the job came to an old colleague of mine, Jim Harner, Ph.D., a prominent Shakespeare bibliographer, to revise and update the MLA Handbook. And so he did. And because he had done it, rather than because it was a professional tool, I bought a copy and read it to see what my old friend had to say. I came across a note in the acknowledgment section in which he cautioned—very strongly—against including animal companions (he called them pets) in the acknowledgments, implying that there was something icky about doing so. I knew he was wrong about that and I didn't want him to have anything so in error in continual print for probably two decades because it would eventually embarrass him.

So I called him up—he was now at UT in Austin—and talked about it with him. By the end of the conversation this very kind, reasonable man agreed that he had spoken/written in error and said that he could change it in the next edition. Now it is officially okay to acknowledge animal companions who have played a role in one's work life.

Our last cat, RiffRaff disappeared several years ago on a beautiful October day. We never found any trace of him. He was seventeen and a half years old and in all the books that I published in those years, I had included an acknowledgment to him. I miss him still but we won't get another cat. We have graves out back of two other cats, Sheila and Silky. So there have been no cats in my lap or at my feet or across my shoulders or gently (or not so gently) nosing me away from the keyboard because one of them wanted attention. But there are certain cats who are animal companions of beloved people and they have kept me informed of their cats' lives through out this time. I want to acknowledge Mr. Fussy and Beauregard, animal companions of Emily and Bruce Toth, Oakie and Fulani, animal companions of Daniel and Marlena Richardson.

And once again I want to acknowledge my mother, Frances Koppelman, who still has good advice for me.

Alison Franks:

And I, too, want to thank my friend and book partner Susan Koppelman, whose vision and passion made this book happen, as we slogged uphill and down dale through all those years between 2001 and the present.

Heartiest thanks to my daughter, Annelise Sklar, brilliant reference librarian and word-processing wizard, for answering so many urgent and panicked questions and for guiding this child of the pre-computer era through many mysteries of book preparation. Her compilation of the index relieved us of a lot of stress. And to my husband Larry Sklar, biotechnologist — a man no stranger to multicontributor projects, be they books, grants, or programs. What better model for collaboration than the professor chosen by his peers to give the University of New Mexico's fifty-third Annual Research Lecture, and his topic is team science. The two of them have held my hand, he literally and she in cyberspace, throughout this book project and have made it possible.

I want to thank Emily Toth and Andrea Lapin for discussions and encouragements about the book project, and Julia Penelope for some education about editing. And I offer a bow of appreciation to my graduate school mentor and friend, Professor M. Jane Young, folklorist, now retired from the Department of American Studies at the University of New Mexico. She may be my junior, but in matters of scholarship she will always be "mom." Thanks also to Brenda Oelbaum for her work on the cover's design.

I do have a current companion animal to acknowledge: Izzy the sixteen-year-old feline tyrant, who comes upstairs to the computer and claws my rear end when she thinks it's time for me to take a break.

Table of Contents

Acknowledgments vii
Introduction 1

1. Collecting the Internet: How Individually Authored Websites Have Generated Nostalgia and a Desire to Collect the Internet
KELLEY C. SMITH FERANEC 9

2. Collecting Materials Born Digital
MARILYN A. DUNN 23

3. Collecting Watches on the Internet
DENNIS MILLS 31

4. Collecting Eyewear on eBay
JEFFREY KESSLER 41

5. The Konnection of the Kelly Kollection: Kelly Doll Collectors and the Internet
JO ANN KELLY GRAHAM 47

6. Gambler's Rush: All That Glitters, Etc.
JULIA PENELOPE 60

7. On Collecting "La Vie en Rose"
TERRY EVERS 72

8. I Want My MP3s: Music Collecting in the Digital Age
ANNELISE SKLAR 81

9. Trading Online Objects on Friendster.com: Cyber Collecting as Socialization
CARSON METZGER 96

10. Tales from the Thrift: Thrift-shopping Enthusiasts Tell Their Stories Online
ALISON FRANKS 108

11. The Venus of Willendorf Project
BRENDA OELBAUM 120

12. Grandmom's Collection
ELANA C. HURWITZ 138

13. Being Collected: Selling Art on the Internet
HAROLD SMITH 147

14. The Past Is Always on Sale: Revisiting *Culture as Commodity: Internet Auctions and Judaica Collecting*
EMILY ALICE KATZ 158

15. Online Museums, Exhibits, and Archives of American Disability History
PENNY L. RICHARDS 168

16. Online Therapy, Obsession, and Entertainment: Adventures in the International Cyber Bazaar
SUSAN KOPPELMAN 180

About the Contributors 197

Index 203

Introduction

It was collecting stories that brought the two of us, Susan Koppelman and Alison Franks, together. In 2001, Susan instigated and chaired the very first Collecting Panels, sessions of talks about collecting, for the Southwest/Texas Popular Culture Association/American Culture Association's annual meeting, held, as it still is, in Albuquerque, New Mexico. Someone sent Alison Franks, who lives in Albuquerque, a copy of the call for papers for this, and it seemed like a good thing to do. Thus the two editors met. It was either at this meeting or at the one in 2002 (Susan remained the Collecting area chair for this one, but for the 2003 meeting, Alison did the chairing) that Susan suggested we collaborate on several books of essays on the collecting topic.

We knew that good or bad, loved or hated, theirs or someone else's, intentional or accidental, a burden or a blessing, everyone has a collecting story. After the first run of talks in 2001, it was clear that one didn't have to be a collector of something to have a collecting story — dealers in collectible items, agents of procurement for collectors, and friends, relations, detractors and admirers had collecting stories, too. The Collecting Area of the SW/T PCA/ACA was rechristened Collecting, Collectibles, Collectors, Collections.

Over the next few years, through various ups and downs, we collected quite a few stories. At one of the SW/TA-PCA meetings in Albuquerque, we approached McFarland & Company, Inc., Publishers, with a packet of the most polished and finalized essays. Editors looked at the lot and noticed that some of them involved the Internet, whether as a place to buy, a place to sell, or a place to learn and communicate about collecting. The press asked us if we would like to put together a book on collecting and the Internet. This volume is the fruit of that suggestion.

As we gathered collecting stories, we became less and less satisfied with a lot of the ideas in the literature about just what collecting is. In fact, we really haven't found an all-purpose definition that satisfies us. It makes perfect sense that no one definition (many of which we have collected, being as how we are inveterate collectors) would be adequate. We love all the definitions but regret those who think their definitions are the final word on what collecting is, means, and is about. Nothing in life that is as rich and as varied and as historically continuous could possibly be described with a single definition.

We can rule out the hoarder in our discussion. Teresa Barnett, writing in Leah Dilworth's *Acts of Possession: Collecting in America*, describes a hoarder as: "The man [*sic*] who accumulates because he accumulates—collecting beyond any possible limits or reason, driven only by his own private, misbegotten, and unanalyzable need."[1] (Christian C. Sanderson was a man, but women can hoard, too.) Stuff saved because stuff must be saved. We need not tarry with the hoarding concept any longer.

Our essayists help us in understanding what we mean by collecting. In her essay "Gambler's Rush: All That Glitters, Etc.," Julia Penelope puts collecting in the context of human anatomy and physicality when she says, "It [collecting] begins when we discover what our opposable thumbs can do. Bipedalism, too, figures in our penchant for collecting because it frees our hands, with those thumbs, for picking up strange shiny objects and carrying them." So we see something we like and we gather it. If indeed collecting begins with the evolution of the opposable thumb, it truly is an "old passion" as referenced in our subtitle.

Penelope adds a physical limitation into the discussion: "There's also a delicate balance between heft and desirability. Sometimes there's simply no way to carry off a find. I've left several beautiful rocks in the field because they required earth-moving equipment." Going outside our own volume again, Philipp Blom, in *To Have and to Hold: An Intimate History of Collectors and Collecting*, adds another limitation, or, in reverse, another criterion for collecting success—the element of commerce. "With trading empires such as the Dutch and Venetian republics came unprecedented wealth, another critical factor for a flourishing collecting culture. In order to take objects out of circulation or to devote oneself to finding useless things, one has to be able to afford the time and resources to do so. Indeed, collections flourished wherever commerce did."[2] Here Blom not only touches on money to buy collectibles, but also the leisure to indulge in gathering things one might not be going to use for practical living. This opens up some of our favorite areas for disagreeing with scholarly definitions of collecting. Some collections really are free: bottle caps found in the dirt; pebbles from the beach and other natural objects personally gathered. Some leisure is not a luxury: "unassigned" time due to unemployment; absence from the workforce due to disability.

Continuing with the theme we introduce from Blom when he says "take objects out of circulation," we have a comment from Leah Dilworth, in her book *Acts of Possession: Collecting in America*. She says, "Collections are quintessentially interior things: they are objects taken out of circulation and brought inside."[3] We know that people can collect objects and use them in daily life as well. One of our favorite books on collecting is *The King's Collection*, a book written for children by Ruth Craft and illustrated by Elisa Trimby. The protagonist king collects many categories of things, and he uses them. "He collected kites. On good breezy days he flew his best one.... He had baking days when he would use all his different biscuit cutters, loaf tins and rolling pins to make star biscuits, gingerbread people, poppyseed twists, Devon cobs and granary rolls." (Wherever our king reigned, the idioms and delicacies were British.)[4] Among our essayists, for example, Susan Koppelman eats off the Stangl pottery she gathered, and Jeffrey Kessler works at the computer with his pince-nez ("Collecting Eyewear on eBay"). The story-telling thrift shoppers in Alison Franks' essay, "Tales from the Thrift," are often collecting things to wear, cook with, or read.

There is indeed the "gather one, then two, then many" element implied in collecting, and we do not dispute that. Some sort of seriality is involved. Samuel Walsh, writing in "Fifth Column," in *CIRCA* 100, an art magazine produced in Dublin, says, "To own two of anything is the beginning of a collection."[5] However, there are different goals and philosophies at work for different collectors. A number of our essayists address these differences. Annelise Sklar, in her article "I Want My MP3s: Music Collecting in the Digital Age," speaks of the completist collector and the specialist collector. Completists want everything ever issued by the artists whose work they collect, every category of dishware in a pattern, every version of a song; specialists, on the other hand, might be most interested in rarities and anomalies, or in highest quality, or in one sub-category of a genre that they just particularly enjoy.

Many commentaries on collecting note that it is common for a collector to start out with being a completist in mind but, for reasons of aesthetics, space, or idiosyncrasy, start weeding the collection with an eye toward specialization. Other collectors, though, remain steadfastly completist and thrive on the beauty of filling in all gaps. We have two essayists, Jo Ann Kelly Graham with her Kelly Dolls and Dennis Mills with his Timexes, who are unabashedly completist.

Another shared quality in collectors is that "thrill of the hunt" moment and the winning moment, whether it involves collecting and the Internet or collecting without it, and our essayists definitely speak of this, whether they are buying something or selling something. Julia Penelope's very essay title is "Gambler's Rush," and she speaks of "hitting the jackpot" and tells us, "For the collector, every day is a lottery drawing." Speaking of his initial successes in "Collecting Eyewear on eBay," Jeffrey Kessler comments, "It has been said that the beginning of any addiction is the thrill of winning. Beginner's luck has hooked many a gambler." Harold Smith, speaking of no longer selling his artwork on eBay in "Being Collected, Selling Art on the Internet," says, "I miss the thrill of a painting sold, the ecstasy of a last minute flurry of bids, and the joy of seeing positive feedback."

So, there is collecting in general, but in this book we examine the impact of the Internet on collecting of all kinds—the "New Technologies" part of our subtitle. This entity, this great, overarching, shape-changing amoeba that most of us live with via our personal computers, provides so much agency for collectors and those that cater to them. The Internet is full of oppositions: it is the most ordered and disordered, accurate and inaccurate, true and untrue, democratic and controlled, private and public entity imaginable. And it is ever-changing, sometimes in the blink of an eye. Websites that seemed so solid are here today and gone tomorrow.

Accessibility is one of the outstanding features of the Internet. Fred Pullen, a Microsoft Partner Solutions Advisor, spoke to the Business and Information Technology Expo in Tucson, Arizona,[6] about the term "leveling the playing field." In the context of business, this term means that the right technology can put a small business and a big business into the same level of opportunity. The Internet can do this for collectors. An adolescent watch-collector has as much access to the lore and information and even offerings of the watches themselves as the professional dealer-specialist. A young museum curator can stay up all night in competitive bidding for a Hank Aaron baseball card along with the professional sports memorabilia dealers and collectors (see Emily Alice Katz's essay, "The Past Is Always on Sale: Revisiting *Culture as Commodity: Internet Auctions and Judaica Collecting*"). Of course, the young watch collector and museum curator are not equals with the well-funded when it comes actually to purchasing high-priced collectibles, as Jeffrey Kessler notes in his piece, "Collecting Eyewear on eBay," and Julia Penelope speaks of the high-priced collectibles available only for the affluent. This puts some bumps back into the playing field.

Even though it feels as though all is revealed and nothing is private on the Internet, this is not true, at least for those of us without the skills or inclination to "hack" into online places where we are not wanted. There remain locked chat rooms, private forums, and photographs for viewing by family members only. This adds at least some dirt clods to the field.

Another feature, and one which stretches our definitions of the known world as based on the five senses, is the element of immateriality. So many images, but none to touch with your fingers, and they can be replicated! Annelise Sklar points out in her essay on collecting of MP3s, that even though the illegal downloaders archive their collections like collections of phonograph records, the non-materiality of the MP3 format makes it hard to believe that the music has ownership and that the downloading is thievery: it's just like listening to the radio. Penny L. Richards, in her essay "Online Museums, Exhibits, and Archives of American Disability History," comments that on the Internet you can go to the museum in your pajamas—there is no building to enter, no one sees you—no need to wash and brush—and there are no hours, so it might be even night-time. Kelley C. Smith Feranec, in her essay "Collecting the Internet," points out the creation of material "stuff" as a spin-off of popular websites: little dolls of a famous Dancing Baby icon, little toy "Hampsters," in addition to T-shirts and coffee mugs. Ironically, when we save and archive things from the Internet, by printing them out or by downloading them and putting them onto disk, we are creating material versions of the Internet immateriality.

The Internet also offers us a non-linear sense of both time and space. Elana C. Hurwitz, in her essay "Grandmom's Collection," says, "Surfing the Web provides a 'stream of consciousness' style of interacting with information that gives the user the ability to jump around, bounce back, and go off in any direction." (And, as Richards suggests, she mentions that this can be by day or at night). Philipp Blom, in his *To Have and to Hold: An Intimate History of Collectors and Collecting*, takes a very linear view of the history of collecting. Regarding collecting in the Nineteenth Century, he writes, "Collections had changed from being instruments of exploration to instruments of conservation."[7] Collectors may rescue, restore and display, but particularly with the aid of the Internet, collecting can always be an instrument of exploration and self-education. As Hurwitz says, the collector is free to explore because the Internet gives the user "the ability to jump around, bounce back, and go off in any direction" after a new wrinkle, a new angle, or even a double-check or a search for feedback.

As for conservation, the Internet provides the most amazing display cabinet, especially with the advent of easy digital photography. Not only do we have whole online museums, such as the ones Penny L. Richards describes, and pieces from the collections of brick and mortar museums, but we have private collections of every stripe to visit online. The thrift shopping enthusiasts in Alison Franks' essay can share their bounty the minute they bring it home, or still *in situ* in the store, using the cameras in cell phones, posting their pictures, with captions, on community forums, or in blogs and online journals. Elana C. Hurwitz has posted her grandmother's collection of toilet paper samples from a 1950s European trip onto a website, where this scrapbook page can be studied, along with toilet paper collections from other sources, by anyone clicking the right address.

Online catalogs, Kelley C. Smith Feranec tells us, began with simple lists, including lists of web addresses that ultimately blossomed into some of the big search engines we use today to do that multidirectional exploring with our collecting. Archiving the ever-changing Internet itself, though, presents special problems, as librarian Marilyn A. Dunn discusses in "Collecting Material Born Digital," and Feranec as well.

Along with transience, a major issue with the Internet is authority. Is it true? Who says so? And just what do they have to prove? All too often we open what we trust will be a benign, objective source on something we are interested in, only to note that whoever is behind the site has a definite agenda, hidden or blatant. Interactive wiki programs, including the famous Wikipedia itself,[8] which in its very citation instructions warns us to be aware of possible misinformation, create even more of a mine field for those seeking solid edification. And of course there is the problem of misrepresentation of goods offered for sale on auction sites and other places for purchasing. Dennis Mills tells how he contacts the bidders on novelty watch items that he knows to be fake, to warn them (usually meeting with resentment or with no thanks at all). We all know the problems about misrepresentation of people themselves online, and of course that is easy in this realm that confuses the intimate and the anonymous, the personal and the impersonal. Brenda Oelbaum, in the notes for her essay, "The Venus of Willendorf Project," comments that we say we are "speaking" to people online, when in actuality we are typing to them and we really don't know who "they" may be.

Even when there is no misrepresentation, the plentitude of online offerings can make quality control an issue for the collector. Terry Evers, in her essay "On Collecting 'La Vie en Rose,'" comments that she'd like to keep the versions she dislikes of that song made so famous by Edith Piaf out of her collection, but that the Internet makes it so easy and offers so much that it is too tempting just to take it all — a completist willy nilly!

The community watchdog approach offered by Dennis Mills is a good place to lead into the biggest plus for collectors that the Internet offers: many opportunities for community with other collectors. Tom McCourt, in an article on collecting music online published in *Popular Music and Society*, claims, "In cyberspace, collecting becomes based not on the linkage of people to objects, but the linkage of individuals to others."[9] This comment covers so many of the collector's favorite online entities, from the auction sites with their feedback mechanisms, online communities , blogs, forums, messaging boards, picture-sharing sites, mechanisms for peer to peer music-sharing, and so much more, including the famous places for "collecting" friends. Carson Metzger, in his essay, "Trading Online Objects on Friendster.com: Cyber Collecting as Socialization," says "This convergence of cyber collecting and social interaction has become increasingly apparent over the last five years in the proliferation and use of online dating and social networking sites like Friendster and MySpace, sites where socialization proceeds through acts of collecting."

But friends are gathered even through sites not officially geared for "friend collecting." In her essay "The Konnection of the Kelly Kollection: Kelly Doll Collectors and the Internet," Jo Ann Kelly Graham details just how embracing an online collectors' community can be. For her and her fellow Kelly Doll collectors, the online KellyKlub is not only a place for sharing lore about their favorite collectible and buying, selling and trading, but it is also a place for the warmest offerings of friendship and support.

And now we would like to pass you on to the collection of essayists and their offerings for this book. The field of popular culture studies has acknowledged the validity of all our voices in describing our culture, passions, and human endeavors, breaking down the divisions between the academic and the "popular" and enlarging the circle of scholarship to include all our expressions of experience. From the very beginning of our interest in collecting stories, we wanted to hear from a diverse group of collectors, rather than only from collectors with academic backgrounds who would tell stories with traditionally defined scholarly writing. In *Collecting and the Internet* we do have such diversity, and every writer is part of more than one world of interest and expertise, as you can see from the Contributors biographies at the end of the book. We do have scholars, both independent and university-affiliated: we also have artists, writers, editors, librarians, museum personnel, teachers, designers, a mechanic, a musician, and even a magician. We have writers with personal and political identities that have been marginalized historically — African American, lesbian, disability rights advocacy and fat liberation advocacy, among others. Here in the book, all the voices come together to talk about collecting and the Internet. We think you will enjoy what they have to say.

Notes

1. Teresa Barnett, "Tradition and the Individual Memory: The Case of Christian C. Sanderson," in *Acts of Possession: Collecting in America*, ed. Leah Dilworth, New Brunswick, NJ: Rutgers University Press, 2003), 223.
2. Philipp Blom, *To Have and to Hold: An Intimate History of Collectors and Collecting* (Woodstock & New York: Overlook, 2002), 20–21.
3. Leah Dilworth, ed., *Acts of Possession: Collecting in America*, (New Brunswick, NJ: Rutgers University Press, 2003), 7.
4. Ruth Craft and Elisa Trimby, *The King's Collection*, (Garden City, NY: Doubleday, 1978), unpaginated.
5. Samuel Walsh, Fifth Column," *CIRCA* 100, (Summer 2000), 5, 11, 15, 19 and 21.
6. Fred Pullen, a Microsoft partner solutions advisor, spoke to the Business and Information Technology Expo in Tucson, Arizona, on October 30, 2007.
7. Blom, 121.
8. Wikipedia (http://en.wikipedia.org/wiki/) (accessed March 18, 2008).
9. Tom McCourt, "Collecting Music in the Digital Realm," *Popular Music and Society* 28.2 (2005), 252.

1

Collecting the Internet

How Individually Authored Websites Have Generated Nostalgia and a Desire to Collect the Digital

BY KELLEY C. SMITH FERANEC

Popular culture is in a unique position today as a result of the Internet. What previously had been promoted by traditional mass media, namely television and print, now has a third medium, that of the World Wide Web, where entirely new parameters apply. Unlike traditional media where products, trends, and information are pushed on consumers, the Internet and Web are radically redefining how popular culture is created, disseminated, and ultimately collected.

Whereas eBay[1] and similar online auction sites continue to alter the exchange and value of traditional ephemera and collectibles—antiques, baseball cards, Beanie Babies—an entirely new phenomenon is occurring online with the exchange and collection of websites themselves. Since the introduction of the World Wide Web in 1993, there has been a steady rise in the number of non-commercial, individually authored websites that have crossed beyond the realm of the digital and made their way into mainstream popular culture. Audiences, then, have not only created communities of culture around such sites, but have also generated nostalgia and a desire to collect the digital information itself.

From individual collectors of Web ephemera to the Internet Archive, from basic lists of URLs to the creation of physical objects based on digital websites, the phenomenon of "Collecting the Internet" is only in its infancy. As the Internet and World Wide Web continue to mesh with our everyday lives and to become further integrated with computers, mobile phones, video games, even television, we will continue to see the rise of Internet ephemera and an increase in the value of Internet collectibles. Therefore, it is important to increase public awareness of the potential value of non-commercial sites in the creation of a new form of popular culture and to highlight the importance of documenting and collecting Internet ephemera as an integral part of the history of the Internet and popular culture of the 1990s and early twenty-first century.

In 1993, with the introduction of the user friendly graphic-based Web browser Mosaic (the precursor to Netscape and, ultimately, Internet Explorer), the Internet was made available to individuals who, with little technical know-how, were suddenly able to both access and contribute freely and enthusiastically to this new medium. The consequential juxtaposition of commercial, academic, and personal information made possible by the graphic browser led to an unprecedented exchange, and to creation of an entirely new form of content.

Digital Ephemera

iStuff, as I've come to describe such digital ephemera, derives from non-commercial websites that, as a direct result of their cult-like status on the Web, have the potential to make their way into mainstream popular culture as consumer products or as elements featured in traditional mass media such as television shows, newspapers, or magazines. As text, image, and multi-media rendered as digital information, iStuff is a new form of expression that has emerged over the past decade parallel with the development of the World Wide Web. Whereas television and print transmit and push goods and services into the home to audiences via a one-way line of communication, the Internet enables individuals to access information at their own pace, build their own Web pages, and ultimately become producers and promoters of their own popular culture artifacts. Personal homepages, fan sites, chat rooms, MUDs (Multiple User Domains that combine the elements of role-playing games and social chat rooms), blogs, and so-called "useless sites" embody some of the best online grassroots culture-making.

Guidelines for identifying iStuff include, but are not limited to the following criteria:

1. it begins in digital form on the Internet.
2. it is originally non-commercial.
3. it acquires accidental notoriety.
4. it attempts to achieve "fifteen minutes of fame."
5. it exhibits elements of exhibitionism and voyeurism.
6. it tends to be humorous.
7. it appears useless or nonsensical.
8. it has developed a fan base.
9. it is distributed virally via e-mail or word-of-mouth.
10. it is ephemeral, can disappear without notice and without a trace.

While not all iStuff exhibits each and every characteristic detailed above, at the core of such digital ephemera lies its beginning as an amateur or grassroots brainchild that is distributed via the Internet. It should be noted, however, that as the Internet and World Wide Web continue to grow and expand alongside technological advances enabling the creation of new forms of content and experiences altogether — 3D Virtual Reality, for example — what constitutes iStuff will constantly require re-examination.

The following is a true story, based on one of the earliest Internet-to-mass media crossovers:

> In 2000, the music world was revolutionized by the release of a new album featuring four unusual musical and dancing talents. The naturally gifted members, recognized the world over for their uniquely synchronized, highly choreographed dance moves, demonstrated their singing capabilities on this, their first ever, musical compilation. Graced with rather unusual vocal ranges, their melodic voices broke through the powerful rhythmic beats and repetitive scores that typified every track, merging voice and instrument seamlessly together.
>
> Unfortunately, this new band never booked a single live performance in their home country, Canada, or anywhere else for that matter. Unlike other typical trendy boy bands of the late '90s, this musical oddity of the new millennium featured talent of a very different sort: not boys, not girls, not humans at all, but hamsters; digital hamsters to be exact. The virtual crew of four, led by Hampton Hamster, made their debut not on MTV, but rather, on computer screens via the Internet, bouncing tirelessly up and down as animated GIFs[2] set to a looping WAV[3] file embedded in HTML.[4]

But how and why would a collection of animated GIFs put together and record a musical CD? And even still, who could possibly care?

The fact of the matter is, however, that millions of people did care. Deidre LaCarte, who created the animated Web site, The Hampsterdance[5] in 1998 in honor of her pet hamster, Hampton, not only managed to attract millions of viewers to her humorous offbeat site in a matter of months, but managed to alter entirely its role from a silly personal Web page to a highly profitable enterprise. After posting the site on GeoCities,[6] La Carte checked the visitor counter one morning only to discover it had risen sharply over the span of four days:

> It had 30,000 people, and I almost fell off my chair. I thought, "There's got to be something wrong with Geocities"... Everyone thinks they want to become rich and famous. But this is not how I envisioned it. Never in my wildest imagination would I ever think my hamster was going to make me famous.[7]

Three years after The Hampsterdance's debut, LaCarte began to capitalize on her site's popularity through the production and distribution of consumer products like T-shirts and music CDs[8] (the title tack, *the Hampsterdance Song*, topped the Australian dance charts at number five in 2001!), culminating in a cameo appearance on a television commercial for the Internet service provider Earth Link.[9] In 2008, La Carte's hamsters continue to produce and market musical CDs and other products.

Like the Hampsterdance, most iStuff sites are created without any sponsorship or corporate funding by an average Web user who simply wanted to participate in the unique experience that is the World Wide Web. In fact, most website creators note that a few hits to their site would have made them happy, and they had no idea that the potential for thousands, let alone millions of visitors was even a possibility. This was certainly the case for perhaps the most infamous of accidental Web stars, Mahir Cagri, the rather naïve, not-so-Web-savvy "I Kiss You!!!" bachelor from Turkey.

Originally intended to serve as a sort of personal ad, Cagri's website,[10] posted as a pseudo personal ad, gained notoriety only after it was mysteriously hacked and its content altered. Visitors, amused by the hacker's changes coupled with the immodest Turk's peculiar photographs, rudimentary English, and outlandish sayings, "I Kiss You!!! I like Sex ... I like to take foto-camera of nice nude models, and peoples," passed the site along to friends and coworkers via e-mail and word of mouth. Within days of its launch, the site received over half a million hits and spurred countless parodies, fan clubs, Web rings, musical and animated tributes, and, let us not forget, merchandising. Cagri became one of the first worldwide Internet celebrities and even made scheduled appearances throughout the United States.

> I was an ordinary person living an ordinary life... But when I woke up one morning on the 3rd or 4th of November, I found all my phones continuously ringing. My lines got locked and I couldn't realize what was happening. Many people from Türkiye and all over the world were calling me to tell their thoughts about my homepage at Internet... I came a well-known person in the world, although I didn't want to be. I became the headlines of many newspapers and TV in different countries.[11]

Other early examples of iStuff include: the Dancing Baby, an animated, digitally rendered baby dancing to music that was originally distributed via e-mail and eventually made its mainstream debut on the Ally McBeal TV show; the Neiman-Marcus "$200 Chocolate Chip Cookie Recipe" that was heavily distributed via viral distribution[12] to everyone's email box at least two or three times; the original "Coffee Cam" which set the precedence for all on-line real-time Web cams and ultimately popular reality TV shows like *Big Brother*; the Mr. T Ate My Balls Web site which eventually had over 600 parodies spoofing its crude title (Bill Clinton, Hitler and Hello Kitty to name just a few who consequently fell prey to the infamous ball-munching antics); Cindy Margolis, pioneer online self-promoter who used her website to drive her modeling (and consequent television) career. All of these examples, though seemingly unimportant, were the driving force behind many of the online innovations we take for granted today. Recording and collecting them will help document and immortalize the somewhat humble beginnings of the Internet and Web.

Physical Collections Made Digital

When one mentions "Collecting the Internet," immediately our thoughts turn to the world's largest and fastest growing online market — eBay. However, eBay is simply an online version of a traditional auction where physical goods are available. While many collectors use eBay to purchase objects to add to their own collections, a variety of collecting goes on both over the World Wide Web via sites like eBay, as well as *by means of* websites themselves. Beyond simply trading physical objects via the Internet, individual collectors use the Internet to share and expose their own unique objects of desire to a worldwide audience. The earliest postings of physical collections were displayed as a simple textual list of objects. Examples of such pages include What's in my desk Drawer,[13] a literal list of various office supplies and miscellaneous objects—wrench, athletic tape, bottle of pain killers—found throughout creator Jason A. Goodman's desk in August, 1995 to La Liste de T-shirts de Steve,[14] in which Steve lists his entire T-shirt collection as of 1998 by genre — generic, music/concert, Internet-related, received as gifts; they are even cross-referenced. Eventually, the introduction and eventual widespread use of graphical browsers[15] (programs that interfaced with the web allowing photographs and dynamic media) enabled collectors to post images of their collections—from dolls and old electric trains, to old Band-Aids,[16] early floppy-disk covers,[17] and even personal collections of belly button lint[18]—creating a virtual extension of prized possessions that could be viewed by anyone, anywhere in the world.

The Web has also enabled collectors to add another dimension to their collections— interactivity. Visitors are not only able to view particular objects but through the technology of the medium can often interact and sometimes contribute directly to the author's collection. In Derek's Big Website of Wal-Mart Purchase Receipts,[19] for example, visitors are able to post their comments directly to the site, enabling them to muse openly over Derek's posted collection of Wal-Mart shopping receipts and the odd purchases he makes. In another example, as a means of combating the endemic "Nigerian Million-dollar Money Transfer" scams (you may have received one of these "urgent" emails from a Nigerian family member supposedly unable to access a relative's funds without the aid of an American citizen), the website www.419eater.com[20] hosts a collection of stories and images submitted by the site creator and recruits visitors who "scambait," or reverse-scam the would-be Nigerian money-scammers[21] by entangling them in a web of time and resource-wasting correspondences.

Digital Collections About the Digital

Collections of websites and iStuff curated by individuals and smaller organizations on the World Wide Web take on a slightly different format from traditional collections. Rather than "physically" possess or host a collection of websites, Web collectors post long, often highly organized lists of links which document their favorite sites. Link lists, developed primarily out of a need to organize the Web, began to appear on personal homepages as a means of demonstrating not only one's personal interests but, most significantly, one's command over the content of the Web. Like collectors of physical objects who place their collections on display, creators of link lists derive a sense of prestige from the depth and uniqueness of their lists.

Link lists can be organized by topic, by community, or by an assigned hierarchy. Examples of basic link lists include My Favorite Links,[22] a typical list of five to ten seemingly random sites featured on Chuck Smoot's personal homepage, and Jason's Collection of Weird Links,[23] a specialized link list developed around a particular genre of unusual Websites. Yahoo!,[24] one of the largest and most successful of Internet search portals, began as a basic link list with just fourteen main topics. Developed in 1993 by graduate students at Stanford as "Yet Another Hierarchical Office Oracle," Yahoo! can be considered a *Wunderkrammer* of lists, displaying what is essentially a highly curated collection of thousands of websites.

Another form of Web collecting takes place via Web rings. Unlike link lists where an individual (or a body of individuals) "curates" the collection, a community of participants helps build and contributes to a particular topic, adding to a string of sites viewed in succession as though traveling through a museum. Often there is a central portal through which visitors gain access to the collection of sites, as in the Unusual Museum of the Internet.[25] Sites that initiate the creation of large Web rings are often those that generate the most nostalgia and maintain a highly developed fan base. Mr. T Ate My Balls,[26] for example, spawned hundreds of parody sites and numerous Web rings on the now infamous topic of ball munching, including the Everybody Ate My Balls[27] Web ring. The popularity of Web rings as a way to view and collect websites has lead to the development of search engines and forums dedicated solely to Web rings: Webring,[28] RingSurf,[29] and Ringlink.[30]

Interestingly enough, digital collections based on Internet content itself began to appear soon after the introduction of graphical Web browsers. Examples of this include sites like The Under Construction Page,[31] a collection and display of "Under Construction" icons that were initially used to denote Web pages that were incomplete or in the early stages of design. From static yellow and black text to flashing, three-dimensional animated displays of "Men at Work," such collections enable us to recognize those elements of the Internet and World Wide Web truly unique to the medium. Similar collections display screen shots of individualized "404 Not Found" pages,[32] bizarre objects put up for sale on eBay,[33] and even early AOL on-screen interfaces.[34]

Of course, there is one inherent problem in using link lists and Web rings as a means of hosting one's collection of websites. Like a card catalog which merely identifies the books housed in a library, there is no guarantee the book will be on the shelf when you want to check it out. Websites come and go with an ever-increasing frequency. Sites are constantly updated, outdated or simply removed all together. Dynamic content is constantly in flux and there are only a limited number of methods of capturing a website at a particular stage in time.

One of the most comprehensive archival projects to date, the *Internet Archive*,[35] has been recording information posted on the Web since 1996. It records websites periodically throughout the year by taking screen shots as well as capturing HTML content of even the most obscure of websites. While only able to present a limited record of every website, the Internet Archive provides free and open access to its collections, enabling researchers as well as the public at large to search and view how elements on the Web have changed over time. By 2002, the Internet Archive had amassed over 100 terabytes (approximately ten billion pages) of information. As of 2008, over 85 billion pages have been archived. With ever-continuing advances in archival technology, the Internet Archive's ability to capture and record the exponential growth of the Web will serve as a monumental tool in researching the history of the medium.

A final method of collecting websites actually involves downloading the content of the site itself, thus enabling the collector to host his or her own perfect replica of the original. Virtually nothing is lost when a site is downloaded; because it is digital, it is possible to retrieve a perfect copy indiscernible from the original. While this is certainly the best method of collecting a website, it is not always feasible. To download, maintain and host websites requires a great deal of digital storage space, both on a physical hard drive as well as on a virtual host if the site is to be accessed via the Internet. In addition, many website authors take certain security precautions that make it difficult to download their work. Downloading a website, however, is often the only way to capture the core of what makes the site unique and valuable — the combination of static, dynamic and interactive content.

How Does a Website Generate Value?

In 1907, economist George Simmil proposed that value "is never an inherent property of an object, but a judgement made about them by subjects."[36] Almost a century later, Simmil's simple definition continues to hold true. Today, what we as individuals using the Internet on a daily basis choose to consider valuable out of the millions of websites and digital elements floating around in cyberspace seems highly dependent on personal, somewhat subjective points of view. Is the site cool? Is it entertaining? Does it generate business and customer retention? Has it advanced the technology of the medium?

It is rapidly becoming imperative, however, to assess the value of websites according to a broader spectrum of criteria. Beyond visibility and technological innovation, other criteria for judging the value of websites should include their economic, historic, or ethical significance.[37] With the rare exception of sites like the Hampsterdance, which have generated considerable revenue from promotional items, few iStuff sites have acquired or will ever acquire economic worth. Rather, the value of iStuff sites should be weighed according to their historical contributions to the development and enrichment of the content of the Internet. As a unique form of personal expression that evolved directly out of the Internet's spirit of free-exchange and freedom of speech, iStuff serves as an early example of the innovative outcome that occurs when individuals are given the opportunity to be creative.

Had information exchanged and posted on the Internet and Web been limited solely to its initial intent (e.g., commercial, military, or academic content), cyberspace would have remained a sterile, dull environment in which the general public would have taken little interest other than to pay bills or purchase things online. Instead, it has become a realm where users who invest time and energy can carve a niche of their own and, particularly in the early stages of the development of the Web, establish new parameters for how the Internet can be used.

The first person to post his or her own personal homepage, for example, set the precedent for millions of people to follow. The whimsical placement of an "Under Construction" icon on an unfinished Web page launched an entire movement of "Under Construction" graphics (which continue to plague the Internet). Individual posts of link lists that tracked "favorite websites" eventually led to the creation of search engines like Yahoo![38] There is an Internet first for every page posted on the Web, with new firsts being created everyday.

An excellent example of an iStuff and Internet first that changed the face of the Internet and Web made pop culture history twice: first when it was broadcast via the Internet in 1993 and a second time when its website was removed in 2000. Touted as the "Internet era's equivalent of Gutenburg's bible,"[39] the world's first Webcam, the Trojan Room Coffee Cam,[40] was disconnected after its decade-long, at-the-click-of-the-mouse appearance. In today's world full of real-time images of everything from refrigerators and doorbells to fish tanks and college girls' dorm rooms, what could possibly be so important about an on-line coffee pot?

As a Slashdot[41] discussion board participant notes, "It's a piece of Internet History that really should be saved... it's a part of the Net's history and lore."[42] Another Slashdot participant, Josh Turiel, describes the Coffee Cam as the "first thing that took advantage of the ability of a browser to handle mixed media in a manner suitable for virtually any platform."[43] Prior to that, Web pages were static, often only text with in-line graphics. As simplistic as it was, the Coffee Cam "was a direct precursor of a lot of things we now take for granted."[44] Throughout the discussion board, participants cry out to have phenomena like the Coffee Cam documented and archived. Another Slashdot participant comments that such sites, in spite of their seemingly useless appearance, "capture the spirit of the net far better than a dozen Gartner analysts thrown in a bin."[45]

It is important to recognize that the Coffee Cam was not just about watching the levels of coffee in an aged and permanently browned pot rise and fall at one frame per second. Rather, its significance lies in the fact that in 1993 (when most of us had not yet heard of the Internet), anyone with a computer could log on and view real-time images from England at any time, from anywhere in the world. It was the notion that something that began as a seemingly simplistic solution to a commonplace problem (running out of coffee) could ignite a technological revolution through the merger of two isolated technologies— the Internet and video— into an innovative application that would eventually inspire thousands of would-be "Web cammers." And, most significant, it was the reality that people were experimenting with machines and technology, creating new programs, and opening up new possibilities— simply because they could.

> "In these times, nostalgia itself has taken on a postmodern flavor. Even things that were clearly ersatz at their inception provoke a longing for tradition from somebody when they go. The first golden arches above a McDonald's. The neon lights of a Las Vegas casino. Even with that in mind, the downfall of the coffee pot highlights the compressed distance between the past and future. The beginnings of the Internet are now artifact."
>
> — Peter S. Goodman, *Washington Post.* Sunday, April 1, 2001

Problems with Storing and Archiving Digital Information

In describing what it means to "Collect the Internet," I often use the example of collections based on television and film which are also time-based experiential media. With the rare exception of owning a film cell or the director's cut, one cannot physically possess a scene in a movie. Sure, we can go out and buy a video or DVD of our favorite actor's latest film; we cannot purchase the actors, the movie set or the actual experience of the film itself. Rather, fans express their fascination, and often obsession, with their favorite shows, films, and actors through the collection of memorabilia: physical objects, posters, photographs, toys, dolls, T-shirts, trinkets, autographs, etc.

Similarly, because websites are digital bits of information, void of any true physical presence, if they are removed from cyberspace, any and all relative information will be lost. As with television and film, iStuff memorabilia is a simple but highly effective means of immortalizing and making collectible a particular website.

Beyond marketing and collecting, however, it should be noted that physical objects like toys and memorabilia have a sense of permanence that digital bits may never achieve. There is a limit to the dogma that making things digital makes them better, easier to handle, and easier to store. While it is true a digital bit takes up significantly less space than, for instance, stacks of paper, digital information takes considerably more work to store, maintain, recall, and preserve. Compatibility issues simply do not come into play when you have a physical object that you can touch, view, and archive without interfacing with software and hardware that is often on the verge of obsolescence.

In spite of the variety of techniques currently employed to document and collect websites, the nature of digital information makes it almost impossible to archive effectively and permanently even the most valuable website. In his book, *Being Digital,* Nicholas Negroponte describes the digital bit as:

> A bit has no color, no size, or weight, and it can travel at the speed of light. It is the smallest atomic element in the DNA of information. It is a state of being: on or off, true or false, up or down, in or out, black or white. For practical purposes we consider a bit to be a 1 or a 0.[46]

Unlike physical objects and archives that have survived hundreds, if not thousands of years, the digital bit often has a shelf life of a mere five to ten years. This is because the recording media are not durable, the hardware used to access the information has a shorter shelf life than the media used to store it, and the task to ensure long-term preservation of digital records is technically difficult — you need specialized expertise, hardware, software and systems documentation.[47] With digital archives, outdated modes of data storage are completely inaccessible. As systems improve and become more efficient, older methods of digitization are lost, leading to the loss of thousands of documents. Thus, "things that have permanent value, but do not appear on paper or physical form, are lost."[48] If a system crashes or becomes obsolete, it is comparable to losing an original to fire.

Toys, T-shirts, memorabilia and similar ephemera based on popular iStuff sites achieve the following: (1) they express the possible value or collectibility of digital objects; (2) they project possible alternative solutions to storing and preserving the digital information; and (3) they serve as a critique of the transformation of the digital into commodity.

Currently, almost any website that receives a large number of hits from visitors will also promote T-shirts, mouse pads and coffee mugs emblazoned with its site logo. While many grassroots sites have turned their popularity into a money-making opportunity, the memorabilia they sell also serves to expand and solidify their community.

The question remains, however, is there a market for iStuff commodities? Who, besides die-hard Internet aficionados, would buy this stuff? Are these items truly considered collectible?

One need only conduct a search on eBay, the Internet's top online auction site, to discover that there is, in fact, a great demand for products based on popular websites. One of the most popular Web icons up for auction is the Pets.com Sockpuppet. Since the failure of the e-business in 2000, online sellers entice buyers with comments like, "You won't find these anymore. Pets.com is gone and soon this will be a memory and WORTH WAYYYY MORE!!!!!"[49] Hundreds of paraphernalia ranging from the Plush Sock Puppet Toy to dog collars, bowls, and even a "Tick Tock I'm a Sock" watch are listed as "Discontinued," "Retired," "Highly Collectible." Other auctions of iStuff included an offer for a *Hampsterdance* 12" vinyl promotional record promoted as "very rare," a "Super Rare" Cindy Margolis promotional postcard and, my personal favorite, the Original Dancing Baby Doll with wiggling arms and head that can be stuck on a car window.

Currently, however, it seems no one is collecting Web-based memorabilia specifically because it embodies a new form of ephemera. Sellers of the Dancing Baby Doll appeal to doll collectors or Ally McBeal enthusiasts, Pets.com sellers target animal owners and fanatic fans of the Sockpuppet itself, and so forth. I believe that in coming years, as people begin to look back on the pioneering stages of the Internet and World Wide Web with nostalgia, the preciousness and value of iStuff memorabilia as its own genre will increase. Furthermore, I predict that sites will be mass-marketed and hyped just as television shows and movies are — toys and memorabilia will surround popular websites and promotional, limited and/or one-of-a-kind items will be distributed to increase the value and collectibility of certain sites.

That the Internet and its contents have historical significance is undeniable. Organizations like the Internet Archive help reinforce the notion that the information that is out there, whether commercial, personal, or nonsensical, has value, and thus should be permanently preserved as public material. As for iStuff, only time will tell how Internet culture will be viewed and received in the years to come. Will popular culture phenomena such as the Hampsterdance be completely forgotten as time goes on and emerging technologies overshadow the naïve and outdated sites? Or will they emerge later as important milestones in the history of the Internet?

Until general audiences recognize the value of iStuff as a new popular culture phenomenon, the genre of humorous, nonsensical, grassroots websites created by amateur Internet users will remain, as they are currently described, "useless." By raising awareness about the social significance and implications of iStuff, I hope to generate interest and enthusiasm for actively archiving and collecting what has certainly been a major contribution to the development and progression of the most influential technology of our time — the Internet. Please visit my website, www.istuff.org, to access more information on iStuff and collecting the Web (Note: istuff.org was created as a part of my 2001 Masters Thesis).[50]

Note: Over time, many of the websites referred to in this manuscript may have been altered or removed. In most cases, it is possible to view their original content at the Internet Archive at www.archive.org.

My iStuff Ephemera Includes

Original Release of the *Hampsterdance*, CD
Hampsterdance, the Album, CD
Hampsterdance 12" vinyl promotional record
Pets.com Sock Puppet
Tick Tock I'm a Sock, Watch
Me by Me, the Pets.com Sock Puppet book
Pets.com flashing safety collar for my dog
Autographed Cindy Margolis 8x10 Photograph
Early postcard advertising Cindy Margolis Web site, CindyMargolis.com
Autographed screenshot of the original Mr. T Ate My Balls Web site from its creator, Nehal Patel
Mahir Cagri I Kiss You music CD
Authentic Wal-mart receipts from Derek Dahlsad, author of *Derek's Big Website of Wal-Mart Purchase Receipts*

NOTES

1. www.ebay.com (accessed February 2008)
2. Graphic Interchange Format, a compression method created by CompuServe for images uploaded to the World Wide Web.
3. Wave Form Audio File Format. WAV files are sound data, the digital representation of an analog signal.
4. Hypertext Markup Language, the programming language for Web pages.
5. http://www.hampsterdance.com (accessed February 2008)
6. http://www.geocities.com — one of the first free Web hosting and e-mail services; acquired by Yahoo!
7. Janet Kornblum, "Hampsterdance.com gets new gig, address," (June 7, 2000) [journal on-line]; available from *USA Today*, <http://www.usatoday.com/life/cyber/tech/cth708.html> (accessed October 2000).
8. Music CDs produced by Deidre LaCarte in conjunction with KOOCH records include: *The Hampstdance Song* (CD single) and *Hampsterdance, the Album*.
9. Internet Service Provider
10. http://www.ikissyou.org/ (accessed February 2008) *Original URL, www.members.nbci.com_XMCM/primall/mahir/new.htm, was removed in 2001.

11. http://www.mynameismahir.com/mahir_bio.html (removed in 2002)
12. On-line "word-of-mouth" marketing or distribution
13. http://cac.psu.edu/~jag164/desk.html (removed after July 2004)
14. http://stev0.com/shirts.html (removed by author on August 13, 2001 with the following statement: "The purpose of this list was for the sole purpose of getting on The Useless Pages. It made it. The Useless Pages is no longer being updated, so there's no reason to keep this page anymore, either.") [Available via Internet Archive: http://web.archive.org/web/20010602034907/http://stev0.com/shirts.html]
15. Although the first graphical browser, NCSA Mosaic, was introduced in 1993, the ability to integrate text, images and sound required some advanced know-how, so many Web users continued to post in text-only formats.
16. http://mybandaids.tripod.com/bandaid_index.htm (accessed February 2008)
17. http://www.cyberden.com/sleeves/ (accessed February 2008)
18. http://www.feargod.net/fluff.html (accessed February 2008)
19. http://lightning.prohosting.com/~receipts/ (removed after September 27, 2002). [Available on Internet Archive: http://web.archive.org/web/20020927201802/http://lightning.prohosting.com/~receipts/]
20. http://www.419eater.com (accessed February 2008)
21. *4-1-9 stands for the section of the Nigerian penal code which addresses fraud schemes, namely Advance Fee Fraud (AFF)
22. http://www.chucksmoot.net/links.html (accessed February 2008)
23. http://www.dimatisah.com/weird.html (removed after July 2004) [Available via Internet Archive: http://web.archive.org/web/20040417185834/http://www.dimatisah.com/weird.html]
24. http://www.yahoo.com (accessed February 2008)
25. http://www.unusualmuseums.org (accessed February 2008)
26. http://www.geocities.com/nkpatel/mrt (removed after July 2004). [Available via Internet Archive: http://web.archive.org/web/19990117025714/www.cen.uiuc.edu/~nkpatel/mr.t/index.html]
27. http://members.aol.com/balleaters (accessed February 2008)
28. http://www.dir.webring.com (accessed February 2008)
29. http://www.ringsurf.com (accessed February 2008)
30. http://www.ringlink.org (accessed February 2008)
31. http://www.acme.com/jef/construction/ (accessed February 2008)
32. http://www.lightecho.net/404page/ (accessed February 2008)
33. http://www.grrl.com/ebay.html (accessed February 2008)
34. http://www.lydiasaoldisks.com/ (accessed February 2008)
35. http://www.archive.org (accessed February 2008)
36. George Simmil, *The Philosophy of Money* (1907, translated in English 1978), 73, as cited in Susan M. Pearce, *Interpreting Objects and Collections* (London: Routledge, 1994), 76.
37. Toby Miller and Alec McHoul, *Popular Culture and Everyday Life* (London: Sage Publications, 1998), 4.
38. Dan Lester, "Yahoo! Profile of a Web Database," *Database*, December 1995, 46–50.
39. Leela Jacinto, "A Coffee Break: World's 'First' Webcam Going Into Retirement," (March 7, 2001) [journal on-line]; available from ABC News <http://www.abcnews.go.com/sections/world/ DailyNews/britain010307_coffee.html> (accessed March 2001).
40. http://www.cl.cam.ac.uk/coffee/coffee.html (accessed February 2008; *The Coffee Cam was disconnected on Wednesday, August 22, 2001, so the site no longer posts live images of the coffee pot)
41. www.slashdot.com (accessed February 2008)
42. "First Ever Webcam to Come Offline," (March 7, 2001) [discussion board on-line]; available from Slashdot <http://slashdot.org/articles/01/03/07/1345210.shtml> (accessed March 2001).
43. Ibid.
44. Ibid.
45. Ibid.
46. Nicholas Negroponte, *Being Digital* (New York: Vintage, 1996), 14.

47. David Stephens, "Digital Preservation: a Global Information Management Problem," *Information Management Journal,* v. 34 no. 3 (July 2000), 70.

48. Ibid, 68.

49. Seller comment on Pets.com Auction Item, "Plush Sock Puppet Toy," posted to eBay, April 2001.

50. Smith, Kelley. "iStuff: The Next Generation of Popular Culture." Unpublished master's thesis, University of Florida, 2001.

2

Collecting Materials Born Digital

MARILYN A. DUNN

Imagine scholars in the year 2050 combing through archives for information about women's reactions to Supreme Court appointees or women's responses to the devastation Hurricane Katrina caused for Gulf families. The crucial challenge confronting archivists, librarians, and historians at the Schlesinger Library today is to anticipate what scholars in the year 2050 will want to know about women of our time. What evidence will they need to form conclusions about the passions, beliefs, aspirations, struggles and roadblocks women faced? Anticipating the requirements of scholars is what the Arthur and Elizabeth Schlesinger Library has done well for over half a century, collecting manuscript materials that include correspondence, diaries, business and organizational records, along with printed materials like etiquette books, advice books, manuals for the newly married woman, and popular periodicals that open windows on the complex forces that shape gender development and expectations.

Schlesinger collections have contributed to more than 11,000 publications about a myriad of subjects from political movements such as the abolition of slavery and the fight for women's suffrage, to social issues like intergenerational relationships, the changing family, women and work, sexuality, and reproductive technology. The Schlesinger has been at the forefront of preserving the evolving record of women as they moved, in the twentieth century, from the domestic sphere into the public sphere. Now, as women enter the cybersphere, the library must lead the way in collecting the dynamic, interactive, and borderless digital expressions of women. In assuming a leadership role in this new frontier, we are grappling with major issues in institutional collecting.

Historically, primary sources were contained in the journals and books that librarians selected and in the paper records that donors offered to libraries. Publications such as books and journals are being transformed by electronic media, and most current library subscriptions are received in electronic formats, purchased through vendors that aggregate many titles into one digital subscription. In the near future, collecting scholarly journals may prove unnecessary as they are so widely held in electronic formats and can be so easily delivered to researchers' desktops. The Schlesinger Library continues to collect periodicals aimed at a female audience and purchased by women or girls in popular venues. Frequently, these are publications that document style, entertainment, spiritual concerns, and other topics in popular culture that future historians will seek. Additionally, the images they hold will speak volumes about women's culture and the role of the media in shaping it.

The extraordinary ambitions of Google and the Open Content Alliance (a competing project sponsored by noncommercial partners) to digitize all books and index all human knowledge have both stunned and excited librarians. Amidst the uncertainty and confusion these projects are generating, a trip to any substantial bookstore provides the confidence that browsing and pleasure reading in paper formats will continue. However, the potential for almost all books to be available in digital versions is a reality that looms over all library planning and collecting efforts. Innovations in the book will assuredly have an enormous impact on libraries of the future, yet just what the impact will be and how quickly it will arrive are unclear. In the near future, book and journal collecting policies will evolve gradually.

However, the same cannot be said for many other kinds of materials that are essential to archives attempting to document the present for the future. Many organizations whose work we document had previously published paper-based newsletters, but are now delivering digital newsletters and email alerts to their members about issues and events of concern and likewise to disseminate editorials and position papers. In fact, newsletters delivered to the library for decades by the U.S. mail suddenly are available only electronically. Women's diaries and appointment calendars now arrive on discs rather than on bound paper and everyone wonders how email will be preserved. The variety and number of informative websites, electronic publications, email correspondence, and new forms of expression, such as blogs, blog-rings, and wikis are causing archivists and librarians to re-examine their practices and create new methods. Perhaps the profession can be judged as too reluctant to take control and be innovative in its approaches to collecting and preserving, but constructing new models and technologies for preservation is a painstaking and complex task.

Most difficult and perhaps most important is electronic correspondence. Today's corporations, philanthropic boards, municipal governments, unions, as well as women's social, political, and economic organizations conduct the preponderance of their business electronically. This has been the case for nearly two decades. Today, countless mothers and daughters share advice and news about family, careers, health, and other personal issues through email rather than by putting pen to paper. Family distribution lists may include three generations of women discussing activities of everyday life and the significance of public events. Collecting this kind of documentation provides researchers with the "stuff" of social history viewed through the lens of women's experience. Formerly, this record was most commonly preserved in paper format, sometimes in audio or visual formats. Considering the evolving technologies of communication that now predominate, how will we continue this collecting practice and preserve the multitude of materials that are born digitally?

Unquestionably, the World Wide Web has revolutionized daily life and communication over the past twenty years—and many more innovations can be expected. Historians of the future will investigate how developments in communication technology affected women: were new developments liberating or limiting? Were there gender differences in the ways that men and women used technology? What were those differences?

Future generations of scholars will require evidence of how both sexes embraced emergent technologies. Schlesinger archivists have discovered that the fortuitous convergence of format and content provides a singular opportunity to document women's uses of communication technologies while allowing the library to enlarge its subject collections as well as expand into new subject areas.

At the top of any list of the important historical events and movements of our era is the pervasive presence of technical innovations. The intersection of science and reproductive technology has broadened women's reproductive options in extremely positive ways, yet the specter of innovation in reproductive technology sparks a myriad of ethical questions. In attempting to find effective, ethical, and available technology to resolve reproductive issues, women turn not only to their physicians but also to an abundance of relevant websites. Many of these publications in electronic format instantiate, exemplify, or represent women's use of technology, while affording evidence for future scholars in a wide range of subjects vital to understanding a major concern in contemporary women's lives.

Electronic formats abound: discussion and bulletin boards, subject-based listservs, and distribution lists. Websites, e-newsletters, and email document virtual communities that form around particular issues, such as Weight Watchers on-line pals, adoptive parents groups, freedom to marry advocates, and women's fundamentalist religious communities.

Which collections are appropriate for the Schlesinger? We believe the key criteria are research value and consistency with the library's mission and subject focus. E-sources offer us the opportunity to capture voices that describe the experience of communities underrepresented in our collection such as African American women, Latinas, and recent immigrant groups including Cambodians, Vietnamese, and Somalis. Additionally, it seems possible that some groups that we have had limited success in documenting, for instance political and religious conservatives, may become more readily available for documenting through electronic media.

Recently the staff at the Schlesinger Library has come to see blogs as a potential bonanza of compelling views and ideas that we want to document and preserve. In collaboration with the Harvard University Library Office of Information Systems, the Schlesinger Library is piloting a program to collect blogs by women. Blogs—short for weblogs—are an on-line medium that suits the hectic pace of contemporary women's lives. Topics prompting discussion in the blogosphere include adoption, infertility, and abortion rights. Additionally, many teenage girls publish blogs that are essentially on-line diaries. Girls embrace this medium to record their spiritual lives, to speculate about their future, to document their physical changes, and to unleash creativity. Social historians interested in the characteristics of girlhood in different historical periods will benefit enormously from the documentation of school and social experience.

For women, as for girls, blogs are replacing paper. In an article appearing in the Spring/Summer 2005 issue of *American Archivist*, prize-winning author Catherine O'Sullivan suggested that blogs continue the tradition of women's diaries of the 19th and 20th centuries. She noted that many blogs address topics similar to those once found in paper diaries, such as identity formation, character-building experiences, and the emotional texture of everyday life.[1] An example of just such a blog is Bluebird Escape (http:www.BluebirdEscape.com)[2] written by an Iranian-American teen telling her story of emigrating from Iran and adjusting to the United States. This blog presents lyrical musings, acute observations, daily activities, self-reflections, travelogue, and photos. A similar capacity for self-examination and expression by women is documented in eighteenth, nineteenth, and twentieth century paper diaries held by the Schlesinger, which makes blogs such as this one consonant with our collections. However, blogs are different from earlier diaries in complicated ways; many are interactive, eliciting responses called "posts" from readers and/or links outside the original site to other blogs, published materials, or websites.

In July of 2006, The Pew Internet and American Life Project issued a study of Bloggers by Amanda Leinhart and Susannah Fox that reported more than 12 million American adults identified themselves as bloggers.[3] A Perseus blog study reported in 2005 that there were 31.6 million blogs on the web and that 10 million weblogs were created in the first months of 2005[4]. Yet there are no standard guidelines or procedures for capturing this new form of public discourse. To collect and preserve rich sources like Bluebird Escape for use by future scholars, the library must be willing to tackle many difficult but not intractable problems. Chief among these is preservation, followed quickly by descriptive cataloging to make the digital material easily accessible and searchable. Of course, the ephemeral nature of digital publications and new issues in intellectual property rights heighten the challenges. Therefore, our pilot program will contribute to the ongoing process of creating "best practices" in digital preservation. Curators have selected topical blogs on reproductive issues such as abortion, adoption, and infertility, as well as blogs by teenage girls, Latinas, African American women, recent female immigrants, and members of the transgendered community.

Although each blog has its own style and format, some may be fashioned after complex websites while others resemble a diary that is self-contained with one voice. Typically, a blog opens with an attractive banner announcing itself and its purpose. Frequently a tab allows a reader to discover something about the author. It isn't unusual to find that a blog may be the product of multiple authors. The center of the page usually contains a "post" from the author with a headline alerting the reader to the subject of the entry that may contain embedded links to a published source like the *New York Times*, or to *Feminist Weekly News*[5] or women's e news.[6]

Most blogs have an archive of previous posts and an area for responses from readers. Many also include a blogroll, which is a hot list of the creator's favorite blogs. Some also contain an RSS feed (Really Simple Syndication) that allows the posts to be pushed out from the site electronically to subscribers who may wish to receive the entry in their email. Blogs can be made more dynamic by the introduction of sound and streaming video or made more attractive by the inclusion of photographs. Readers may browse the blogger's archive and add a post on an entry that is several months old. Such blogs pose many questions and require decisions about systems that crawl through the internet and retrieve the sites. How and what do we use to capture the material? How frequently must it be captured to ensure the integrity of the site? And to what extent should links to outside sources be followed? That is, should the outside sources be documented at the first level only, or should their links also be followed? Varying iterations of blogs are not unlike multiple editions of books; however, each edition of a book remains stable within its boards once published while blogs may change minute to minute as reader's respond to entries that may be months old and stored in the blog's internal archive. Furthermore, blogs can be extremely ephemeral — a large complicated site that has been dutifully maintained for two to three years may disappear overnight.

Therefore, preservation must be expeditious and collectors rely on a particular kind of web software known as a web "spider" or crawler" or "robot" for searching, locating, and copying the blog targeted for archiving and preservation. Usually it is set up to visit and copy specific blogs at regular intervals and has the pre-determined information about how far out links should be followed. Once the blog is copied and retrieved, how is it stored and how is its content preserved for future generations? These are daunting questions that libraries and consortia of libraries are working collaboratively to answer and thereby arrive at standards that would allow preservation in a kind of special library called a "trusted digital repository."

The widespread awareness of the ephemeral nature of blogs is evident in words like "authenticity," "integrity," "trust," "reliability," and "fixity"-words that populate the conversations and literature on this topic. Once a blogsite has been copied, it must be stored, described, and preserved, presumably to last for decades or even centuries. Can a researcher be sure that this is the authentic site as it originally appeared? In other words, how can this intangible media be "fixed" in time and space for future display in ever-changing technical environments? Can a site's integrity be maintained? How is a researcher certain that the data has not been in part corrupted and/or deleted? The vulnerability of the medium also causes concern that a site may be inadvertently erased or lost. To address these problems, trusted digital repositories have accepted the charge to manage all the processes that guarantee the continuation of a specific byte stream and the architecture that dictates how data is displayed on the screen.

Trusted digital repositories are necessary for the preservation of all kinds of electronic media that women create and use — email, text files, graphics as well as sites that may combine all of these, such as a blog. Being such a repository also involves the creation of metadata that incorporates the activity previously understood in libraries as "cataloguing." Essentially, metadata determines how the site is formatted by recording its informational structure and architecture. It also describes the content in terms of characteristics that can be searched both currently and in the future. Embedded in this process is the assumption that the site may be migrated many times in the future as software and hardware change. Metadata also records information that will be invaluable to future researchers such as the provenance, context, donor information, and restrictions on use.

In order to provide the appropriate metadata to preserve the blogs in our pilot program, decisions about the arrangement and organization of the sources were required. Will future historians search for collections on topics or wish to look at blogs created in particular geographic areas or historical periods? For example, how will scholars approach the study of the September 11th attack on the World Trade Center through blogs? Will they analyze the event, focusing on ethnicity, gender, and geographic region? Librarians will decide whether it is preferable to treat blogs as individual unique entities or artificial collections with a common theme or common purpose.

At the same time, librarians will try to imagine where and how a historian will search. For instance, will research be done in a familiar search environment like traditional library catalogs or on internet search engines like Google and Mozilla Firefox? The search environment chosen might influence the choice of descriptive phrases or keywords that are selected as access points for future researchers.

Another complicating factor is the limited understanding of intellectual property rights as they pertain to this new medium. Can libraries and archives collect and preserve blogs under the ambiguous provisions of title 107 of the copyright law that governs fair use? Does the highly public venue of WWW publishing imply that the material is available for the taking? Librarians assume that we are obligated to seek permission from the blog owner to copy and retain their blog indefinitely; but we have no assurance of an answer. Is written notification of intent sufficient? Although it is nearly impossible to contact them for permissions, do secondary authors commenting on a post by the blog owner or another respondent have an expectation of copyright protection? Blogs such as abortionclinicdays (http://abortionclinicdays.blogs.com/),[7] written by two women who have worked at an abortion clinic for more than twenty years, often contain passionate arguments or anecdotal stories with detail. Here defamation may be at issue, as it may also be if a blogger writes about specific people, such as an employer, a parent, or an institution like a hospital. Violation of property rights and defamation present the risk of litigation, and that, in turn, may influence the choice of blogs that could be preserved. Considering that one group of bloggers, teens, targeted by the Schlesinger for collecting, is under the age of consent, we fear parental permission may be problematic.

Some blogs contain advertisements and links for commercial properties and owners may be compensated for the use of space in their blog. Certainly libraries like the Schlesinger have no intention of depriving bloggers of any advantage, either financial or intellectual, nor do they intend to republish any material. Does the intention then to preserve for the use of scholars fall within the fair use clause? In addition to the financial interest of the blogger, does the manufacturer or owner of software that facilitates the publication of the blog on the World Wide Web have rights that need to be protected? Programs such as eblogger (www.eblogger.com),[8] LiveJournal (www.livejournal.com),[9] and others provide the software that bloggers use with ease to record their ideas and opinions. Does capturing and archiving intellectual property such as this software exacerbate the already thorny issue of rights? As technology develops and changes over time, the facility of the software may be changed, causing librarians to contemplate not only the technical difficulties of keeping sites accessible but the legal difficulties as well. There are many questions about these new publishing venues and little consensus in answering them.

The great gift of blogs is that they inspire and provoke women who may never have had an opportunity to make their thoughts, feelings, judgments, and talents public, an opportunity to contribute to the public record of our time. For too long women's voices were suppressed, or at best muffled, depriving history of half of its story and self-knowledge. However, in 2004 at least 47 percent of blogs were published by women and of those a large percentage were personal blogs, many published between the years 19 and 29[10]. At a time when women are the majority, but are shockingly underrepresented on courts that may narrow their reproductive choice, in legislatures that make decisions about health-care available to them and their families, and on editorial pages and television news that discuss minimum wage, women's contributions to the public debate will be available on blogs. While the problems appear daunting, the reward is well worth the effort to surmount them.

NOTES

1. BlueBirdEscape. http://www.bluebirdescape.com, 23 October 2007.
2. O'Sullivan, Catherine. "Diaries, On-line Diaries, and the Future Loss to Archives; or Blogs and the Blogging Bloggers Who Blog Them." *American Archivist* 68.1 (Spring/Summer 2005): 53–73.
3. Lenhart, Amanda, and Susannah Fox. "Bloggers, a portrait of the Internet's New Storytellers," http://www.pewinternet.org, 23 October 2007.
4. Perseus Blog Study. http://www.vovici.com, 23 October 2007
5. *Ms Magazine*. Weekly Feminist News, http://www.msmagazine.com/news/news.asp.com, 23 October 2007.
6. Women's e news. http://www.womensenews.org/, 23 October 2007.
7. Abortionclinicdays. http://abortionclinicdays.blogs.com, 23 October 2007.
8. Eblogger. http://www.eblogger.com, 23 October 2007.
9. Livejournal. http://www.livejournal.com, 23 October 2007.
10. Herring, S., I. Kouper, and E. Wright. "Women and Children Last, Construction of Weblogs" in "Into the Blogosphere" edited by Gurak, L., S. Antonijevic, and L. Johnson, et al. http://blog.lib.umn.edu/blogosphere/women_and_children.html, 23 October 2007.

3

Collecting Watches on the Internet

Dennis Mills

As a child I was fascinated by machines of all kinds, and, yes, I took things apart that I couldn't get back together again, angering my parents. But I especially liked cars and bicycles, and with the extraordinary ability to understand comparatively simple machines, I became quite competent at repairing bicycles, as long as the repair wasn't too complex, by the age of 11. I rarely got paid for these repairs as my friends could barely pay for the parts!

I was given a box of old watches by a relative for Christmas 1957 at ten years old, and I became determined to get some of them running, mostly as a challenge to my ability to figure out a new machine. At first they were too tiny and complex for my beginning skills, so I saved enough money from mowing lawns to buy a new Timex Self-Wind, Viscount model. It is chrome with a black dial and green luminous hands. I thought it was beautiful! I loved the colors and the fact that the dial has rings that run around the dial under the numbers. It was subtle but attractive. I still have it. It's more handsome than other Timex Self-Winds of that year. Next I got a used Bulova — "17 Jewels" is engraved on the movement — with a stainless case and black dial, for my birthday. I don't remember which birthday and I don't remember who gave me the watch but I still have the watch and I still love it.

In 1960 I bought a Westclox pocket watch, Scotty model, new, at a local drugstore, in Hickman Mills, Missouri. The drugstore was the kind rarely seen today — an old-fashioned independently owned store run by the actual owner. Back in those days all the money I could get my hands on went into watches. Those watches represented dozens of mowed lawns. (Well, not ALL the money I could get my hands on. Some of it went into bicycles. When I was twelve I bought a three speed English lightweight Raleigh.)

Then I started to figure out the tools required to repair watches. The primary tools I needed were obvious to me — a variety of very small screwdrivers and tweezers of various kinds to pick up the tiny parts. I needed heavier tweezers for manipulating the relatively big parts of pocket watches. I needed thinner and lighter ones for dealing with wrist watch parts. I needed very specialized tweezers for straightening hair springs. As a kid, decades before the Internet was invented, I had no idea where to find these tools. I bought the little screw drivers and the tweezers at the same drugstore when I had bought the watches.

But the tweezers had to be filed to fit and that's when I learned that sometimes when you can't find the exact tool you need, you can modify an existing one. I'd been wearing eyeglasses since I was eight years old and so I had some old broken glasses, frames intact but the right lens broken out. So I replaced the missing right lens with a magnifying glass I bought at the same drugstore and so created a tool to make visible the tiny watch parts. Even if I had known, as I later learned, that all these tools were available to professional watchmakers, I would still have had to invent them because I didn't have the money to buy a professional's tools.

Working with these simple tools, I began to fix some of the old watches I still had in that box. In the process I began to understand the mechanical marvel they represented and how they worked. They are made with precision that is still hard to believe, millionths of an inch in the case of the better ones and highly polished parts to reduce friction. I found the gear train and other parts of the movement to be relatively easy to understand and diagnose. The real challenge comes in trying to diagnose escapements, as that is the part of the watch that actually regulates its timekeeping. The interaction of the parts of the escapement is complex. When the escapement is running properly it is a blur of motion, and when not running defies one to figure out what is wrong. The better quality old ones, from about 1800 to the 1950s, were frequently Damascened[1] and engraved.

When I was 15 I got a job cleaning watches for a local jeweler after school and on weekends. He had more work than he could handle and I proved to him that I could do the work. In those days, people got quality watches repaired. This was before throwaway quartz watches. I had been coming to his store to buy crystals for the old watches I was repairing and I would show him the ones I had repaired and we would talk.

One day he offered me the chance to clean a watch that had been brought into him for repair and cleaning. I took it home and brought it back clean and running well. So he offered me the job and I began to learn about the more specialized tools for watch repair. I acquired some more broken watches for my collection, including another black dial Timex Viscount like the one I had purchased new — my only duplicate. Most of the broken watches were Timexes that people had brought in and when they discovered that it wasn't economically practical to repair them, they'd abandoned them there or traded them in on a new watch. These were the broken watches I bought. When I went to college I quit that watch cleaning job, as I didn't have time for it anymore.

The next opportunity to get more watches came when I was in the Army, in Germany. The PX had a bunch of watches that had been brought in for repairs and never claimed. I bought most of them for the cost of the repairs.

After the army, the next chance I got to acquire more watches was when a friend told me of a watchmaker who was retiring and selling watches, parts, and tools. I bought his remaining inventory. This allowed me to repair many fine watches and increase my skills.

In the 1980s and 1990s my wife Susan and I found a new way to stretch our legs on long car trips. We stopped at antique malls. I began to find a few watches that way, if they were bargains. By then I had learned enough to recognize a bargain when I saw one — most of the time. I was slowly developing a focus for my collection and I only bought watches that filled a hole in it.

Up to that point the collection did not have a clear focus. It consisted of many Swiss watches of varying quality along with a few old American pocket watches of mostly high grade quality and beautiful workmanship. The workmanship was the end result of centuries of progress by watchmakers to improve the construction, precision, parts interchangeability, accuracy, and beauty of both the movement and the case. The decoration consisted of Damascening of the plates of the movements and winding wheels, polishing of screw heads, escapement parts, and pinions. The cases were engraved with many pastoral scenes, horses, locomotives, or anything that pleased the buyer. Two or more colors of gold were sometimes used on the case for decoration. Also gold inlays on silver cases were used.

My favorites in the collection were the early twentieth century American wrist watches that had been created by the manufacturers from ladies' small 0 size pocket watch movements installed in the new strap watch cases, as those first wrist watches were named.

None of these early watches, pocket or wrist, was practical for daily wear, as they are not shockproof or waterproof. So I was limited either to wearing relatively new Swiss wrist watches, or to risk damaging irreplaceable antiques. I had a few Timexes in the collection and wore them a lot because of their ruggedness. Then came the greatest chance I had to create a coherent collection of watches, which had been mostly overlooked by other collectors: the Dollar watch which I will describe in detail later.

Until I discovered the online marketplace, my ability to collect was extremely limited to chance encounters. I couldn't really develop a focused collection in terms of either contents or boundaries because my options for finding watches were so few. I had a job, a family, and a house to maintain. Our finances were tight and there were no extra dollars for trips to exotic places to search for desired collectibles, watches or any other kind. I couldn't hire agents to search out what I coveted. I was limited by the circumstances of my life to remain a dilettante collector.

But then I discovered that the great democratizer of collections and collectibles had come into being—the Internet marketplace. Now I had as good a chance to define and work towards completion of a watch collection as any millionaire with time to wander the world at leisure looking for old watches. Now what mattered was my ability to master the new challenge of learning to search successfully, learning to discern the truth about what was being offered, learning how to bid successfully, etc. Now I could begin to define the dimensions of what I wanted to collect and be reasonably certain I could meet my goal.

EBay was my first chance to see and bid on an extremely large variety of watches of all types. Such a variety had never been available to me or to millions of other people.

Whether people were serious collectors or just wanted a cool watch, eBay was the place where they could find their wishes come true. This was the place for collectors and vendors of watches who were neither wealthy nor professional. This was a place for people to find bargains on a watch that otherwise they would never have found. Because the high priced watch sellers didn't think Dollar watches were worth collecting they weren't available in antique shops or jewelry stores. The only places Dollar watches were available were at the national watch collectors' conventions—and there you'd pay top dollar for them—along with travel and hotel and restaurant expenses. The expensive access to this limited market made Dollar watches unavailable to a person of average means. There have been and still are Dollar watch collectors but their collections end when Timexes become available. Timexes are a direct continuation of Dollar watches. But Timexes are still not considered a "collectible" category. So if you wanted to specialize in Timex collecting there was no place at all to go.

Then along came the Internet, along came eBay, and now everything was different. People who weren't professional watch sellers or collectors were just selling old watches that had been lying around for decades. They were cleaning out ancestors' attics. They were selling the unfashionable contents of grandma's jewelry box. They were buying up retiring watchmakers' surplus watches and sometimes even their parts and tools. And they were listing all of these disparate disconnected items on eBay. Early on eBay had a category that included watches but over the years the categories have changed, becoming more specific and reflecting more clearly the interests of buyers.

In the beginning of my searches on eBay, about 1997, the sellers really had no idea of what market might exist for these old watches, some of which ran but most of which didn't. They had no idea of what to ask for them either. And their ability to describe the watches was limited (and, for most of the sellers, still is) and uncertain. Non-watch collectors, non-watch aficionados, simply had no accurate descriptive language to use in describing what it was they wanted to sell. They were guessing, sometimes wildly, at what it was they were offering. And the buyers had to guess, too. There was a sort of "shaking out" period when the pickings were plum.

And just as the sellers of these old watches were novices at selling so too were the buyers novices at collecting. There were and are a lot of things to learn for the novice watch collector at eBay and its competitors, learning to detect fakes being the first thing. The number one fakes that I ran into in terms of expense were cheap Dollar watches that had had the dials repainted to include stereotypical racist figures such as Aunt Jemima or Little Black Sambo. These are offered for sale as a subset of what are known as "character watches," which were defined by the first of their kind: Mickey Mouse watches. The category of character watches came to include a vast variety of characters, from Superman to Elvis, from Cinderella to Hopalong Cassidy, from Tinkerbelle to Spirew Agnew. The sellers then touted the black character watches as original 1930s and 1940s artifacts and aimed their advertising language towards the expanding market for "black collectibles." However, no such watches had ever been produced by any watch company.[2]

When some of these watches were up for auction on eBay and had bidders, I would contact those bidders and tell them that what they were bidding on was a fake. The response I got from this was usually — nothing. No response. Sometimes I got a response saying "I don't care" or "It's none of your business" or something along those lines. I never seemed to contact anyone who appreciated it so I stopped doing it.

I contacted them because I didn't want the fakes to become known as authentic through the fact that they had been sold — and then resold as authentic. If this were to happen long enough, often enough, no one knows if they are authentic or not. The "authenticity" of the fakes gains momentum. I didn't think it was fair play. And I, as an eBay user/citizen, thought I had a responsibility to inform potential buyers of the inauthenticity of what they were bidding on. Although I assumed there was a way to notify eBay's corporate structure of the existence of these fakes, I didn't know how to find that way. But more than that, I was an expert in this particular kind of collectible and I felt a citizen's obligation to police our own neighborhood.

In addition to those selling outright fakes, there were and are the dishonest sellers who misrepresent deliberately the watch being sold, such as saying it's a self-winding watch when it's not. Or a solid gold watch when it's only gold plated. Or substituting dials ("dial" is the correct name for what many people call the "face" of the watch) that belong to a more valuable watch onto a cheaper watch and then trying to sell it as the more valuable watch. The only way to detect these crooks is by knowing really well the products they claim to be selling. And that knowledge is hard won.

And then there is the research needed to learn what those poorly pictured and inadequately described potential finds really are! For the better grade of American watches, lots of reference books exist and can be of great use if you want to collect Elgin, Waltham, Seth Thomas, Dueber-Hampden, Howard, Illinois, Rockford, South Bend or South Bend Studebaker, Stevens, United States Watch Company, Hamilton, Fasoldt, Columbus, or Ball Watch Company. Besides these bigger companies producing high quality watches in the United States since 1830 (and none of them are in business in the U.S. anymore although several of the names continue to be used on watches made elsewhere), there were any number of small companies making all grades of watches in the United States and there were a few inexpensive but not Dollar watch category manufacturers, such as New York Standard, New England Watch Company (whose output was split between Dollar watches and intermediate grade watches), and Trenton Watch Company.[3]

But I wanted to collect those rugged watches made by Timex and their ancestors and sometimes competitors: Ingersoll, Waterbury, Westclox, New Haven Clock, New England Watch, Ingraham, Ansonia Clock, and International Watch Co of New Jersey, (not IWC of Swiss origin). All of these manufacturers made Dollar watches. Some literature was available for the early Dollar watch makers. But almost nothing was available for the early Timexes.

The term "Dollar watch" came into use when, in 1892, Robert Ingersoll introduced the first watch to sell for a dollar. Robert Ingersoll had the idea to shrink a desk clock small enough to put inside a pocket watch case, and because the clocks of the era were non-jeweled and inexpensively made, he thought that shrinking one small enough to fit in a man's pocket would allow him to sell the watch for only one dollar. So he went to one of the largest makers of clocks in the country — Waterbury Clock Company of Waterbury, Connecticut — and persuaded them to start manufacturing those first large sized pocket watches. They were a huge success.[4] They were crude, but they gave the average working person a chance to own a watch that was tough compared to the cheapest, or for that matter, most expensive watches made by the Americans or the Swiss. Drop one of those and it broke the balance staff and quit. Drop the Ingersoll and the balance probably would survive and the watch would keep right on going.

So I began looking for those watches on eBay and finding them for very reasonable prices and not too much bidding competition. I was able to create a nearly complete collection of those Timex ancestors, in a few years of buying and repairing. I began to find the substantial differences between the quality of watches produced by the various manufacturers. I learned that watches made by Ingraham and New Haven Clock Company were the best two companies because they produced the most accurately engineered and well made watches. Westclox made both very good quality watches and some pretty junky watches.

Westclox also lasted the longest as a company, producing watches in the United States from 1899 to 1990. Some smaller manufacturers of Dollar watches, such as the International Watch Company of New Jersey, produced watches every bit as bad as Ingersoll's which, true, didn't break when dropped, but which were not dependable and accurate. The Dollar watches produced by the New England Watch Company, while comparable in price to its competitors, were not as durable or rugged as any of them. Ansonia Clock Company made Dollar watches but they are not common and are hard to find. But the examples that I have of Ansonias seem to be of excellent quality. Of course, as with all of the Dollar watches I've collected, I took apart the Ansonias and cleaned, oiled, and adjusted them.

I learned that Ingersoll watches made by the Waterbury Clock Company from 1892 all the way through to and after World War II (until the old Ingersoll movements were all used up and entirely replaced by the new Timex movements) were very inaccurately made. When I acquired them, they required many careful adjustments, polishing of pivots, and demagnetization of the steel parts. They had required that ever since their manufacture. Even after all that, they still weren't very satisfactorily running watches. Each one took a tremendous amount of time for me to repair. There had been complaints when these watches were new about the poor quality but they came with a one year guarantee and the company stood by that and lost a lot of money correcting these watches. This left Ingersoll, in spite of the fact that they had sold millions and millions of watches, in financial straits by the time of World War II. It was government contracts for fuses for bombs that saved them financially. The thing that finally solved their financial problem was the purchase of the company during World War II by a consortium that came to be known as U.S. Time Corporation. This company became Timex.

For a while there was a Timex forum that I found when I was buying Timexes on eBay. Another buyer told me of the existence of this forum and I was excited at the thought of being in contact with other collectors of Timex. The forum was an extension of some individual's website. I learned a lot more about Timexes from the participants—and I told what I knew. Trading knowledge and comparing "finds" was fun. We told each other what we were looking for and sometimes a member would pass on information about a sought after Timex that was available, if not on eBay somewhere else on the Internet. One day it stopped taking new posts and it has never returned to active status. The old posts are still there, still accessible, and still useful to a novice.[5]

Although I'm still looking for some of those rare early Dollar watches (I have holes in my collection and I have the obsessive nature that craves to be a completist), the emphasis of my collecting changed to finding early Timexes. That was challenging. I didn't know what they looked like, and the sellers rarely knew what they were selling. I was fortunate to find Timex repair manuals on eBay with pictures for some of the 1959 to 1970 models and also to find on eBay magazine ads for the 51, 53 and 55 years with partial lists of models made. I found these manuals and ads in my early searching by putting "Timex" into the eBay search engine. I set up my search to eliminate modern Timexes in order to get the number of watches and other things relating to Timex down to a reasonable number. Before refining my search, the greatest number of hits on a Timex search was for quartz, recently made, or new models. These models I excluded from my search because I wasn't interested in them. I was looking for early Timexes. You have to make some sense out of a collection, establish some boundaries. If I had chosen to try to collect all the models of modern quartz Timexes, I would have had to build an immense museum. We're talking here about millions and millions of models. Well, maybe only thousands and thousands.

Beyond the information I could glean from the magazine ads for Timex watches and the service manuals, I had to deduce the rest on my own. I figured out that there are at least two ways to identify the year when a Timex was made. Between 1953 and 1962, a date code is stamped either into the metal on the back of the watch or ink stamped on the inside of the back of the watch. The date stamp is not straightforward at all. The date stamp will be something like this: 7F35. The year is the transposition of the last two numbers. How did I figure this out? Brain power! I knew "35" couldn't be the year because Timex wasn't making watches in 1935. After much observation of old Timex watches, I broke the code. But I'm keeping that a secret — beyond what I have just written about how to tell the year. Being able to identify what you've collected is important. You have to know what you've got.

It wasn't until 1959 that Timex published pictures of the various models and explained how to decode the information about the watch. They continued to publish that critical information through 1970. After that they only tell you how to repair the various movements that were in production. They do not tell you how to identify the watch you've got via the medium of pictures. They still tell you how to decode the code on the dial of the watch. If you see a Timex on eBay manufactured after 1970 and you want to know what it is, the only way to do that is to ask the seller to get a powerful loupe and read and send you the numbers at the bottom of the dial. And that assumes that the code is legible. Sometimes they would put the watch together and part of the watch case overlapped the numbers and you can't read the code unless you take the watch apart.

Prior to 1959 the only way to identify a Timex is if you find pictures of it in old magazine advertisements that show you what it looks like and tell you the name of the model. If you have the year of the magazine you know the year of the watch. However, not all Timex watches were ever in ads.

For instance, I have a rectangular 1952 Timex with a gold filled case and I have no idea what model it is. I probably never will find out what it is. It's also an oddity because it has "06T25" stamped on the back and that translates to a 1952 — but 1952s don't normally have a code stamp. It is a mystery.

The coding system that Timex came up with in 1962 for the 1963 models is explained in the manuals, starting with the Timex Parts Catalogue #10. The new system is tremendously more complicated and it completely identifies the watch from numbers printed very small at the bottom of the dial, on either side of the number or marker for "6 o'clock." You need to wear a ten power loupe to read them. The number printed on the bottom of one of my watches is 65177265. This translates as follows: "65" is a Timex 21 manual wind. The third digit, the "1," denotes the color of the bezel. And because it is a number "1" we know that it is a chrome plated bezel. Generally speaking, odd numbers are chrome plated and even numbers are gold plated. And the fourth digit denotes sweep or non-sweep second hands with plain dial or Radiolite dial. The "7" here denotes a sweep second hand with a Radiolite dial. The fifth and sixth digits denote the movement number. The "72" in the fifth and sixth places tells us that the movement code is "72" which is a 21 jewel manual wind Timex. The seventh and eighth digits are the last two digits of the year of manufacture; in this case "65" is 1965. This system continued on at least until the end of mechanical watch production in the 1980s.

From what I've written above it might seem that there is no watch in the category of early Timexes that I can't identify. But that wouldn't be true.

I could continue this by describing in great (and loving) detail each of my 370 Timex watches. I could provide pictures of each of them — front, close-up of front to reveal tiny details on the dial, back, inside both close-up and far. I could even take them apart and photograph each of the components. But somehow I have figured out that my dear readers don't really want an encyclopedia of my Timex watch collection. I can't imagine why they don't — but I have been assured that they don't.

So, after eleven years (starting in 1997) collecting these early Timexes on eBay, I now have what I believe to be an almost complete collection of mostly men's mechanical models made from 1950 to 1970, in good running order. Approximately 370 watches in total.[6] I know there are some rare hard-to-get ones missing. I don't lose sleep over their absence, but I do keep looking for them.

Notes

1. Damascened is a form of decoration on metal that was developed in Damascus, Syria, as a by-product of creating a superior sword. The more intricate the pattern, the better the sword is considered to be. They began using the process in the eighteenth century using engraving tools to create a similar pattern on the brass or nickel of watch movements. It became more elaborate and more decorative as the skills of the engravers improved. It isn't done to any significant degree anymore, even on the best watches, except as a special request. Now it is done on the metal parts of guns. Engraving and damascening are done by the same

people but they aren't the same thing. Damascening is very shallow while engraving creates grooves.

2. Fakes and reproductions of black memorabilia are rampant and the warnings about them are included in some reference and scholarly materials about black collectibles. For one example of this, see Larry Vincent Buster, "Spotting Fakes and Reproductions," *The Art and History of Black Memorabilia* (New York: Clarkson Potter, 2000), 60–61.

3. See Roy Ehrhardt and William "Bill" Meggers, *American Pocket Watches: Identification and Price Guide: Beginning to End—1830–1990* (Kansas City, Mo.: Heart of America, 1987). I found this useful guide for identifying American Pocket Watches in the gift store at The Time Museum located in Rockford, Illinois in the Best Western Clock Tower Resort and Conference Center. "The Time Museum, an international collection of time-measuring devices, was open to the public for almost 30 years. It was closed in March, 1999." After three years of the collection being on exhibit at the Museum of Science and Industry in Chicago, the collection was sold by Sotheby's Clock and Watch department. See the Time Museum website, http://www.timemuseum.com/ (accessed February 25, 2008). The Ehrhardt and Meggers book is out of print although a few copies are available on amazon.com starting at $149.00. I paid $15 for it new.

4. The story of the early manufacture of these Rob't H. Ingersoll and Brothers dollar watches is told in much greater detail than I have room for here in *Timex: A Company and its Community 1854–1998*, (N.p.: Timex, 1998). This book is useful for company history but no help for identifying watches.

5. Vintage Timex Watch Forum, http://www.network54.com/Forum/102266/, accessed February 26, 2008.

6. Besides these 370 men's mechanical Timex watches, I have collected about one hundred Timex women's watches from the same period. Long before I met my wife, those were the watches she was buying for herself. But she didn't keep them once they stopped working. Now I find them on eBay, repair them, put a custom colored dial on them to match her outfits, and present them to her, one at a time, on special occasions such as birthdays, Valentine's Day, anniversaries, and the publication of a new book. Although my son and his wife only like quartz watches, I do give Timex mechanical watches as gifts to lots of different people: my beloved granddaughters Jasmine and Sarah Cornillon, my young cousin Rachel Wenzel, my dear young friend in Nogales, Susannah Armenta, my foster son Patrick Hinkebein and his lovely wife Michelle, my mother, my mother-in-law, my good friend and St. Louis attorney Gary Krautmann who has saved me from endless parking tickets, my dear Tucson friend Dr. Alan Goldberg, Esq., my life-saving doctor John Polacheck, and most recently to the rising young star, winner of the first season of America's Got Talent, the then-twelve year old Bianca Ryan. I gave her a 1969 lady's Timex color-flix when my wife and I met her at the first concert venue in Phoenix, Arizona, on her first concert tour, the summer of 2007.

Timex color-flix have a three colored dial divided into pie shaped sections. And instead of a second hand, they have a translucent seconds disk divided also into three different colored pie sections. As this seconds disk rotates it makes for a continuously changing combination of colors on the dial. They have black minute and hour hands for the reading of time and silver cases. Bianca, now fourteen, emailed me recently to tell me she had taken her watch to school to show her friends because she thinks it's so cool. Naturally, I am thrilled. If you aren't already familiar with the voice of this prodigy, check out her videos on YouTube.

4

Collecting Eyewear on eBay

JEFFREY KESSLER

I think it was thirty-five years ago when I bought a pair of gold-rimmed, wire glasses. I didn't need glasses at the time. I could see just fine, but I wanted a theatrical prop to make me look wise when I did my mind-reading act. They were wonderfully comfortable to wear and not expensive at the time, (thirty-five dollars as I remember) very light, with rotating nose-pads that fit wherever placed. Flexible earpieces curved behind my ears and gripped the glasses to my face.

So, looking through the clear glass, into the eyes of a woman who thought the Queen of Hearts was freely chosen and existed only in her mind, but that I decided on hours before in my dressing-room and revealed to her before the audience in a mysterious way, I looked very wise and the woman was stunned.

I was living in L.A. at the time, gigging at the Magic Castle, a famous private club in Hollywood for magicians and fans, and around town, doing a combination of sleight of hand and illusions and some mind reading stunts. I wasn't above a birthday party or bar mitzvah. I got the birthday boy up and made him a hero by blowing a trick and letting him catch me up but, of course, there was a double-cross. I did the cruise ships. The money was good but it was like going to prison. I got on a boat and right off the dock I was homesick. The ships were beautiful, the food never ending, and we glided over a serene and silent ocean, under thousands of stars, to glorious dawns. But after my first performance all the passengers knew who I was and I had no peace. They'd come to me in the dining room and expect me to produce barnyard creatures in the middle of my meal. It was very wearying, having to be "on" all the time. So I'd do a show for the crew, down under the decks, and get to know the cooks and dishwashers and oilers and bunkermen. I met them in the mess, passing around bowls of food, and they asked me questions about where I'd been and what I'd done.

Lots of these below deck characters were freaks, with multiple earrings and tattooed to the limits of their flesh. They the passengers never saw and might not board if they did but with them I could lay back and groove till I had to go updecks and do a show.

As I went through subsequent incarnations these glasses went from one old-stuff drawer to another. The lenses broke and fell out and the frames got shoved in the back of drawers and forgotten until my youngest, thirty-four years later, dug them out and revived them for a Harry Potter look.

Then the time came when drugstore glasses didn't work for me anymore and I had to see the guy who writes prescriptions.

Those old frames were back in a dusty drawer and I pulled them out. After all these years they held their shape and I marveled at this sturdy construction, seemingly so delicate, that survived thirty-five years of trashing and neglect.

I put them on and checked myself in the mirror but, needing lenses to focus, I only got a dim idea.

Eyeglass frames are costly. Forty dollars is cheap, sixty more normal and they go a long way up from there. Here I had a beautiful pair of frames, bought thirty-five years before, that I liked and needn't spend a dime buying. It was a no brainer. I checked the Internet and found similar frames selling new for one hundred sixty dollars.

So I had a prescription made for these old frames. As soon as I put them on I was at home. Even with the lenses being glass rather than plastic, they weighed near nothing. I could twist the frames, adjusting the lenses to my eyes, and shape them to my head while the flexible ear-hooks hugged them to my face.

In the mirror I saw my great uncle Harris, a master tailor who learned his craft in the old country and wore such frames as did his sister-in-law, my grandmother. I wrote a check and thanked the technician for a wonderful job and then she informed me that if I lost them or ruined a part or needed a screw for repair or bent an ear-piece not to come to her. This made me worry. I'm not always the most careful guy. I've sat on glasses, fallen asleep while wearing them and woke with a broken hinge. I've had them vanish — as if inanimate objects sprouted legs and wondered off.

These glasses are my lifeline to see my children, the computer, the road, lunch.

So I want you to experience my dilemma. If these glasses got lost or trashed I'd be up the well-known creek.

The impulse that took me to eBay was my need to see.

I had limited experience with Internet commerce. I'd bought books from Amazon, a sweater from Joseph A. Bank, a dozen bar towels for my kitchen, and tracked down my favorite cooked cereal (Hearts of Wheat), no longer made by its big producer but still ground in a small mill in the east. So I began to scout eBay cautiously to learn its mysteries.

As a logical start I typed in "Old Glasses" and was rewarded with four thousand four hundred fifty-six (4,456) things to buy, shot glasses, stained glass windows and lampshades, soup bowls, beads, rabbits—and even some eyeglasses to be found by diligent study.

So I tried "eyeglasses" but that gave six thousand seven hundred twelve (6,712), a further burden of one thousand sixteen (1,016) items to look at.

"Antique eyeglasses" brought the hits down to one hundred eighty-one (181). "Vintage eyeglasses" upped the count to nine hundred-twelve (912).

Scanning the photos in every category I was able to home in on what I sought. Glasses similar to mine were offered singly and in lots, often with separated parts.

The craft of changing screws for eyeglasses or fitting parts together didn't daunt me. I'd trained as a watchmaker and, though I'd left that craft, I kept my tools and the magnifying optics that made tiny parts big and, after watches, glasses were a snap.

Early on I bought eyeglass lots not useful to me. The sellers didn't say they were fashioned for children and I hadn't the knowledge to ask. I guess kids grew out of them fast and needed larger frames so these come in the best, as if little used condition and wonderfully filigreed around the bezels. The ear-pieces are too short for me and the lenses too small for my face, so they are useless except for putting in my collection bowl because I don't know any child needing glasses who would want these lovely frames.

Buying these glasses in lots proved easy and not expensive. The frames on my face today, allowing me to see this computer screen, came as part of a lot of frames and ear-pieces costing eighteen dollars.

About this time I learned the proper name for what I'd been calling ear-pieces was "cable temples" in the trade, distinguished by the flexible, segmented, metal-wrapped hook that bends behind the ear.

I consider the price of eyeglass frames one of the great rip-offs of the modern market. Sixty-five dollars is typical for plastic frames made in China for probably thirty cents and they are not light, sturdy, flexible, and unlikely to fall off as mine are, nor are they gold-filled or so good looking.

While buying these lots I chanced on unexpected things. One was the pince nez, glasses unconnected to the ears but that pinch on the nose. They came to me by accident. I didn't know I was buying them. They came as incidentals in some lots I bought. They were of two kinds; one connected the lenses with a watch-spring that could be spread. Nosepieces, delicately rimmed in cork or shell, pinched the nose. Another style used a spring mechanism that needed to be pinched in front so that the nosepieces spread open. Once spread, the pince nez could be placed precisely on the nose.

By chance, one of these pince nez worked perfectly for me when I was working at the computer so I got used to wearing it when online. I was surprised by how comfortable it was and how reliably it hugged my nose. Like most of these glasses, it came with a hole in the outer, lower corner of one of the lenses, sometimes connecting to a decorative metal clasp for threading a ribbon to be worn around the neck so the glasses can hang when not needed and are protected from accidents that could knock them off.

Some, made for ladies, had delicate chains attached ending in a hairpin or hook for behind the ear. Some had the chain going into a small, metal, round box that pinned to the clothing and into which the chain could retract when tugged like a window shade.

Such glasses can be seen on old photos of Teddy and Franklin Roosevelt and in old movies, sometimes on a motherly old granny and sometimes on the villain. Considering their lightness, comfort, simplicity, and practicality, I wonder why they ever went out of style.

While noodling through the subject of every kind of eyeglasses, I found lorgnettes. These are seen in films as glasses not fitted to the nose or face, but attached to a handle and used mostly in scenes of ladies at the opera. An interesting feature of the classic, fine lorgnette is that the lenses fold against each other, the bridge-piece being a flat spring, and hook together by a decorative clasp. While these were of only passing interest to me, I chanced on a kind of folding lorgnette that had no handle but were fitted with nosepieces like a pince nez. They folded like the classic lorgnette and hung like a beautiful dollop at the end of a lorgnette chain. These chains come in varying qualities, the finest of white or yellow gold with lovely links, the upper loop going around the neck and meeting at the corners of a small, ornate triangle or jump ring, then to a single chain from which dangles the lorgnette.

A fine lorgnette chain can go on eBay for one hundred twenty-five dollars or more.

Digging around on the Net, I learned the proper term for these glasses is Oxford Lorgnette. The legend is that in the early eighteen hundreds a professor at Oxford invented this lorgnette by removing the handle and adding nosepieces. No matter how much digging I've done, I've never found the name of this professor, nor any historical verification for this persistent story.

It has been said that the beginning of any addiction is the thrill of winning. Beginner's luck has hooked many a gambler. I bid on an Oxford lorgnette and hit the jackpot for forty-five dollars the first time out.

I wasn't to learn until after other searches that a leather Oxford lorgnette case in good condition was dear to come by. But this first lorgnette came in a fine black case. I was to learn lorgnettes of this kind most often have round lenses; this pair had beautiful ovals and came with a lovely chain. These fourteen-carat white-gold glasses fold with perfect precision and the clasp holds them solid until a flick of the thumbnail snaps them into shape like a magic trick.

This was so easy. The value was so much greater then my cost. There was nothing to it. Right?

In trying to match it, I've learned some things about stalking and winning items from eBay and some of these lessons have been hard.

The first hurdle to the item is finding search words that work. In this case, "Oxford lorgnette" is nearly useless though I check it regularly just in case. "Pince nez" works part of the time, "pinch nose" in French, as does "nose pincher." Sometimes "classic glasses" works though you have to scan through lots of thumbnails and any wise seller would include "vintage" and "gold."

Once I find an item I want to watch, I save it to a file on my desktop called "NOW" and label it by the date the auction ends. By checking this file daily I easily keep track of the glasses I am interested in. EBay has a function that keeps track of bids but I started my method before I knew about this and find mine easy. Also, doing it as I do keeps the seller from knowing I am looking.

As I watch, I use the function that lets me peek into the histories of the bidders. This is very revealing. If the bidder has a history of going after this kind of item, I might expect real competition. If the buyer is just noodling around I might expect him or her to drop out (I've been fooled) and often I bump into the same buyers interested in glasses.

Clearly there is an advantage to jumping in at the last moment and getting in a winning bid before a competitor has a chance to top it. Programs are available (Squirrel and others) that bid for you at the last moment to trump the competition but I have never used one. There is also the option to enter a maximum bid that is revealed to the competition in increments. As the increment is beat, a kind of chicken game can occur.

I have proved my genius at this by winning an auction of what I knew to be worthless parts, but the seller's photo showed a nice-looking Oxford lorgnette, stuck among the trash, as if the seller didn't know its worth. Turns out he probably knew. This was my first clue that, unlike the beautiful lorgnette of my first score, some were crap. The catch didn't work. The spring was bent. The metal was cheap. It came with no chain. Money down the drain.

This and other experiences have made me wary as I've bid on and won other lorgnettes. I have seen that when a spectacular example is offered on the Net, collectors, otherwise unseen, are on it like Wall Street on a dollar and the bidding often goes beyond my reach.

My last buy was for seventeen pair of cable temples, old but unused. These old temples are better than the new ones I can get for fifty dollars a pair. As soon as I jumped in the competition emerged from the woodwork. Bidding was furious and I learned I was not alone among those who sought this kind of temple. I watched the computer at two in the morning as the bidding rose alarmingly. At the last moment I bid two hundred twenty-five dollars and won at one hundred ninety-nine including shipping. This made my cost just under twelve dollars a pair and I have a lifetime supply. (I'm wearing a pair now.)

So I continue to watch the auctions, hopefully wiser and smarter about getting what I want, lusting after a "steal," and collecting fine eyewear so I can see the world.

5

The Konnection of the Kelly Kollection

Kelly Doll Collectors and the Internet

JO ANN KELLY GRAHAM

When you are seven years old the German Black Forest is very, very dark even in the middle of the day. I had always been comfortable there; in fact, I had felt protected and comforted by the trees meeting over our heads as I traveled the German roads with my family. That day, however, was different. The dark and looming spruce trees were ominous as we drove to the orphanage. My brother, sister and I were crying because we were about to lose many of our toys. My littlest sister was too young to know what was happening, but the rest of us were heartbroken at our impending loss. For me it was the loss of a doll collection that I treasured. I would not truly realize the full impact that this day would have on me for many, many years.

My father began my doll collection when I was very young—probably three or four. Every time he went on a business trip he brought me back a doll. The small six or seven inch collector dolls so popular in the 1950s were available in airports and dime stores and other places convenient for a traveling father. When we moved to Germany in 1955 the collection grew in size and interest as he brought back dolls from the many nations in Europe and North Africa that he visited. I clearly remember running to greet him upon his return in anticipation of the next addition to my doll collection. I had dolls from other important events too, like the time I had to get stitches in my scalp after a car accident and the day of my first ballet recital. The dolls in the collection were special to me, cherished, cared for, displayed, and admired. These were not "play dolls." The play dolls were bigger baby dolls, for the most part. There were three or four of the baby dolls, and my sisters and I and our friends played with them all the time. The ones that Daddy brought back were collection dolls, and now I was about to lose all of them. Well, not ALL of them but certainly most of them.

My parents had decided to return to the United States. Germany was not a healthy climate for my sickly brother and frail youngest sister and both were often ill with pneumonia. Because their return to the U.S. was voluntary, the U.S. government would not pay to move us home as they had paid to move us to Germany. That meant a huge expense for a young couple with four children, seven years old and younger. We needed to reduce what we had to ship home. Since the furniture, dishes, sheets, and towels could not be left behind, it was decided that many of the toys could be. And the German orphans, of which there were many so soon after World War II, certainly needed all the toys my parents chose to give them.

So on this gloomy Saturday my parents loaded what seemed like all my doll collection into the trunk of our car and drove to the orphanage deep in the Black Forest. I am sure they disposed of some of my brother's and sisters' toys at the same time but I don't remember it. I only remember the heartbreak of losing my dolls. Each little doll was so precious to me, had its own personality and was wrapped in its own special memories. The smaller they were, the better, in my opinion, and I especially liked the three and four inch dolls that could fit in my pocket. I remember crying and begging to keep the dolls but to no avail.

When we reached the orphanage I jumped from the car and ran to the trunk. Still crying and begging for a reprieve for my treasures, I watched as the trunk opened. All the dolls were there in a jumbled pile. I spotted two that were special favorites—one in a yellow dress and one in a pink silk dress and large silk sunbonnet. I grabbed them quickly and begged to keep them. I am unclear about what happened next. Some days the memory is that I was told to put them back and secreted one of them in my pocket. Some days the memory is that my father finally said "you can have one only." There was no question who got to stay with me. The little pink dress girl with the long blond hair. I don't remember where she came from but she was one of the smallest and fit well into my hand and pocket. I continued to cry all the way home and I never forgot the dolls that were now gone.

Was this incident the beginning of my need for a doll collection? I don't know. Was saving the little doll with the pink dress and long blond hair a precursor to my obsession with Kelly dolls? I don't know. Whatever the psychological significance of the event, I know that I never collected dolls or much of anything else again for more than thirty years.

Like all young girls I had a Barbie doll (and actually also a Lili, Barbie's now very valuable German precursor). My mother and grandmother made clothes for Barbie and Lili for my Christmas and birthday presents. But my Barbie and Lili were passed to my younger sisters, and I did not collect dolls.

Occasionally, maybe once every few years even into adulthood, I would buy a tiny baby doll, three or four inches long, that I found by chance and bought on a whim. I especially liked the ones that came with clothes and accessories like a cradle and a blanket and bottle. It made them seem more real, and I did not have to use my less than colorful imagination to build a world for them. They were always cheap foreign plastic—"Made in China" or "Made in Japan"—but somehow they called to me and fulfilled some need. I did not play with them and usually put them in the back of a drawer only to be seen and briefly loved when I cleaned out the drawer once or twice a year or looked in the far back corner for a missing item of clothing or jewelry. It was nice to know that they could fit in my pocket or purse but I never took them anywhere. After all, I had become a highly paid, highly effective, senior level corporate executive—and such people do not play with and are not seen with dolls!

Then one day in the fall of 1994 I took my twelve year old son to a mall toy store in Plano, Texas. I remember it like it was yesterday. While he shopped for video games and books and swords, I browsed the doll aisle. There on the very bottom shelf was a bright pink box holding a little doll with long blond hair. She was four and a half inches high and came with a change of clothes and a bed and blanket and bottle and other accessories. She had a bright pink, bunny footed sleeper, and I fell in love. She was Kelly, the Baby Sister of Barbie. I had to have her and was pleased to find that the set was only about $7.00. It never occurred to me that this was the beginning of an obsession that has brought me friends through out the world and opened me to a world of knowledge I could not have imagined even existed. It was years later before it occurred to me that her first name—Kelly—was the same as my maiden name that I have used for forty-eight of the fifty-seven years of my life. Somehow this coincidence was never important and definitely *not* the reason that I loved the little doll, all her renditions, and all her friends.

I really thought that this first Kelly doll would join the other two or three little dolls in the back of the handkerchief drawer, but somehow she slowly wedged her way into my life. Several months after my first purchase, I was again at the toy store and found another Kelly doll. This one came with a bathtub and robe and towel and many other accessories. She was also only $7, and I had to have her. Was this the germinating of a completist collector? I suspect such was the case. I know that by the time I found the third Kelly doll set several months, maybe a year, later there was no question that I had to have it. I had the first two and the potty training doll would complete the set. Or so I thought!

My obsession with Kelly had not completely taken over my life—yet! I began to occasionally check the toy aisles at Wal-Mart and Target to see if there was a new doll to be found. If there were new dolls I always bought one of each but I did not make special trips or out of the way trips or otherwise hunt for the dolls. I had no idea that there was a way to learn what dolls were being issued or when they would appear or how they could be acquired through trade or purchase on the private market. I certainly never thought that there were people who specialized in selling these little plastic darlings! But the obsession was starting to creep into my soul. If these little dolls had new play sets, (i.e. a bedroom or playroom or schoolroom or playground) I bought it — after all I had to be complete.

While I was not wealthy, I was fortunate to have a very good job and to have the discretionary cash that allowed me to purchase the dolls where and when I found them without concern for overdrafts or unpaid bills. The open market dolls were and still are inexpensive ($4 to $7 each) and something that I could get my brain around in terms of "having all of it." My collection grew, and the dolls moved from the back of the drawer to a shoebox in the closet. Soon the shoebox became a small plastic crate under the bed. I seldom had time in my busy schedule as a single mother and career woman to actually play with the dolls (whatever solo adult playing with dolls is!) but I got pleasure opening the crate and looking at them and occasionally smoothing their hair and changing their clothes.

In 1998 I met, and a short six months later married, a wonderful man. Before the wedding he and my teenage son were getting along well and developing a great relationship. My son knew of my doll collection (obsession was one of his kinder terms) and was often with me when I shopped for the dolls, although he was an unwilling participant in the doll portion of the trips. As I packed the dolls for the move to the new home that we would share with my husband, my son came to talk with me. With the most serious demeanor I had seen on my teenager in a long time, my son asked, "Does Ron know about your dolls?" I said I didn't know but I didn't think so. I hadn't tried to hide them but didn't think I had discussed them with him either.

My son heaved a huge sigh of relief and said, "Oh good, I really like him and I wouldn't want him to find out before the wedding. He might change his mind." While I thought the suggestion ridiculous, I realized my son was deadly serious. He perceived my collection, then numbering about fifty dolls and three or four sets of furniture, to be an aberration, something only a crazy person would want to have and certainly not something a sane, middle-aged woman would have. My son sincerely believed my soon to be husband would view my hobby as a deal breaker. I dismissed his concerns but did not bring up my doll collection to Ron either.

Once married, my schedule became even crazier. A much longer commute, a greatly increased demand for business travel, and the addition of many more household responsibilities added to an already stressful life. But it seemed that the crazier and more stressful things became the more I had to have my dolls. I had favorite stores in cities where I traveled often on business. I knew I could usually find a recently released doll at these stores that might not yet have arrived in the stores at home. I would make excuses to slip away from my meetings and then take a quick drive, hopefully to find a new doll. I would debox the dolls in the store parking lot and hide them in my suitcase in the trunk of the rental car (thank heavens they are small) before returning to my colleagues. I always took a few dolls and several changes of doll clothing with me on business trips. At night alone in my hotel room I found changing the tiny dolls' clothing and combing their hair very soothing after a long and stressful day of catching planes and making presentations.

I worked at the time for a large, very macho lumber company. As the first and only female in upper management I was often outnumbered at meetings thirty to one by men. How my coworkers would have guffawed and teased if they had known I was playing with dolls while they watched the baseball game on TV. I suspect they would have been both puzzled and shocked. I know they would certainly have considered it evidence that I was unfit for duty! When not traveling I often planned weekend shopping trips or my commuter route home to assure that I went to stores I knew would be the first to get dolls scheduled for release.

Late in 2000 my son introduced me to eBay. I had been vaguely aware of this new economic medium but had not visited the site. Ironically, my son introduced me to eBay because of a doll. He had been driving home from college for the holidays and heard about the Pregnant Midge phenomenon. This friend of Barbie had years before married Alan. Now, Midge was expecting a baby and Mattel introduced the doll to a wide range of public reactions. Despite her permanently painted-on wedding ring, conservatives claimed Mattel was destroying the morals of little girls by exposing them at an outrageously young age to the facts of life. Midge's magnetic belly removed to reveal a tiny baby inside who could be swaddled and placed in the included crib. Without the magnetic belly, Midge returned to her svelte pre-pregnancy self. Liberals saw the move as daring and realistic and welcomed it.

Fearing a conservative backlash Wal-Mart pulled the dolls from its shelves only days before Christmas, causing a flurry of buying of all the dolls to be found anywhere. The news media made such a fuss that the dolls became high dollar collector items overnight and were selling on eBay for over $275 each (normal retail about $12). Hearing this, visions of high profit sugarplums danced in my college son's head and he showed me eBay in the hope I would underwrite his attempt to buy several for resale on eBay. I never bought a pregnant Midge, and the furor soon died down but I found that eBay sold Kelly dolls and hand made Kelly doll clothing.

With the help of eBay the Pandora's Box was opened, and Kelly claimed a large and permanent place in my life. I tentatively bought a few Kelly dolls and clothing from eBay over the next few months. Emboldened by the anonymity of the Internet, I contacted one seller with a question about her item. She was warm and friendly and after learning of my love of Kelly dolls suggested that I join KellyKlub, an Internet chat group of Kelly doll collectors. With her recommendation I was accepted into the group and quickly learned far more than I ever knew existed about these dolls.

I studied Internet sites devoted to Kelly and all her friends, sites that cataloged and identified her clothing and fashion accessories, sites featuring picture stories of imaginative Kelly adventures, and sites devoted to repainting and redressing Kelly in a wide variety of costumes and demeanors. I became online friends with many of the other collectors and several times a day I read dozens of messages posted on KellyKlub. Once in a while I also corresponded privately with other collectors. I found out that there were people who knew more about this little doll than I had dreamed even existed. I found out that my collection was by no means the complete collection I had assumed. I found out that the community of doll lovers came from all over the U.S. and all over the world, from all economic levels, ethnicities and religious persuasions, from both genders and all sexual preferences, from all ages and all marital statuses, some who are childless, some with young children, some with grown children and some with grandchildren. But regardless of whether they had small children, most of these people did not play dolls with their children; they collected and coddled and obsessed about their own dolls either alone or with their adult friends.

I decided it was time to properly organize my collection. I printed out the thirty-plus pages listing all the Kelly dolls ever issued and began to organize mine. I got them dressed back into the outfits they had been sold in, and placed them into Plano boxes. The Plano box is a flat, rectangular plastic container designed to hold any type of small parts such as fishing lures, buttons, bolts and screws or anything else that needs organizing. The Plano 3500 is made with a flexible configuration that can be set to hold a dozen Kelly dolls in twelve perfectly fitting compartments. (A non-doll friend of mine calls them caskets!) When I had more than twenty Plano boxes it became clear that something other than random placement was needed if I were to find a doll easily when I needed to reference it to answer a question from one of my Internet pals. So the dolls were reorganized and placed in order of release (manufacture) by Mattel. That is when the unthinkable became obvious fact — I did not have them all! The completist was not complete! *This* situation must be rectified and soon!

Fortunately, the Internet, through eBay and my new dolls friends, held the answers. Over the next several months I bid and won many online auctions for the dolls I needed. Harder to find dolls were often bought directly from other collectors who had extras. Some collectors directed me to doll related websites and stores where I could find what I needed. My once tentative approaches to

Internet strangers became direct and confident. I *had* to get all the dolls and the only way to do it was through these people.

That is where a whole new world of friendships opened for me. I found that KellyKlub members often had a lot in common beyond the dolls: recipes were shared, resumes were rewritten, common problems with husbands, houses, parents, children, bosses or illness were commiserated about and advice was given and received. Personalities, behavior patterns, and personal idiosyncrasies of members could be seen and traced. It was clear (and my later academic study confirmed) that true friendships grew between individuals and the group. Often members looked first to the group for help and support in time of crisis reporting miscarriage, divorce, illness, unemployment, or deaths of loved ones. The group responded with messages of support, sympathy and concern, and frequent offers of prayers. Members shared happy times, too, including pregnancies and births, graduations, new houses, new jobs, and new cars. Everyone got Happy Birthday greetings when the electronic announcement heralded the special day and was followed by dozens of personal best wishes.

At first I looked askance at this "hokieness," but when my own birthday came and I was flooded with Happy Birthday emails, I understood the warmth that could be communicated and felt through a keyboard and screen. I was sometimes shocked at the things that people discussed online and I am still much more reticent about my personal life than some of the group members. But I also know that my Internet friends provided incredible friendship and support when I became an empty nester or lost my father to cancer.

Slowly at first and then with more gusto, I contacted KellyKlub members outside the group forum. I traded, bought, and sold dolls and began to share parts of my private life with them and to learn of theirs. One day a member posted that she had a limited supply of a very hard to find doll and would be willing to sell them at cost directly to members. I quickly responded and, reaching agreement on cost and postage, I electronically transferred the money to her through PayPal. By using PayPal my address was passed to her, but I had no idea where she lived and didn't really care. When the doll arrived only a few days later I was shocked to see she lived in another Dallas suburb not more than twenty miles from me. Sending her a thank you email I mentioned our proximity and we slowly discovered we had a lot in common. Several weeks later when we had come to know each other better I invited her to come to my home to see my Kelly collection which was by now well over 400 dolls strong and carefully organized in Plano boxes. To my happy surprise she agreed and came the next Saturday afternoon. After several hours of talking and looking at dolls and sharing doll stories and personal histories we discovered we are much alike. One of my closest, dearest friendships was born that day. We have spent much time together since. Our husbands enjoy each other and both enjoy car racing. We have even vacationed together. All because of a little doll and the Internet connection it brought us.

In January 2003 I decided to stop working. At only fifty-two I was really not retiring but I was no longer going to work in a highly demanding executive job. My husband and I agreed that I would resign and I decided I would like to go back to school to pursue graduate work. I also began to travel more and to spend more time on the Internet investigating Kelly and her friends who had become my friends.

As I began to enjoy these friendships I was curious to see what other members were like in person. My travel gave me the perfect opportunity. As I went to different areas of the country visiting family members, I asked my online friends in the area if they would like to meet for lunch or dinner as our schedules permitted. Other online friends contacted me to tell me they were coming to my area and would like to meet me. It was a new idea for these long time friends to actually meet in person, to actually hear a voice when they had only seen words, and most of all to attach a face to the personality. I have met many people I like very much, some who have become even better friends and others I would just as soon never see again. But each rendezvous gave me insight into why and how these women loved their little dolls. I learned how they played with their dolls, displayed their dolls and why. I learned that I was very unusual among doll collectors in that I primarily concentrated on just Kelly dolls with only very small, partial collections of other dolls. Most unusual was the fact that I had no interest in collecting Barbie dolls.

I quickly knew why—there was no possible way that I could ever, ever, ever have a complete Barbie collection. There have been tens or hundreds of thousands of different types of Barbie dolls released since her arrival in America in 1958. I could not possibly find, afford or store all the dolls in such a collection. But a complete Kelly collection was obtainable and I was determined to get one and to keep it complete.

My Kelly collection (or more properly my Kelly Kollection since all k or c sounds become K to KellyKlub people) now numbers over 1000 dolls. As far as I know, based on all the documentation I can find, I have all but four of the Kelly dolls issued anywhere in the world. As the owner of one of the best collections anywhere I have a great responsibility to my friends in the Kelly world and have become a reference of sorts for many. Among those 1000 dolls are about 200 that are considered One of a Kind (OOAK). These dolls were acquired in swaps organized over the Internet, purchased on eBay, at doll shows or at conventions, ordered from doll craftspeople throughout the world and received as gifts. Each is unique and is a doll that has had its face repainted or its hair restyled or its clothing replaced or any combination of the above. And this OOAK collection is unique in that the vast majority of it was obtained via the Internet. Long discussions take place fine-tuning the doll, discussing options and pricing, and making decisions regarding the details of the doll, but all these discussions are through email with people whose voices I have never heard.

Following my "retirement" I returned to college to seek a graduate degree in Cultural Anthropology. As I progressed in my studies, I needed to select a specific topic that would be my area of study, specialization, and expertise. For many cultural anthropologists this is a group of native peoples living in a distant place in primitive conditions. But I have never been a "mud and bugs" kind of person, don't like camping and find no romance in outdoor toilets and gritty meals. Not only did my personal responsibilities prohibit a yearlong study stint in a distant location but I also had absolutely no desire to spend that time with "mud and bugs." Furthermore, since I was not pursuing this degree to progress my career I wanted to choose a topic that was enjoyable and interesting to me.

Discussing this quandary over lunch with a close Kelly doll friend I had met on the Internet, my topic took shape. Why not investigate and document the culture of the Kelly doll collectors on the Internet and how the Internet has drawn together diverse and dispersed individuals who would never have met just a few years ago. The Internet was certainly a burgeoning area of anthropological study, and I certainly had a head start on my research. It was a great idea! I received professorial approval and set to work.

Gathering more detailed and consistent data from my friends was tricky. I had gained their trust and friendship through years of effort and was well known in the internet community of Kelly doll collectors. I didn't want to risk the friendships I had made. Most of all I wanted to make sure everyone knew that I was not doing this just to be a gossip or spread private information about them. But after explaining what I was up to and promising anonymity and confidentiality (and prizes), most of the active members of the internet group (several dozen) responded to my detailed surveys. The information I gathered provided more insight into the world of these electronically connected Kelly doll collectors, why they collected these little dolls, and what the dolls added to the lives of their devotees.

The group members represented a wide range of ages (twelve to seventy-seven), incomes ($15,000 per year to over $300,000), races, occupations, and creeds. They came from most states in the United States and several foreign countries. Of course, location is not an issue on the Internet, when my next door neighbor is as close as a friend in Australia. Although 95 percent of them are women there are several men in the group and a few of them are heterosexual. All these varied people in various places electronically came together every day to discuss their doll collections and their lives.

While gathering demographic data was interesting, it wasn't too surprising since I knew these people and their dolls well. What really gave me insight into my friends' motivations were their reasons for participating in the Kelly doll groups. Their reasons were often the same as mine — stress relief. I found that although they might not tell me this in person or admit it to our friends in the chat group many of my friends found, like I did, solace, relaxation, and an escape from day to day problems and stress. One friend said "I think dolly groups help us get through the tough times, we connect at a childhood level, and it's simple, easy, relieves stress and is fun! It is like we are in our own world where nobody will laugh at us for collecting dolls." Another said "It is a way of relaxing and enjoying life with some of my friends. I find friendship among the members there and joy that I am not alone. This Kelly Klub group has opened my world to others just as obsessed as I am about collecting. My friends, family and coworkers don't get it, but my Klub members do" (Graham, unpublished thesis).

Probably one of the most poignant comments came from a heterosexual male friend who ended his career in law enforcement due to a disabling injury. He said the following:

> As a boy and young man, playing with dolls in the 1960s and 70s would have labeled me as mentally unbalanced. Therefore, I was forced to keep my inclinations very much a secret. I now belong to an online group called "Men with Dolls" where I can freely discuss my hobbies with others of like mind in relative safety. This form of camaraderie would not exist were it not for online doll forums. Granted that my Kelly dolls are a bit outside the norm but they are not only accepted, but appreciated by many other men. When I posted my first Kelly tales several other gents posted pictures of their own Kellys that they had been keeping secretly among their toy soldiers and overly endowed female dolls. I was very surprised to find how many fellows cared for the wee tykes. As an adult woman the stigma to you is not so great, but for a boy or young adult male the consequences of enjoying this sort of hobby can be catastrophic. I am not so alone as I once thought [Graham, unpublished thesis].

I had known on a gut level that the groups were important to me, but now I began to think about how and why, to think about not only how I could find rare dolls or learn about the latest product from Mattel, but also why I checked my emails so many times during the day. These people, many of whom I had never met in person or even seen a picture of, had become my dear friends and part of my life. While I was much more restrained than some in sharing my personal frustrations and problems, I often commiserated with them regarding theirs or offered advice and solutions that had worked for me. As my birthday rolled around I felt the real warmth of the online wishes, instead of being blasé. As my son graduated from college and went off to seek his fortune, I received advice and sympathy from other empty nesters. And always there was help finding another doll that they, or I, needed to complete the collection. But I would not know what great friends they were until tragedy touched me. Then my friends rose in support and prayer and love and helped me through a very, very hard time.

In October 2005 I visited my parents in Colorado as I did two or three times every year. They were quite elderly and well into their eighties but things seemed to be going well and their health seemed to be better than that of most their age. I made plans to visit again in the spring when the weather was warm enough for my thin Texas blood. After a week's visit I cried, as always, when I left for the airport. I always worried I would not see them alive again and tried to sear their image waving goodbye into my brain.

But I was back in Colorado sooner than expected. In late December my brother, who lives with his family only a block from my parents, called to say that Daddy was not feeling well. This was not something that my mother had shared with me during our twice weekly phone calls. She had not wanted to worry me. By Christmas my father was "a zombie" and could not drive. He seldom left his bedroom and refused to see a doctor. In early January my mother and brother made two appointments for Daddy to go to the doctor but he would not go, saying that his back or ribs hurt. When he finally went to the doctor and tests were performed there appeared to be no diagnosis matching his symptoms and the doctor was lackadaisical at best in his attitude. My brother called again and said, "I need you to come and handle this. Maybe someone will listen to you." As the oldest child I have always been the most assertive sibling and have never been intimidated by doctors or their worlds. Having been once married to a doctor I understand the "lingo" and know how to maneuver through the medical system. More than that, for some mysterious reason my father would not argue with me when I told him what needed to be done, although he argued with everyone else and refused their requests or direction. Of course, I was on the next plane to Denver and my travel dolls were safely tucked into my suitcase—just in case.

In less than a week I received the news from the doctor that we had neither expected nor wanted. Daddy had liver cancer and only a few months to live. The task fell to me to tell my father and my siblings and my son. As they and my world fell apart, I had to be strong and a little doll helped me to do it. The next five months were a blur as I shuttled repeatedly between Colorado and Texas staying longer and longer each time, coordinated visits from widely dispersed family members, arranged hospice care and medical care, and served as a calm place in the storm for many.

What helped me be the rock that so many in the family needed? Well, probably a lot of things but two very big helps were my dolls and my online doll friends. Driving instead of flying I could bring a few more dolls with me. I set up a shelf in my parent's guest room where a few dolls were displayed and often at night when my parents were finally sleeping, I would re-dress and hold the dolls.

Of course, I shared the crisis with my online friends and they all offered support and prayers and concern and suggestions and caring—caring that was very real, and that I felt in every message. While not discussing it in the public forums, I often poured out my frustrations with other family members and my situation in individual emails to my collector friends. Their emails of support and sympathy in return truly helped me make it through this difficult time. I continued to bid on eBay items and actually won a very rare doll and wardrobe set that was sent to me in Colorado.

My father did better than expected despite refusing all treatment for his disease. I hoped that I would be able to attend the annual convention of Kelly doll collectors scheduled for the third week in May. Many weeks earlier on a brief trip home to Texas, I had rushed to finish my convention gifts and dolls and given them to my nearby doll friend to take to the convention on my behalf. If I could get away from Colorado for just a few days I could go to the convention. My sister agreed to come and relieve me so that I could go home and then to Cincinnati for the gathering. But as the time grew close, Daddy suddenly failed significantly and it became clear I needed to skip the convention for more important priorities. I was the one doing the cooking and cleaning and nursing and managing medications. I had to be there and there was no one else who was emotionally prepared to do it.

When I announced my decision at the eleventh hour, my Kelly friends sprang into action with support and love to help me participate in the convention vicariously via the Internet. My gifts were there and my dues were paid so my place at the table was saved. Every gift I would have received in person, and some special ones I would not have had otherwise, were put aside to be brought home by my friend. The auction brochure was emailed to me and I could bid on special items from afar. I received convention updates several times daily complete with photos of all the activities and gifts I had garnered from the other conventioneers. Friends printed banners saying "We Miss You Jo Ann" and held them in group photos that were promptly sent to me in emails. I received several phones calls daily with well wishes and updates.

As my father slipped into unconsciousness, my husband could not be there, my son could not be there, most of my siblings were not there, and my mother was lost in her own grief. But my Kelly collector friends were with me, offering support and prayers and love throughout the days and nights. My frequent visits to the computer buoyed me up with strength to continue to support those around me. And several times a day I snuck into my room and spent a few stolen minutes with my dolls. Just holding them or looking at them for a few moments calmed me. Enjoying their beauty for a few minutes was a little nugget of joy in the midst of all the sorrow.

The day after the convention was a travel day. Tough on everyone. My supporters were incommunicado on airplanes. That evening I received a call from my Texas friend telling me that she was home safely. It was a welcome break from caring for others. She had all my gifts waiting for my return. We both knew that my return would not be before my father's funeral. As she recounted the last details of the convention my mother approached and said simply, "I think he is gone." The phone call was over.

There is no sufficient way to thank my Kelly friends for their love and support. There is no sufficient way to explain how this little doll helped me through such a very hard time. I will never be able to thank my Kelly friends for the joy and caring and love they bring me daily. Oh, I might send them a doll that they are missing or know the stock number of a rare doll when they need it most, but I will never repay the love and concern and sympathy and prayers that these online collectors shared with me and that enveloped me and held me up in this hard time.

Today I still collect Kelly dolls. I still have one of the best collections in the world. Many of my rarer dolls were photographed and included in a book documenting all the dolls. My collection of Kelly doll clothes has recently been photographed for use in another book about Kelly dolls. I still talk to most of my friends every day via email rather than in person. I still am fortunate enough to have Kelly doll collector friends who mean more to me and have done more for me than I can ever repay. They brought me through my adult German Black Forest, and I have emerged into the sunshine with my doll collection intact and my head on straight, thanks to their love and support and knowledge.

6

Gambler's Rush: All That Glitters, Etc.

JULIA PENELOPE

Some may disapprove my sweeping generalization but I think everyone collects something, at some point in our lives. It begins when we discover what our opposable thumbs can do. Bipedalism, too, figures in our penchant for collecting because it frees our hands, with those thumbs, for picking up strange shiny objects and carrying them, also freeing our mouths to repeat juicy tidbits of gossip (which some of us also collect). Walking on our hind legs, rather than all fours, makes it harder to see what's on the ground, but aren't there always trade-offs?[1]

The decorative objects archaeologists continue to find in the former dwellings of our early ancestors testify to how deeply this urge to gather and collect pretty things is embedded in our species. Collecting, I believe, begins in childhood with simple curiosity or delight, or both. *What* is *this?* All of us begin curious, and the most fortunate never lose that quality. As we grow we become increasingly mobile and our horizons broaden. We gather odd objects and treasured mementos in shoeboxes, cigar boxes, glass jars, plastic bags (aren't zipper bags nifty?), whatever comes to hand. There's also a delicate balance between heft and desirability. Sometimes there's simply no way to carry off a find. I've left several beautiful rocks in the field because they required earth-moving equipment. The divide between those who collect and those who don't comes when some decide they prefer to travel lightly; others of us just run out of space.

Among the first things I remember collecting were a fossil herbivore's tooth, many, many shards of colored glass, odd marbles, a kitten, three turtles, numerous four-leaf clovers, peacock feathers, alligator teeth, porcupine quills, seashells, and a large chunk of shiny green rock I found under the magnolia in our Florida back yard. I erroneously identified it as malachite because it had the same swirling, layered whorls described in my rocks and minerals book. (I found out recently that it was probably glass created by the meteorite that fell to Earth 65 million years ago near what is now the Yucatán peninsula.) Beautiful things, small creatures, detritus that might be made into other things, all these fascinated me. And still do.

Pockets, too, although a more recent development, also help. My pockets are always full of the dirt from objects I've stashed for later examination. I started wearing men's pants at an early age because the pockets are larger and deeper than the tiny, shallow things stitched into women's clothing. (Still, designers just don't get it, as though women don't have interesting things we want to carry home.)

I admit it: I'm a primate. Whatever glitters, including pyrite (fool's gold), attracts my wandering eyes. I'm particularly fond of the bizarre, the absolutely weird. My museum of strangeness—my "cabinet of curiosities"[2]—is my coffee table because I can see every item, and so can my friends: the fish made from a curving ram's horn by the addition of a carved wooden head and tail; the metal sculpture of a long-stemmed flower with a feeding hummingbird hovering above a beautiful chunk of red lace agate; the clay box with a fashioned trilobite for a lid; a T-shaped opalescent bivalve; a round thing I bought at an estate sale that looks like a fossilized cantaloupe. Wonderful things, some still-unidentified things.

Space, as well, enters into the equation: most of us have just so much space we can devote to our avocation, whether it's stamps, coins, matchbooks, swizzle sticks, shot glasses, microcrystals, ammonites, fossils of the Lower or Upper Cretaceous; dolls, porcelain figures—only porcelain dogs, only greyhounds, antique roses, heirloom vegetables—only heirloom tomatoes; any bottles, only whiskey bottles; art glass—only Murano, or Fenton, or amethyst glass, or cut glass; art pottery—only Roseville or Frankoma or Van Briggle or Gonder. For example, I have a friend who collects outstanding recipes even though he hasn't cooked for himself (or anyone else) since the 1970s. He doesn't hesitate to seek out a restaurant cook whose pecan or lemon chess pie is the best he's tasted, or offer to trade an equally valuable recipe should the cook balk.

Class, a taboo subject in U.S. culture, is likely the most significant factor because our financial situation dictates what we can afford to collect and how much space we can devote to our acquisitive habit. Like most of the choices we make during the course of our lifetime, what we can "choose" to collect is severely limited by our economic class—our financial resources.

Theoretically, people collect what they can afford to collect; the wealthy don't care what something costs if they want to own it. But, of course, their collecting isn't indiscriminate either and, although they might conceivably collect whatever appeals to their fancy, they, too, make decisions concerning their collecting interests. Although old wealth and new wealth, the nouveau riche, may collect the same things—artwork, classic cars, statuary—the nouveau riche know that they have something to prove because they weren't born into old money.

Those who inherit old money also inherit the collections amassed by antecedent generations and so have a leg up, as it were. To some extent the inheritors build on what their ancestors entrust to them. They may also explore new collecting avenues to satisfy their own sensibilities. The newly privileged, in contrast, must begin from "scratch." Whatever their differences, however, both old and new wealth can afford what humbler collectors cannot: they can retain professional advisors with the "right" connections who are knowledgeable about which collectibles, artists, or cultural objects will be sound, appreciating investments.[3] While I would be among the last to assert that the rich derive less aesthetic pleasure from their collections, their purpose is more financial than aesthetic, and their spiritual satisfaction is more often the knowledge that they own something no one else can.

Perhaps the most well-known collectibles for the wealthy are works of art, Hollywood memorabilia, and the possessions of the rich and famous, all of which can sell for millions of dollars at auction. For example, when Jacqueline Onassis's estate was auctioned off, the winning bids far exceeded the presale estimates of value.[4] Her costume jewelry set a record for exceeding a presale estimate of $39,000, selling for $2.5 million, and JFK's MacGregor wood golf clubs, valued at between $700.00 and $900.00, sold for $772,500.00.[5] The 40-carat diamond ring given to Jackie by Aristotle Onassis was bought by Heinz CEO Anthony J. F. O'Reilly for $2.6 million. Imagine having that kind of spare change. (Better yet, imagine how many people that much money could feed.) The name, a specific identity, determines value.

Among the best-known collectibles are the elaborately jeweled eggs made by Fabergé, brought to prominence in 1885 when Czar Alexander III ordered the first imperial Easter egg. The czar was so taken with that first Easter egg that he ordered an Easter egg every year thereafter. His successor, Nicholas II, ordered two Fabergé eggs every Easter between 1895 and 1916, giving one to his wife and one to his mother.[6] There are currently four varieties of jeweled eggs being made by Fabergé (enamel, crystal, porcelain, and musical). Contemporary musical eggs bring the highest prices (from $3,000.00 to $3,500.00), followed by the enamel eggs, which start at only $450.00 but can cost as much as $3,000.00.[7] I've seen Fabergé egg collections at estate sales but they're considerably beyond my budget.

Stamps and coins for the most part are inexpensive enough that many collectors start when they're children, but when they reach the stage of trying to gather a complete collection that includes rare coins or stamps, the investment quickly escalates. In November 2007, for example, an anonymous collector paid more than $30 million for about 1,000 prototype coins, some made in the 1700s, that were never circulated by the U.S. mint, a sum well beyond the finances of most collectors.[8] The coins span centuries, from 1792 to 1942, and the seller spent 10 years gathering them.[9]

Prototypes, like antiquities and art, introduce yet another important factor in collecting — time. It takes time, sometimes hundreds or thousands of years, for objects to acquire their greatest value, and only the very rich can hold onto such things for years. Eventually the most valuable coin and stamp collections become estate items and are passed from one generation to the next or bequeathed to a museum or other earnest institution.

This is not to say that the things collected by those of less means cannot acquire value. Time is also a factor with bubblegum cards and matchbook covers. Because they cost little or nothing and are easily stored, preservation often gives such collections the time required to increase their value.

Other aspects of our environment are also significant. For many of us, it's a parent's interest or enthusiasm that stimulates us to begin collecting as children. I was a sickly only child, and spent more time at home in bed than I did in school. To occupy my mind and my hands while she was at work, my mother started me collecting stamps, dog figurines, and coins, all things I could manage in bed. (She collected Chinese cloisonné, Mercury Head dimes, and, late in her life, roses.)

There are collectors, and there are ... avid collectors. I am an avid collector. I've collected rocks and fossils, for example, since I was nine, and now have four tons in milk crates stacked in my back yard. I wish I could display all of them, but flat surfaces are now at a premium.

While most of us continue collecting into our adult years, we often begin to specialize, to define more narrowly what we can afford and what we're willing to carry home. For the average collector of modest means, this is as much an economic decision as it is aesthetic or preferential, a decision based on our gradually acquired knowledge. As we learn more about the objects we collect, the parameters that define our interest shrink and become more focused.

Recently, I've indulged my lifelong fascination with glass, that amazingly flexible fusion of silica, lime, and soda. Remember those shards of colored glass I collected as a child? Now I collect whole pieces. Although I've dabbled with varieties of glass over the years—cut glass, cobalt glass, ruby glass— none of them really absorbed me. Then a few years ago a friend introduced me to a kind of art glass called controlled bubble (or *bullicante* in Italian). Among the great makers of controlled bubble objects are the glass blowers on the Venetian island of Murano, where they've been making fine glass objects for centuries. People all over the world collect Murano art glass.

I began with controlled bubble objects but became fascinated with the art of glass blowing and, for a while, broadened my interest and collected different types of art glass: opalescent and iridescent, jack-in-the-pulpit vases, satin glass, blue satin glass, black glass, and so on. Mind you, I am not indiscriminate. When I started, I had rules: no animals, no pink glass, no paperweights. Then I found two Art Deco–style iridescent pieces—a handkerchief vase and a compote—in a local antique mall; both had exquisite iridescent pink feathering. Each had the initials OBG acid-etched on the bottom.

Knowing what you have—being able to identify an object's provenance (origin) and, when possible, the artist—is what determines its value. At first, I thought that the letters OBG were the artist's initials. I searched the Web, but found only one site, Oregon Blown Glass, which makes hand-blown bongs and pipes. I doubted that the Oregon factory had produced objects so far removed from their advertised specialty, and remained ignorant until about a year later, when I bid on and won what the eBay seller described as a clear orchid vase with green feathering that was marked OBG. It was the first time one of my Web searches had found what I was looking for. I had no idea what an orchid vase was, nor did I care. Once it arrived, I found that holding it was an extraordinarily sensual experience, something I shared enthusiastically with lesbian friends. "Hold this," I urged, "doesn't it seem to warm as your hands caress it?"

Still I had no identification for OBG. Then, in May, 2003, OBG items suddenly began to show up regularly on eBay. I surmised that OBG glass was starting to come out of estate collections, although it's also possible that OBG art glass was sold on eBay all along, before I began to look for it. The sellers, with one exception, were (erroneously) identifying OBG as Oregon Blown Glass, probably because they also found the company's Web site when they tried to identify the maker. That single exception identified OBG as Ornamental Blown Glass Studio, which is still located in Lynnwood, Washington.

Now I collect only OBG art glass (okay, okay, and bullicante made by the Murano artist, Barbini) and I've broken all of my rules, especially the one about no paperweights. Ornamental Blown Glass made a lot of different types of paperweights. And some of their products are pink. In addition to the sheer pleasure OBG art glass gives me, much of the thrill has come from inferring information about the studio—I've found nothing about Ornamental Blown Glass studio in my books on the subject—on the basis of the style and chronology provided by the glass objects themselves. For example, my collection of more than 100 pieces at first spanned only the years between 1986 and 1995. For a while, I had gaps at 1988, 1994, and 1995; I've finally obtained pieces made in those years, and in 1996 as well, so OBG was productive for 10 years that I know of. OBG has made a lot of paperweights; of my collection, more than 50 are paperweights. But they've produced a variety of Art Deco–style vases with delicate feathering, something I'm also finding in their paperweights, as well as bowls, perfume bottles, starfish, and what one eBay seller identified as a "perfume burner." (I have no idea!) Most of the unusual items OBG produced are dated 1986 or 1987, which seem to have been their most creatively expansive years. I've also learned that not all OBG art glass is signed, as I'd once thought, and that first "orchid vase" I got on eBay? Beware of eBay dealers' identifications of what they're offering. That "orchid vase" is actually a perfume bottle that no longer has its original stopper.

This narrowing of focus has had consequences. I ran out of flat surfaces for display about the same time mergers in publishing began to result in the closing of reference departments. (As a freelance copy editor, I specialized in dictionaries and encyclopedias, and reference works have traditionally been the loss leaders for publishers.) The simultaneous loss of available space and freelance income pushed me to become a seller on eBay in order to generate cash flow, and what I sold also opened up flat surfaces. Shortly thereafter, on the urging of another seller, I opened a shop on Ruby Lane, a virtual mall for antiques, fine art, and collectibles (http://www.rubylane.com/shops/eyesnglas).

Because I was now selling at two venues that were very different in structure and cost, I became increasingly dissatisfied with eBay, its buyers and sellers, and its listing costs, which have continued to rise. Buyers on eBay are looking to pay as little as possible and as far below the actual market value as they can get away with. In order to do this, they "lurk," watching an item they want, until hours or minutes before the auction ends. Fortunate the seller who's the beneficiary of a last-minute feeding frenzy. More often, fewer bids mean a lower price. and a single bidder wins the item at its starting price, which can be less than the seller paid for it. I know sellers who list all their items at a starting price of 99 cents regardless of what they paid for it. Add to this the fact that eBay charges sellers at both ends of an auction: anywhere from 15 cents to $4.00 to list an item, depending on the starting bid (I usually pay 35 to 40 cents), 15 cents per photo (the first one is free), various charges for additional features such as a Gallery listing, bold-face font, listing an item with a reserve price (a percentage of the reserve price), and a percentage of the final sale price.[11] And eBay now owns PayPal, which charges sellers a percentage of sales to buyers who use the service. After eBay and PayPal have collected their fees, the seller is lucky to walk away with anything.

Ruby Lane, in contrast, is the most seller-friendly of the virtual malls. There is a one-time setup fee of $75.00 that must be paid before one can open a shop on Ruby Lane, and sellers pay 30 cents to list each item. After that, monthly fees for maintenance—$15.00 per month flat fee for up to 50 items or 30 cents per item for 50 or more items—and advertising ($20.00) are assessed. For example, on February 1, 2008, I paid a maintenance fee of $111.00 for 370 inventory items and the $20.00 advertising fee for a total cost of $131.00. During the month of January, I sold 9 items for a monthly sales total of $397.00. So I pay at least 60 cents for each item (listing plus maintenance), but I can add up to 9 photos for each item I list and Ruby Lane takes nothing from my sale price. In addition, there are various bonuses and other features I can take advantage of including one month a year when no maintenance fee is charged (a considerable savings for me considering the large inventory I have) and a monthly Featured Items maintained by Ruby Lane where I can feature any item of my choosing for free. Also, I have the option of allowing potential customers to make an offer for an item if they don't want to pay my price and I can accept, counter, or decline the offer, a feature that often enables me to make a sale—and a profit. The customer has gotten a deal and I've made a sale. Is the selling experience different on eBay and Ruby Lane? You bet!

There are two other differences between selling on eBay and selling on Ruby Lane: First, the pace is very different. Because an auction on eBay can last anywhere from 3 to 10 days, the pace can be frenetic, especially during peak periods of consumption like November and December, with only the possibility of some reward for one's efforts (see fn. 11 in this regard). Recall that I only sold 9 items on Ruby Lane in January 2008, which results in a much more leisurely pace. Second, the only time I deal with the administrators of Ruby Lane is when I pay my monthly statement. Otherwise they leave sellers pretty much alone. eBay reserves to themselves the authority to order sellers to remove auction items they don't approve of. On Ruby Lane, while there are stringent guidelines for what sellers can call antiques or collectibles, anyone—another seller, a Ruby Lane browser—can call a seller's attention to something questionable about a listed item, for example, its age or provenance, by clicking on What's This? It is then the seller's responsibility to correct the error by revising the description, remove the item altogether, or appeal the accusation.

The serendipitous decision to open a shop on Ruby Lane has broadened my scope and the wider application of a theory about collecting that I call "the gambler's rush": the surge of adrenaline; the giddy, light-headed buoyancy; the shivery nervous pretense of feigning indifference; the heart-pounding anxiety of negotiating a purchase; the heady exultation of obtaining a fine item at a bargain-basement price.

I am shameless. Other collectors, including museum curators, will claim higher motives: preservation of artifacts from lost cultures, preserving historical continuity or extinct animals; making objects available to the general public; building an estate to hand down to one's progeny; investing for the future or as a hedge against the next depression.

Oh yes, some will claim that they're only thinking of posterity. Perhaps a few will admit to the slightest pleasure in mere acquisition or sensory delight but the gambler's rush is something every archaeologist, yard-sale enthusiast, or collector of fine art recognizes. What else could the paleontologist feel when she unearths the complete skull of a new dinosaur after months (or years) of digging through hot summers if it isn't the sudden realization that she's "hit the jackpot"? Isn't the curator's combination of hope and anxiety to acquire that newly discovered Picasso drawing akin to what Joe Sixpack is feeling when he has five winning lottery numbers and is waiting for the sixth ball to drop? For the collector, every day is a lottery drawing.

I'm not only an avid, passionate collector, I'm an unashamed hedonist. The gambler's rush, I've learned, provides a great high at every point in the collecting cycle: the find, the buy, the sale, and the payment (there's delayed gratification as well). Finds can occur anywhere on any day: at a yard or estate sale, an antique mall or a thrift store, on eBay, or when I finally identify something I already have. Being able to provide information about an object's provenance is where the profit margin lies. It's how I increase its value.

There was the Swedish vase I bought for $10.99 at an antique store — the price was right and I loved it. When I got it home under a good light, I discovered the firm's logo and the maker's acid-etched signature along the outer edge. Yes! Or the art pottery aquamarine peacock wall planter I bought for $5.99 because I'd never seen anything like it. While showing it off to friends one night, the light happened to hit it just right and there, under the thick glaze, was the maker: McCoy Pottery (highly collectible art pottery). Yes! One time, I spotted a beautiful shallow bowl tucked away in an antique store. Acid-etched on the bottom was the maker: Hadelund, a famous Swedish maker of art glass in the twentieth century. Yes! Paid $16.00 for it; sold it for $65.00 (eBay). Got high again.

A lot of eBay sellers, me included, often don't know when we have something valuable. I won a beautiful art glass vase in an auction on eBay. The seller couldn't make out the acid-etched signature, but I could: it was Orrefors, the name of another famous Swedish maker of twentieth-century art glass. (*That* I've kept.)

Start to finish, there are a variety of possibilities during the collecting process that can provide the "gambler's rush":

Suddenly realizing that you can accurately identify something without looking it up;
Finding something, finally, that you've looked for, for a long time;
Cheap find #1: Being able to identify something and paying much less than what it's worth;
Cheap find #2: Buying something for almost nothing and, after bringing it home, discovering that it's valuable;
Obtaining that final piece that completes a collection;
Selling something for much more than was paid for it;
Selling something that will replace a cherished item that was broken or lost;
Selling something to be given as a gift that has been long sought after.

My favorites, I admit, are the cheap finds.

I'll settle for one high per item. My best rush comes when I can buy cheap and sell high. The best! Take my word for it. One gambler's rush came at an estate sale on a farm near Lubbock. I bought two Murano shallow bowls, one for $10.00, the other for $5.00. The one I paid $5.00 for has its small silver label, which identifies it as the work of Salviati & Co. Estimated value with that label? $125.00. And I shamelessly tried to get the dealer to give me the second bowl for $5.00, too, but he refused. Those Salviati bowls brought me more highs when I sold each of them for $65.00 (Ruby Lane). My most exciting estate-sale find was a small clay figure, a Native American woman, less than 2 inches high, with seven tiny children crawling over her. What drew me to her was her open mouth, a big round "O"; I thought she was screaming because she was burdened by so many children! At just 34 cents, the price was right (I bought three items for one dollar). When I searched the Web to identify the clay figure, I discovered that she was actually a Cochiti Pueblo Storyteller made by an artist at either the Jemez or Acoma pueblo. That's why her mouth is open and the children are climbing all over her: she's telling them a story. I sold her for $85.00 (Ruby Lane). When I asked the buyer whether she collected Pueblo storytellers, she told me that the storyteller "spoke" to her. (I didn't ask why, fearing a long narration about all of her own children.)

In my short career as a seller, I've probably had more than my share of highs. I've mentioned the McCoy peacock wall planter, which, it turns out, isn't pictured in any of the books my customer had. (She got her high, too, I hope. An undiscovered McCoy design!) There were the two Blenko glass cubes that went for $104.00 on eBay; I paid about $14.00 for each of them. A piece of my grandmother's costume jewelry sold for $56.00, and a set of Sulawesi marriage jewelry I bought at an estate sale for $8.00 sold for $78.00 (both on eBay). When I put something up for auction on eBay, I never know whether there'll be even one bidder; often there isn't. But when several bidders want something, ah! Watching the price escalate is a high!

There's a reason why I call these experiences the "gambler's rush." Like an addicted gambler, I focus on the highs, but there are risks. For every exhilarating high, there are many lows. I'm still too new to buying for resale to know with certainty which items will sell well. There are some things I've bought, like Homco porcelain figures, that I can't give away on eBay. For one thing, I'm still learning not to base a buying decision on whether it suits my taste, which is, I've learned, kind of "out there." They say never buy something you don't like, but I've found that, in order to sell, I have to take some chances.

Some of those chances have been costly. Listing on eBay costs money and it adds up fast. The first picture is free, but selling glass and pottery usually requires at least three pictures because I must show the condition of the item's base and, in addition, show any damage to it. Buyers and sellers on eBay are strangers to each other, and providing visual evidence of the condition of art glass is one way to establish credibility with other collectors. Not everyone is so scrupulous. Because selling on eBay is now so expensive, many glass sellers show only one picture and describe whatever damage or production flaws there might be.[1] Every picture after the first one costs 15 cents, so simply listing an item can cost anywhere from 95 cents to over $4.00. (The cost doubles if a seller lists an item in two categories.) Items that don't get any bidders mean money down the drain. Sometimes I'm lucky to get back my cost for an item; often I'm not lucky at all but I keep rolling the dice, looking for the next big payoff.

I've also been taken, big time. At a local auction house, there were three identical small mold-blown vases with six naked women dancing under hanging grapes. The style of the work and the kind of glass, I thought, were characteristic of one of the great makers of art glass in the twentieth century, the French artist René Lalique. Sure enough, there on the base was one of his well-known signatures, R Lalique. Talk about a rush! I was beside myself. I broke out in a cold sweat and my hands shook. Anxiously, I waited until those vases were brought up. And I paid $100.00 for the three of them. I was sure I could get hundreds of dollars for each one.

After I brought them home, I started doing my research. When I cleaned them, I had my first doubts about their authenticity: under the auction house's stickers on each was an obviously abraded spot where something had been scraped off. No one removes information from a piece of art glass because it helps to identify and authenticate the item. Artist's signatures and maker's labels—visual evidence of provenance—increase the value of an item. Further, I was unable to find a similar vase in any of my books on Lalique's work. To confirm what I was already fairly sure of, I took the vases to a local jeweler who sells art glass, including contemporary Lalique products (the firm in France is still producing his designs). After only a cursory glance, she confirmed my suspicions. They were Czechoslovakian reproductions.

Well, you might think that reproductions also have their value, and that's true: Czechoslovakia is another country well-known for its art glass. Each of these vases could, conceivably, have brought about $400.00. Unfortunately, I certainly could not sell them as genuine Lalique. Without an outlet for them, I listed them on eBay as Art Deco vases without mentioning Lalique's name, and got $10.00 each for the two I sold (they were pink) and kept the amethyst one because it does have value, and it's a reminder—now I look under the dealer's label to see what's hidden.

First I'm a collector, and I think that's true of many sellers. That's how we're drawn into selling. Perhaps we run out of space for our collection or we've decided to specialize so we make room by selling what we can live without.

I'm a collector, not a hoarder or a packrat. I've thrown out countless things I wish I'd kept, like all my lesbian trash novels from the 1950s, bought and hidden in my room while I was in high school. I tossed them in a garbage can when I moved to Los Angeles and they couldn't go with me. I decided to restrict my art glass collecting to just two makers, OBG and Barbini's exquisitely precise bullicante art glass. I am passionate about those pieces, and I derive giddy pleasures from them, not because I own them, that is merely a precondition for the real pleasure I get from looking at them, touching them, holding them, cataloging them, and rearranging them. Every new addition to those collections requires that other pieces be moved and examined for their most advantageous placement: How does it look in this light? Next to these pieces? And the collecting process continues.

At bottom, I collect because of the pleasure my collections give me. I am aware that others propose nobler, more virtuous reasons for collecting but I know that, like me, they've experienced the gambler's rush.

Oh! Did I mention that it's addictive?

NOTES

1. In 1999, the discovery of a unique hominid skull, dated to between 3.5 and 3.2 million years old, was carefully pieced together from 30 skull and tooth fragments by Meave Leakey. The discovery forced anthropologists to abandon their assumption that it was a larger brain that drove the evolution of the Homo species. Bipedalism, it is now thought, is actually responsible for the evolution of our brain, not the other way around. She named the species *Kenyanthropus platyops*, "flat-faced man of Kenya." Available online: Wikipedia, s.v., "Kenyanthropus platyops," http://en.wikipedia.org/wiki/Kenyanthropus_platyops.

2. During the sixteenth and seventeenth centuries, collectors, especially the nobility of Europe, created "cabinets of curiosities" in which they displayed assorted found objects including preserved animals, horns, teeth, tusks, minerals, clockwork automata, works of art, and objects from what were, to them, "exotic" cultures. Originally, the word *cabinet* referred to a room, and such cabinets of curiosities were the basis for the establishment of museums. See, for example, Oliver Impey and Arthur MacGregor, eds., *The Origins of Museums: The Cabinets of Curiosities in Sixteenth- and Seventeenth-Century Europe* (Oxford, UK: Oxford University Press, 2001).

3. The Chicago Palmers (Bertha and Potter), for example, collected the work of many artists now recognized as among the greats—Monet, Renoir, Cassatt, Degas, Whistler, and others—during the late eighteenth and early nineteenth centuries. Although they supplied the money, their purchases were made on the astute advice of Sara Tyson Hallowell (1846–1924), "the first American woman art curator and agent" (see Kirsten M. Jensen, "Her Sex Was an Insuperable Objection: Sara Hallowell and the Art Institute of Chicago" (masters thesis, Southern Connecticut State University, 2000).

4. "Jacqueline Kennedy Onassis Estate Auction Index," *USA Today*, April 29, 1996, http://www.usatoday.com/life/special/jackie/ljack000.htm (accessed January 28, 2008).

5. "$772,500 Golf Clubs Par for Jackie Auction," *USA Today*, April 26, 1996, http://www.usatoday.com/life/special/jackie/ljack034.htm (accessed January 28, 2008).

6. Wikipedia, s.v. "Fabergé Egg," http://en.wikipedia.org/wiki/Faberge_eggs (accessed January 28, 2008).

7. Fabergé Web site, http://www.fabergetheperfectgift.com/catalog.html?src=overture&OVRAW=faberg (accessed January 28, 2008).

8. A prototype coin is also referred to as a pattern coin, a design judged to be inferior to the one actually chosen for production. In other words, prototypes are one of a kind.

9. "Coins Sell for $30 Million," *USA Today*, http://www.usatoday.com/news/offbeat/2007-11-18-coins_N.htm (accessed January 28, 2008).

10. Just as I was finishing my revision of this article, eBay announced that, in response

to sellers' requests, insertion fees would be lower as of February 20, 2008, and a Gallery picture would be free as of the same date. Insertion fees are based on the seller's starting or reserve price, whichever applies. The eBay announcement and chart for the sliding scale is available online, http://pages.ebay.com/sell/update08/basic/index.html?ov=004KO (accessed January 30, 2008).

11. There are, as well, hidden costs to sellers that eBay customers may not be aware of such as the current cost of the fuel that takes us to yard sales, estate sales, and thrift stores, then to the post office in order to ship an item to a customer, the cost of packing materials (also quite high these days), which sellers often hide in inflated shipping rates, our time spent looking for items to sell, packing sold items, and going to the post office (where we frequently stand in long lines) to ship, not to mention our investment in a library so we can identify items in our area(s) of interest. Selling online is not for the faint-hearted.

7

On Collecting "La Vie en Rose"

TERRY EVERS

The sound of a song can lift you up and carry you to a special place, somewhere very far away. And for me, there is one particular piece that stirs my soul and lifts my spirit: "La Vie en Rose." For over forty years, my fascination with collecting this song has led me into more record shops, music departments, and Internet sites than I can remember. But why I collect this particular song is something I've not given a great deal of thought to until recently. After all, "La Vie en Rose" wasn't sung by anyone whom I would term a favorite singer. As a typical young girl growing up in the 1960s, I was a fan of the Beatles and the Dave Clark Five and most of the other mop-headed singers who came roaring across the pond during the British invasion. I loved Elvis and all things rock n' roll and even folk music. But smooth crooners of the time, like Andy Williams and Frank Sinatra, were strictly uncool for my friends and me. After all, that was more our parents' style of music. So when I heard "La Vie en Rose" for the very first time, sung on national television, it was completely exotic to my ears, like nothing I'd ever heard before. And no other song has captured my imagination in that way since.

Just thinking about that Sunday evening in our suburban Dallas home back in the 1960s when I initially heard "La Vie en Rose" reminds me of how powerful a childhood memory can be. Our family ended every week with the Sunday evening ritual of gathering in our family room, which adjoined the kitchen. We four children did our homework while our father would rest in his favorite recliner from his week's labor, leafing through one of his Reader's Digest abridged novels that he so enjoyed reading. A few steps away, my mother would stand in the kitchen assembling lunches for school and work the next morning, often pestered by one of us to cook up some special sweet treat we could munch on. But the main emphasis on our Sunday evenings was crowding around the television set to watch the *Ed Sullivan Show.*

On one of those evenings, I was sitting on my knees at our green-formica kitchen table, poring over a cutout cardboard shape of the United States. Piles of salt dough dyed in a rainbow of colors were positioned on a long sheet of waxed paper on one side of what would become a topographical map for my fourth-grade geography assignment. As I struggled to get the consistency of the salt dough just right, so that the Rocky Mountains would stand up properly and not sag into the Great Plains, I was aware of my mother standing at the kitchen sink, using a long wooden spoon to beat a pot of fudge that she'd just removed from the stove. I could hardly wait for a taste of my favorite chocolate candy as I pinched the salt dough repeatedly to get it to stand up. This geography assignment was particularly frustrating. It required intense concentration, the salt dough was smelly and messy, and my knowledge of where the states were located in relation to each other was sorely lacking.

Despite the distraction of that delicious-smelling fudge, I was so focused on the map that I hadn't noticed who was singing on the *Ed Sullivan Show* that night, not until a man's voice broke out in a jaunty French lyric accompanied by a piano. At that very moment, my mother dropped the wooden spoon into the pot, began humming the tune, and grabbed my hand. Her voice brimmed with excitement as she sang, "Duh, da-dee-duh, duh-duh-duh, da-dee-duh, duh-duh-duh, la-dee-duh la vie en rose." She lifted me off my knees quickly and we began dancing around the kitchen to the music coming out of the television, she in her pink chenille slippers and me in a pair of white bobby sox.

There are so many things I remember in precise detail about that evening: the smells, colors, and textures of the kitchen, and the delighted look on my mother's face as she waltzed me around the room and sang. But what has eluded me all these years is the identity of the man who sang "La Vie en Rose" on the *Ed Sullivan Show.* At times I'm convinced the singer was Jimmy Durante. And I can just visualize him pounding out the tune on his piano as he rasps out Luh-VEE-on-ROSE-ey, in the same inimitable fashion that he sang "Inka Dinka Do." Other times I'm convinced the singer must have been Maurice Chevalier. My father often said, "Yore mama jes loves ole' Moe-Reese Chevrolet," in his strong Dublin, Texas, twang. Did my father say these words out loud that night? I no longer remember. But irrespective of who was singing, what I remember most vividly was how much fun I had dancing with my mother across the kitchen floor as she sang to me.

There is something peculiar about a song that sets you on a journey to collect a multitude of recordings by different artists. Until recently, I never fully considered why, of all things, I'd seek out one particular song. But, collect it I did. At fifteen years of age I bought my first recording of "La Vie en Rose" on an album of Edith Piaf's music. I played that song over and over on my stereo until the record wore out. In the evenings when my sister and I would do the dishes after dinner, I'd sing "La Vie" along with Piaf, making up my own French words to accompany her. On one of those nights of singing and drying dishes, I tried gargling with water to imitate the guttural warble that distinguishes Piaf's voice, nearly choking. After that, I was satisfied to stick to my interpretation of the French lyrics, much the way small children hear words they don't understand and simply make up a parallel vocabulary. I doubt that the words I sang resembled the French words in the slightest. But I belted them out anyway, as if I were center stage at Carnegie Hall with Mr. Sullivan listening from the wings, just as he did with Jimmy Durante or Maurice Chevalier or whoever was singing that night when I first heard the song.

Piaf's rendition was more than a sonorous tune for me. Something in that song stirred a desire to travel to a romantic world where people spoke a language as beautiful-sounding as French, where glamorous dark-haired women walked casually down boulevards past accordion players under streetlamps, and where people sounded as if they were gargling when they sang. In my youth I dreamed constantly of going to France. My father had been there during the war, but he rarely spoke of it, which only heightened the mystery of this faraway place. Like many young men of his generation, his Normandy experience defined his silence whenever, many years after he returned home, we children would ask him to tell us about France and the war. Everything about that country was so exotic to us young Texans, for most of the children of my acquaintance rarely ventured outside of our state, much less traveled all the way to Europe.

As years passed, and when I became old enough and resourceful enough to travel, I found myself in bookshops and record stores in various countries, leafing through album covers searching for renditions of "La Vie en Rose," usually without success. I found more recordings by Piaf than anyone else. And Louis Armstrong's version appeared often in his albums. But it wasn't until the advent of the World Wide Web, which presented a universe of information at my fingertips, that I became aware of just how many other artists made recordings of this song. Suddenly, through the Internet, I could read about and listen to innumerable performers who interpreted the music in a wide range of styles— traditional to torch, jazz to operatic, samba to swing.

The Internet is a cavern of information. As I learn more and more about navigating its nethermost reaches into cyberspace, I am amazed at how much music around the world is right at my fingertips. Now I can search "La Vie en Rose" on Google.com, and there are well over a million paths to explore in order to find out who performed or recorded a particular rendition. A couple of years ago, my ability to acquire new versions of the song expanded enormously with the purchase of a Macintosh PowerBook G4 with the iTunes feature. The iTunes music store currently allows on-line purchases of an individual song for only ninety-nine cents without having to invest in an entire compact disc and the accompanying playlist of songs, most of which I don't care to own or listen to.

When the Internet phenomenon shattered cyberspace and forever changed the way we communicate, I wasn't exactly a believer. I just didn't think the Internet would be much good for anything. That is, until the Nobel Foundation in Stockholm informed me about the gold medal.

The day before I learned about the gold medal back in the early 1990's, I was sitting in my university office listening to the pleas of our computer technician, Chris, begging me to approve a brand new communications system for our small staff. It was called e-mail, and I rejected the idea out of hand. Chris bent down on one knee to plead with me that e-mail was the way of the future.

I argued with him. "What good is it," I countered, "to waste time typing notes to each other when I can go right outside my office door and talk to anyone on the staff? If I send them an e-mail, I can't be sure that it will be read as quickly as I need it to be. The whole effort will be a waste of time."

He was insistent. "But it's not just the outside office you'll be able to communicate with, but anyone in the world."

"Anybody?" I asked, half mocking.

He nodded his head firmly. "Anybody. Anywhere."

Well, I was determined to show him otherwise. I considered his claim carefully. "All right then. If you say we can contact anyone in the whole wide world, let's start with the Nobel Foundation."

Much to my surprise, he didn't blink. Moving his hands over the computer keyboard, he found the web address in Stockholm with a few quick clicks. "What do you want to ask them?"

I thought carefully. On my desk was a proposal for a new medal honoring outstanding teaching on our campus. We wanted the medal to be prestigious in its meaning and design. Not too small, not too large, not too heavy or light. So I wondered what a Nobel Prize medal weighed. As I typed the question, I thought that this would be the litmus test of whether or not communicating in cyberspace was going to be worth anything.

I was quite certain that those few clicks on the computer would be headed straight to some cyber-dump in outer space. And I went home that afternoon satisfied that I'd put to rest this silly attempt to bog down the communications systems in our small office with e-mail. Ours was a busy place, and I felt anxious to get on to the other important matters stacking up on my desk.

Imagine my astonishment when I came to work the next morning and turned on the computer. There it was: a reply from the Nobel Foundation in Stockholm. Two hundred grams and 66 millimeters in diameter of 18-karat green gold, plated with 24-karat gold.

I almost fell out of my chair. This Internet contraption was good for something after all. It struck me that if I could find the address for the Nobel Foundation on the Internet, and the weight of the medals the King of Sweden hangs around the necks of every Nobel Laureate, I could find out anything in the entire world. Details, facts, narratives, poetry, literature, science, music: it was all there as if by magic.

And that was my first step down the road leading to a musical cyber-search for my "La Vie en Rose" collection.

Recently, I stopped to consider why I was so invested in collecting this one song. So I was excited to learn that early in 2007 a biographical movie about Edith Piaf entitled *La Vie en Rose* by Olivier Dahan would be released. I looked forward to understanding how Piaf's life experiences inspired the music that had me scurrying for the last forty years through record stores around the world and across cyberspace on the Internet. Finally, Dahan's bit of celluloid would reveal, I hoped, the essence of Piaf's inspired creation, and I'd gain some insight into my fascination with one particular song. But, in that respect, the film was an astonishing disappointment.

Before I headed into the theater, I knew from reading the biographical notes on various album covers that Piaf had had an extremely difficult life. In Texas, we have a particular word for such circumstances—hardscrabble. But my notion about Piaf's hardscrabble life had been exclusively a romantic one. I imagined that such an achingly beautiful song like "La Vie en Rose" must have welled up from some tender and wistful places deep in her heart, conjuring the cruelty of a dashing but indifferent French lover. I had no idea just how hardscrabbled Piaf's existence really was.

For over two hours, Marion Cotillard's portrayal of Piaf swept away every romantic idea I'd had about the young French girl who grew up to become the most iconic singer of France. According to the film, Edith Piaf was abandoned in her earliest years by her parents. She grew up in a brothel in Normandy where her father's mother worked as a cook and where Edith was cared for by prostitutes. After contracting meningitis at the age of three, she was blind for four years. Some time after she recovered her sight, her father returned to take possession of her. She was compelled to follow him around while he performed as a street acrobat. And it was on the streets that little Edith sang in public for the first time.

In her teenage years, Piaf continued singing on the streets of Paris in the company of her half sister, Mômone. When she wasn't singing, she and Mômone alternately entertained and consoled each other over their impoverished, squalid lives with chronic drunkenness. At seventeen, Piaf had given birth to her only child, Marcelle, who died of meningitis at the age of two. As if that loss were not grievous enough, Piaf staggered from one disastrous relationship to the next.

Finally, it appeared that Piaf had a chance to be whirled away, at last, from the degradation of the streets. Her savior was the nightclub owner Louis Leplée, who brought her into his club and molded his new singing discovery into La Môme Piaf (Little Sparrow). He decided that she would wear the small black dress that became her trademark and taught her how to carry herself onstage and command an audience. Just as Piaf's career was taking off in the right direction, Leplée was murdered. Shockingly, Piaf was initially implicated, although she was eventually acquitted. Her prior association with mobsters who were thought to have killed Leplée nearly ruined her reputation.

Piaf's love life was marked agonizingly with a number of traumatic affairs. At one point, she fell in love with a married boxer, Marcel Cerdan, the French middleweight champion. But their liaison ended in 1949 when Cerdan was killed in a plane crash. Piaf married twice after that, but between the trauma of those marriages breaking up and painful injuries she sustained in several car crashes, she became addicted to painkillers and alcohol. By 1963, Piaf was only forty-seven years old and racked with liver cancer. By the time she died that autumn, she had grown into a ghastly presence: broken down, demanding, physically ravaged. But still singing.

At least that is how the film presented Piaf's life. By the end of the movie, I no more knew what inspired her masterpiece "La Vie en Rose" than when I'd stood outside at the Loft box office to buy my movie ticket. I was certainly disappointed, but not in the acting, which was superb, nor the singing, most of which was Miss Cotillard's excellent lip-synching of Piaf's recordings, nor the dizzying editing, which jumped backwards and forwards from her early years to final years to middle years and then all over again. Instead, it was simply that I couldn't connect Piaf's erratic and often boorish behavior with her wonderful music.

As the film ended with Piaf's voice booming "Non, je ne regrette rien," I sat listening to a woman behind me blowing her nose and wiping her tears. And I wondered, why was she crying for Piaf? Did this woman pick up on something that I missed? I've always considered Piaf's music to be exquisite, but how could such inspired creativity come out of a person who appeared so spiritually bankrupt? Doesn't even the smallest amount of regret come from the simplest humanity of self-examination?

But then, I didn't understand what Piaf meant when she sang "Non, je ne regrette rien." Since the film was in French, it's likely that some of the more powerful and poetic threads in her life may have been lost in translation. So whether it was the quality of the subtitles or the over-dramatization of Piaf's excesses is not for me to judge. After all, I'm not a film reviewer; I am simply the collector of a single song.

Today I have thirty-one recordings of "La Vie en Rose," even though it is possible to purchase many more versions from at least twice that number of artists. For the most part, these other renditions don't hold up to the magic of hearing the song for the very first time. The ability to collect versions as easily as clicking a few keys on the computer is tempered by a resistance to clutter my collection — a truly pleasant symphony of sounds and voices. To my ear, half the renditions I've heard are either poorly performed or simply sound uninspired. I am tempted to buy them all the same, but I am satisfied to wait a while. The ease of Internet shopping erases a lot of cognitive dissonance I feel in forgoing these additions to my collection, at least for the moment.

As beautiful a song as "La Vie en Rose" is, there are some versions that are simply painful to my ear and are not part of my collection. Ute Lemper sounds as tentative as a frightened child at a public recitation. Claudia Beechman's delicate voice reminds me of a hummingbird skittering across a hot pavement. A favorite singer, Dionne Warwick, sounds tired, compared to the brilliant energy that infuses her other work. I want badly for Tony Bennett and k.d. lang to either sing a new arrangement of their duet or record individual tracks. And I want Al Simmons to stop growling and sing "La Vie en Rose" like a love song.

At least I think it is a love song. I've never bothered with understanding the lyrics, but my collection reflects my preference for romantic interpretations sung in French. To know the meaning of those words would diminish the sense of mystery, so I listen to the words sung in French in blissful ignorance. These selections range from the Piaf's Waif Sparrow sound, for which she was so famous, to versions interpreted by steel drums, bossa nova rhythms, jazz singers, crooners, pop stars, opera singers, orchestras, harpists, and world styles. There is a genre for every mood: jazz, vocal, electronic, pop, classical, New Age, Latin, folk, easy listening and ultra-lounge. Some interpretations are real standouts, like Bette Midler's recording. Louis Armstrong's raspy vibrato is a great and old favorite, second only to Piaf. Each time I hear the riveting first few notes of "La Vie en Rose" played on Chuck Mangione's trumpet, I drop what I'm doing and come to a complete standstill. When Marcie Castro, who sounds so much like Judy Collins when she hits a high note, sings this song, my eyes fill. James Galway's magic flute swirls my imagination, and I imagine the softness of the illusionary veil affixed to my hair on my wedding day.

I also collect a sub-set of "La Vie en Rose" just for my mother, sounds from her era that evoke the forties and fifties, like Marlene Dietrich, Mantovani, Jo Stafford, Tony Martin, Ray Conniff, and Jerry Vale, to name a few.

All this sudden access, at my fingertips, to this entrancing song amazes me. But despite all the information that is out on the Internet about "La Vie en Rose," what still escapes me is the identity of the man whose voice entranced me with that wonderful song when I was a young girl. There are still so many avenues to explore to find out who he is, like researching the Ed Sullivan websites where the weekly line-up of stars and the songs they sang is noted. Perhaps one day it will be possible to watch these shows again on my computer. Then I can see that man's performance, and when I hear his voice, I will remember. At least I hope so. I wonder if, with that discovery, will that be the final rendition of "La Vie en Rose" that I collect?

Recently I asked my mother if she was aware that I collected "La Vie en Rose" and, more importantly, if she remembered who sang it on the *Ed Sullivan Show* the first time I heard it. Furthermore, could she shed any light on what inspired me to collect this same music over and over? Her response was a look of surprise at first. Then she shook her head. Did she at least have the same memory as I had of our kitchen and the fudge and the salt dough map? Again, no. "But," she says, her eyes twinkling, "I do remember exactly where I was the first time I heard it."

Her experience of hearing "La Vie en Rose" is markedly different from mine. She recalls that it was the late 1940s and the war was over. She had accompanied her aunt to the Crystal Ballroom of the Blackstone Hotel in downtown Fort Worth, filled with young men in dress military uniforms and ladies in elegant formal gowns. When the orchestra struck up "La Vie en Rose," she remembers thinking that it was the most beautiful song she'd ever heard in her entire life. She still feels that way today. That evening she danced with her cousin, an Air Force lieutenant, who was home on leave. There was so much my mother was happy about that night. Her husband (my father) and all the young men in their families had survived the war that secured freedom and peace in Europe and Japan. Now that her husband was coming home soon, they would begin their married lives in earnest after being separated by the war. Was that what I saw in her eyes the night she and I danced around the kitchen?

Since that conversation with her, I've wondered more about why I keep searching for different recordings of "La Vie en Rose," and why it is so important that I uncover the identity of the man who sang it the first time I heard it. Is my collecting a way to get back to that innocent moment of my youth when I was looking forward to so much? Or does the song represent the springboard I mounted to catapult me towards being a grown-up and towards the start of my dream to explore the world? On reflection, it may be an unconscious longing for our family ritual on Sunday nights at home, when we were all still together. Our family was intact then. Our parents and we four children were all young and healthy and enjoyed the same pleasures in togetherness every Sunday night. Ten years later, premature deaths began to re-shape our family; now there is just my mother and three children.

My mother is much older today and struggles through these final infirm years of her life. But when we talk about "La Vie en Rose," the sparkle in her eyes makes me think she is back in the 1940s in the Crystal Ballroom in Fort Worth, dressed in a beautiful evening gown, dancing with her cousin.

I think that sparkle is what I saw in her eyes all those years ago—a look of sheer joy coupled with my youthful intrigue to seek a romantic world. For whatever reason, this song anchors my recollection of a tender evening back in our home in Dallas. My two brothers are young and robust, vying for the fudge-covered spoon that my mother has just dropped into a pan. My father is relaxing in his armchair, reading quietly as my sister sits nearby watching the television screen. And my mother begins singing "La Vie en Rose" in her pretty alto voice as she swoops me from my chair. That memory comes back to me in quiet moments when I play through my collection. As soon as I close my eyes, I can feel my mother's happiness as she holds me by the hands, our feet gliding across the linoleum floor. And we're twirling and we're twirling and twirling.

8

I Want My MP3s

Music Collecting in the Digital Age

ANNELISE SKLAR

Aficionado. Fan. Addict. Collector. For the Gen X/Gen Y cusper, music is life, from cassette tapes to CD-Rs, from elementary school radio/alarm clock to teen car stereo, whatever format it takes along the way, songs have always been there for them. Lifetime sound clips might be: New Jersey teen mall idol Tiffany looping in tinny mono on the tape deck of a suburban pre-adolescent; a large collection of hair metal tapes marking the days at the end of the 1980s and early 1990s; flannel-clad grunge gods defining angst-ridden adolescence in the early-mid 1990s; and pop-punk backing those high school years in the late-mid 1990s. In college, these cuspers planned road trips around seeing bands and had a stream of traveling bands sleeping on the living room floor.

For the cuspers, elementary school brought *Dial MTV* (the precursor to today's *TRL: Total Request Live*) and the weekly Top 40 countdown on the radio. Music came on tape until those first CDs in antitheft cardboard long boxes. High school brought memberships with Columbia House and other mail order catalogs and CD-buying in local record stores. Friends made each other mix tapes for their cars. With the prevalent personal computer came burned copies of CDs, sometimes in traditional audio format and sometimes in MP3 format, the blank CDs purchased in bulk spindles on sale. Friends sat at the computer with a spindle of blank CDs, duplicating each other's CD collections. Then the Internet exploded in the late 1990s, followed by the first DSL connections.[1] No longer limited by 56.6 kilobits per second (kbps)[2] or slower file transfers, the early-adapter audiophiles signed up for free screen names with Napster, a popular free MP3 downloading service at the time, and it was immediate obsession. Now it is MP3s stored on an MP3 player, the computer hard drive, and the occasional USB flash drive or burned data disc for transfer between computers.

As technology has evolved, the music collecting game has changed, too: some collectors stick to vinyl, some collect all physical formats, and some are quite happy with a partially or wholly digital collection in the form of MP3s. Sound recordings, including vinyl records, tapes, eight-track tapes, and compact discs, and now including digital formats like MP3, are some of the most popular items to collect. Record collecting is associated with music fandom, and the record collector inhabits a particular subculture of the fan lifestyle. To rabid record collectors, vinyl is distinct for its physical size,[3] which allows for "artsy album covers and graphics, insightful liner notes, and distinctive label packaging"[4] and for its scarcity in the mainstream, which "forced collectors to walk a little farther, look a little harder, and at times pay a little more money."[5] For the avid collector, records are symbols of fandom that, as Auslander notes, "become objects to collect and stockpile, not [only] to hear."[6] Marshall suggests that "'Complete' seems to be a new buzzword in popular music—consumers want a 'complete account' of the recording sessions,"[7] and record collectors want it all: every recording available by their favorite artists, starting with the "official canon"—often in a variety of technological formats—and then expanding to the one-of-a-kind live sets, out-takes, and alternate versions usually found on bootleg releases.

MP3 and P2P Technology

Napster was the first of the well-known peer-to-peer (p2p) file-sharing services. Basically, the program allowed a computer user to access and search select files on other people's computers and vice versa.[8] Napster, with its simple artist/song title searches, made it easy to find and swap music files known as MP3s.[9] The MP3 is almost the vinyl record's dialectical opposite: Where vinyl is large, MP3s have no mass at all. Records can only be played in a space where one has a record player; with the right equipment, MP3s are portable. Records must be bought, usually at specialty record shops; MP3s are ripped from other media, swapped over p2p networks, or downloaded from websites. A copy of a record means loss of sound quality; a copy of an MP3 is virtually identical to its parent MP3. And at generally between two and five megabytes (MB) per file, MP3s are too large to copy to floppy disks (which hold only 1.44 MB) or transfer effectively over a telephone line[10] (though it can be done, just not quickly), but they fit easily onto one's hard drive, a CD (700 MB) or DVD (4.7 gigabytes), and they transfer fairly quickly over a broadband connection.

Unlike physical media, MP3s cannot be rendered unplayable with scratches (though files can be corrupted or accidentally deleted and the technology on which they are stored may be physically damaged), and unless one loses their MP3 player or computer, they cannot be physically lost (though the less computer savvy may have trouble finding exactly where on their machine they stored the file). On the other hand, an MP3 offers few opportunities for accompanying artwork, and I dare avid fans to find a way for their idols to autograph their MP3s.

Nonetheless, as Sterne notes, while "MP3s exist as software, people tend to treat them like objects."[11] He suggests that because MP3s collections are often described analogously to record and book collections "the MP3 has been ascribed the status of a thing in everyday practice"[12] and can be studied in a manner similar to that of other recording container technologies, as, after all, "the point of recording something is not simply to reproduce the event later on, but also to move the recordings across space."[13] The evolution of sound recording formats—and opposition to it by those who are perfectly content with their current technology—is nothing new. Since the 1970s, we have seen the introduction of and frustration with 8-tracks, cassette tapes, CDs, and all sorts of digital files, including MP3, and, as Plasketes comments, "No doubt there were those who bemoaned the loss of their Edison cylinders when shellac became available."[14] The general trend, as McCourt observes, is that "Each subsequent format has less physical presence while allowing for more storage and greater possibilities for user programming."[15] In particular, as Bishop explains, the popularity of, first, home taping and the cassette recorder in the 1970s, 1980s, and 1990s and, then, the CD burner in the 1990s and 2000s changed the way fans interact with their music. Whereas before fans could only obtain recorded music from its officially sanctioned source, "For the first time in the history of the music industry, consumers could now actually dabble in production. And through Internet file-sharing applications, the consumer could now also achieve a certain amount of distribution that was previous [sic] unavailable."[16] As Jones and Lenhart note, though, "The key difference between home taping and file sharing, of course, is not to be found in the number of songs copied, but in the *availability* of songs for copying."[17] In other words, with home taping, someone in the fan's immediate circle of acquaintances had to have access to an original to copy as there was obvious sound degeneration in a copy of a copy. With p2p networks, once one person rips a song and makes it available, anyone can copy it from that copy—or from someone who has made a copy or a copy of a copy—and the sound quality doesn't noticeably degrade. In short, as Robinson and Halle summarize, "Napster encouraged a new horizontal playing field that, in theory, gave music to the online public."[18]

Legal/Ethical Aspects of MP3 Collecting

There was just one small problem with Napster: most of the music was made available through the violation of federal copyright law.[19] So it was only a matter of time before several major record companies, represented by the Recording Industry Association of America (RIAA), filed a class action suit against Napster, as they did in December 1999. At first, the action merely gave the service additional publicity and increased its popularity. Then, in July 2001, a judge issued an injunction that ordered the shut-down of Napster's services.[20] But crafty entrepreneurs with similar services had already lined up to take its place. Some people switched over to Audiogalaxy (popular from 2001 until 2002)[21] and continued to download music almost uninterrupted. When it, too, disappeared, many downloaders went on to experiment with using other p2p services such as Gnutella (with interfaces such as Morpheus, BearShare, and LimeWire), FastTrack (the most popular interface for which were Grokster[22] and Kazaa[23]), DC++, BitTorrent, and SoulSeek.

Record companies oppose p2p song trading because under copyright law, artists and record companies—or whoever holds the copyright to a particular song—have the exclusive right to distribute their songs. Copyright violations undermine their profits. The International Federation of the Phonographic Industry determined the global value for pirated music in 2000 at $4.2 billion,[24] although "Piracy figures are often used for their rhetorical impact rather than as a reflection of reality."[25] Also, while it is true that CD album sales have declined since the rise in popularity of MP3 technology,[26] it's also true that American consumers saw only the slightest increase in their disposable income at the beginning of the new millennium.[27] It should be noted that the widespread popularity of MP3 downloading and portable MP3 players (the Apple iPod in particular) finally influenced record companies to create their own avenues for legal downloadable music. The Apple iTunes Store opened in 2003 and became a huge commercial success. There are now many online outlets for legal downloads, usually charging approximately $1 per song.[28] However, most of these legal files include digital rights management (DRM) technologies, which prevent users from doing the things they like best about MP3s: sharing or trading them, downloading them to multiple playback devices, or burning them to CDs. They may or may not be compatible with the user's software of choice or files from different services. For many users, Sterne suggests, "it is probably easier to install a Gnutella client and acquire illegal files than it is to manage two separate MP3 collections and two separate playback programs."[29]

With no tangible product, the line between individual intellectual property and cultural property is, first of all, hard for most people to grasp, and, secondly, not legally uniform though the entire world.[30] For many, listening to music on the computer feels no different than listening to the radio, except that, in an era where radio is increasingly monopolistic and individual stations across the country are more or less interchangeable, MP3s give one the option of on-demand programming without the commercial interruptions. Copying an MP3 feels like photocopying something (which, obviously, is not always legal, either): it does not interfere with the original work and most collectors are certainly not passing the work off as their own music or making any money off of it. Not surprisingly, then, Jones and Lenhart discovered that 78 percent of early downloaders believed that file-sharing was not stealing.[31] After all, as Sterne suggests, MP3s are "perfectly and lovingly shaped for the very purposes to which it is not supposed to be put: the MP3 is perfectly designed for illegal file-sharing."[32]

Collectors

So who are these collectors of free and, most likely, illegal MP3s, anyway? Several previously published investigations provide data. Jones and Lenhart, in analyzing early Pew Internet and American Life Project studies, found that in April 2000, 21 percent of respondents who used the Internet had downloaded music. By February 2001, the number had grown to 29 percent, most likely due to increased news coverage of Napster. These early downloaders were predominantly male (roughly twice as many were male as female) and approximately half were under thirty, which is not surprising since those are the demographics most likely to have had access to the technology at the time. Early downloaders also typically had a college education and above-average incomes, though the slightly later surveys "found that greater percentages of the lower income population downloaded music and that they made up a greater percentage of the music-downloading population as a whole," most likely because more and more people started owning computers and high speed access. Jones and Lenhart also note that the demographics of music downloaders are similar to those of the home tapers from twenty years before, who were predominantly male and/or between the ages of twenty and thirty-four years old and/or who had at least a high school education and/or "above-average" incomes.[33]

A more recent survey, from January 2005, from the Pew Internet & American Life Project had somewhat similar findings. Men are still more likely to download music than women (25 percent of male Internet users vs. 19 percent of female Internet users), and downloaders are more likely to be young (40 percent of eighteen-to-twenty-nine-year-old users— those Gen X/Gen Y cuspers are in here — download music whereas only 18 percent of thirty-to-forty-nine year-old users, 13 percent of fifty-to-sixty-four year-old users, and only 6 percent of the sixty-five-plus users are downloaders). Not surprisingly, Internet access plays a key role: half of all Internet users now have high-speed access at home, and 29 percent of home broadband users download music.[34]

News reports of individual music downloaders the RIAA sued for copyright infringement (starting in 2003) provide more detailed ethnographic information. Many of those first named in lawsuits were the middle-aged parents of downloading teens, sixteen of whom later appeared in a Pepsi/iTunes cross promotional Superbowl ad. The most famous of these teens was then twelve-year-old New York honor student Brianna LaHara, who had approximately

1000 songs on her computer. She and her mother settled with the RIAA for $2000.[35] Among other MP3 collectors revealed by the lawsuits were: a fifty-four-year-old mother from San Francisco who downloaded digital copies of the Golden oldies she owned on CD because it was an easier way to make playlists on her computer,[36] a Hunter College student,[37] a fourteen-year-old girl (or, more specifically, her father), a twenty-one-year-old woman (or rather, her mother), and a nineteen-year-old roofer who claimed to also buy at least two new CDs every week, all from the Boston area,[38] a thirty-nine-year-old sheet metal worker from St. Louis who paid a subscription fee to Kazaa under the impression that his downloads would then be legal, and a Jackson, MO, woman who then had to file for bankruptcy after she was sued.[39] All of those sued had a common element: they claimed to be music lovers.

Marshall notes that "The literature on fandom has helped show that being a fan is not a passive experience but rather a continual process of meaning creation"[40] unique to each fan. The same can be said for MP3 collectors, who are, after all, a subset of music fans with no ties to a particular genre. I would argue, however, that there are two distinct types of MP3 collector: the completist, who wants the entirety of their favorite artist's oeuvre or the gamut of their chosen genre, including bootlegs and other oddities, and the selective collector, who wants only certain songs, rather than artists or complete albums. For the completist, the joy is in the details: owning every album with every song in album order, perfectly arranged files, and a generally impressive *complete* collection. For the selective collector, the joy is in the mix: finding the right song for the right occasion or even letting random order dictate the mood rather than vice versa. For this collector, collecting is about having only the things that one actually likes and purposefully omitting the rest. McCourt remarks that "While mechanical technology enhances the possibilities for reproducing an original artifact, digital technology increases the possibilities for modifying an original."[41] For the selective collectors, MP3s return music collecting to the song level, along the lines of a collection of 7" 45-rpm singles. The order and arrangement is no longer set by albums and their creators; audiences can select exactly what they want to hear and how they listen to it, combining tracks from their entire musical collections in what basically becomes the equivalent of an ever-changing, perpetually looping mix tape. The listener, plugged into iPod headphones while walking down the street or listening to music while working or gaming online becomes "Theodor Adorno's nightmare: the 'distracted' consumer of mass culture."[42]

Collecting Motivation

In the case of (free) MP3 collecting collectors can participate without actually spending a lot of money. Most scholars and collectors agree that economics are one of the motivating factors behind MP3 collecting. When I asked one anonymous collector responding to my informal online survey why she collects MP3s, she responded: "Why? The question should be why not? I end up still buying CDs, but most of the time I want to preview a band or album before I shell out the flippin [sic] twenty bucks they cost."[43] Bishop suggests that, in MP3 swapping, "the world's music consumer has found an option to the price gouging of the industry. The CD-R offers a previously unavailable choice, a response to the economic oppression perpetrated against consumers by the world's wealthy"[44] and notes that "in 'low-income' societies throughout the world, music pirates are not seen as the bandits ... [but] are, in many cases, Robin Hoods, freeing music from its economic raptors and returning it to the people."[45] In their study of how the MP3 format affects music habits, Dujmovic and Mellegard quote a subject who puts it more bluntly: "Why spend 30$ [sic] on two CDs when you can have 30, 50, 100 or more with a 30$ [sic] internet connection?"[46]

Sterne suggests that the "status of the MP3 as a valued cultural object which can circulate outside the channels of the value economy is one of the fundamental, enabling conditions for the intellectual property debates that surround it."[47] Marshall observes, however, that "the industry's concern with questions of supply (who owns these recordings?) has neglected important questions of demand (why do people want them?)," and that "recording industry statistics do not take into account the variety of different meanings and uses that pirated music takes in the day-to-day lives of many people."[48] Mp3s are usually easy to acquire: the collectible items in question are free and generally readily available — anyone can have any music their heart desires with only the click of a few buttons. Ownership of a particular record or genre of records allows the owner entry into a particular fan subculture.

McCourt claims that "Each [new sound recording] format also has reduced the listener's physical interaction with music, which allows music to acquire an increasingly ambient status" but,

> Paradoxically, the lack of materiality in digital files heightens our sense of "ownership," as well as our desire to sample, collect, and trade music in new ways. Possessing digital files is a more intense and intimate experience than owning physical recordings, based on: the desire for compacting..., the desire for immediacy..., [and] the desire to customize.[49]

He says that, "With an iPod, flow is determined exclusively by the user,"[50] noting that the song is no longer tied to an album, and users are constantly "recontextualizing it through mix CDs or playlists."[51] However, Dujmovic and Mellegard observed two diverging means of storing MP3 collections. Some of their subjects had "virtualised" [sic] their CD collections into MP3s. Others "commodify the MP3s they download by burning them onto CD."[52]

For those with the proper technology, though, MP3s offer many options.

They are portable and can be copied easily. With a storage capacity, depending on the size of the hard drive, of up to 15,000 songs in a physical space approximately the size of a cassette tape (and sometimes even smaller!), portable MP3 players have more or less rendered their forbearers, the Sony Walkman cassette player, Discman, and their generic equivalents, obsolete relics of a past age. Following suit, many portable devices—mainly cell phones and personal digital assistants—include MP3 players.[53] Suggests McCourt, "The popularity of MP3 files and related formats, as well as music in the form of telephone ring tones, indicates that access and convenience are increasingly more important than artifact and sound quality."[54]

Collecting Behavior

Collecting behavior is unique to the individual collector, but several key behaviors have been identified. McIntosh and Schmeichel developed an eight-step model to describe behavior common to all collectors[55]: "First, people decide to collect some classification of things," in this case, MP3s. "Second, they gather information about the objects," such as information about particular bands, genres, albums, or songs. In my own informal survey of anonymous MP3 collectors, most reported that they heard or heard about new artists through means such as internet radio, recommendations from friends, reviews, or mention of the bands in magazines, and then they go online and search by artist. Some collectors also find new music by browsing the files of users who appear to have similar taste in music.

Third, collectors "'court' one or more of the objects by forming an attachment to them and devising a plan to obtain them," which means they decide there's one in particular that they want. "Next, they hunt for the objects(s)," which would be running a search for a particular artist, album, or song, though most collectors reported that they search by artist rather than song title because they want to hear multiple songs by the same artist. This is then "followed by acquisition of the object(s)," or actually getting it, in its entirety, downloaded, which seems straightforward but often entails waiting in queue as others download the song first, hunting again for that one song missing from an album or for files of similar quality.

Next is the "reaction to the acquisition," which could be listening to the song and either enjoying it or being disappointed at how awful it is or even a simple "Yay! I got it! Time to move on." Finally, collectors will "display and catalogue the object(s)," either burning their MP3s onto a CD or arranging them into playlists or folders by artist, album, genre, or some other category for other people to see when they browse the collector's files, or some combination of the above. At last, the collector will "move on to other objects that are classified as belonging in the collection."[56]

Social Aspects of Collections

McIntosh and Schmeichel also observe that "by the time that object becomes part of a collection the owner views it as valuable in symbolic terms, not utilitarian ones."[57] In other words, even with MP3s—and certainly with physical sound recordings—at least part of the joy of collecting is in what owning the album (and being able to show off that one owns the album) represents rather than merely using/listening to it. As with physical record collections, the prized possessions are usually the rarities: the bootlegs (alternate tracks, live sets, early radio interviews, and the like), the extra bonus tracks included with only a particular version of the album, and digital copies of items that are harder to convert to MP3 such as tape- or vinyl-only releases or anti-piracy encoded releases. McCourt suggests that, "In cyberspace, people collect lists rather than objects"[58] and that, "As aesthetic imagined communities, or 'taste tribes,' become more formalized and concretized via online tools, playlists may serve the function that CDs serve now,"[59] indicating ownership of the items, which, en masse, in turn indicates expert knowledge of the genre and membership in the appropriate music fan subculture.

Though the mental image of MP3 collectors is one of the Internet junkie at home alone with his or her music and computer, the social aspect of MP3 collecting is actually a quite meaningful part of the process as well. McCourt suggests that "In cyberspace, collecting becomes based not on the linkage of people to objects, but of the linkage of individuals to others."[60] After all, p2p networks by their very nature work based on (often anonymous) trade. In their anthropological study of early Napster users, Giesler and Pohlmann found that "Napsters's file sharing system suggests the creation of a complex and contradictory subculture of consumption challenging the interrelations between technology, culture and consumption,"[61] and they mention that it is considered bad etiquette to download files without sharing one's own files with the rest of the community.[62] They explain the process as gifting behavior, but describe it as "parasitic gifting."

> This principle suggests the MP3 transaction to be classified as a gift transaction between donor and recipient. However, it is one that requires some technical broadening that acknowledges four important consequences of digitized information in the digital networks. First, a gift is always a perfect copy of an MP3 file stored on the donor's hard drive. Second, a donor is usually a recipient and a recipient is usually a donor at the same time but not to each other. Third, it is the recipient and not the donor who initiates a gift transaction. Fourth, donor and recipient are anonymous and gift exchange is usually not reciprocal.[63]

They use the adjective "parasitic," because people are "gifting" music, but for their own gain—so that they might get more music for themselves. They put up music for the taking, but only because they in turn are taking what others have put up. No one loses anything in the gift exchange because only a copy is exchanged. The exchange is usually not one-to-one, because the person putting up an offering is then downloading offerings from a number of other people. The person who wants the file usually initiates the transaction, unlike more traditional gifting in which the gift-giver does the initiating.

As MP3 collecting has become more commonplace, the social behavior associated with it has become more complex. Obviously, the act of one user's computer connecting directly to another user's computer in peer-to-peer swaps generates the potential for associated computer-mediated communication and virtual community. The original Napster, Kazaa, and current flavor-of the-month SoulSeek all included instant messaging functions, the idea being that those users might need to coordinate the trading transaction and that those with similar tastes in music might want to talk to each other about it or other things they might also have in common. Some people even post lists of their MP3 collections on web sites so that they may trade with other fans, too. Not surprisingly, then, recent services like SoulSeek now include chatrooms where users can chat about music — or anything else that suits their fancy — while they hunt for and download files. At the same time, though, while collaboration is necessary to perpetuate the peer-to-peer system, as McIntosh and Schmeichel note, in general, "There is a strong element of competition in collecting."[64] MP3 collectors will often remove their "special" files (often the rarities or ones that will most definitely get a user sued, threatened personally by a band member, or at the very least flamed by another user) from their shared folders and only share them with special friends.

In fact, while there was a large decrease in self-reported p2p users,[65] many MP3 collectors are incorporating good old-fashioned copying of music from and/or for people one already knows in "real life" into their collecting routine. My informal study found one collector who sometimes sends songs to friends who are DJs for local underground radio stations. Another collector notes that "a good bit of my music was ripped from friends' cds, off the network in college, or from free sites" though she tries to pay when she can "because I know it supports the artists." Yet another collector explains that she and her friends will sometimes share in person, through private shared accounts, tools like yousendit, private webspace, or on the network drive at work. She also sometimes borrows cds from the library to make MP3s.[66] The January 2005 Pew study had similar findings: 20 percent of Internet users were found to share files with others privately through email or instant messaging and 15 percent claim to have copied files from someone else's MP3 player.[67]

Changed Behavior

In my informal survey of anonymous MP3 collectors, most reported that they collected more varied genres than they previously purchased. Several said that their musical tastes have broadened because of the ability to collect such a variety of music. Most also reported that they own MP3s of music that they never would have purchased — but are glad to own, nonetheless. Most collectors still buy music. For example, one collector claims that she buys more music than before because she wants to give her money to independent artists, but she doesn't buy mainstream music for the same reason.[68]

In their study, Robinson and Halle found that "two-thirds of the 1,135 college students surveyed reported that rather than stealing, downloading music is a sampling procedure that allows them to make educated choices about what music to purchase."[69] Likewise one of my own respondents says that she still purchases CDs, "perhaps not as many as I did before, but the ones I purchase now I'm more informed about ... so I don't tend to buy something and then sell it back to a used record store almost immediately. The biggest difference about what I have now and what I had before I started downloading music is probably the live shows and unreleased things you can find online. It's always fun to find something that no one else has."[70] Similarly, Jones and Lenhart found that 21 percent of early downloaders claimed to later buy CDs of the music they downloaded "most of the time." 48 percent said they did at least a few times.[71] They also found that 28 percent of early downloaders said that they were downloading music that they already owned in another format.[72] For example, one of my anonymous respondents claims that he will "only buy vinyl now. I haven't bought a CD since 2003."[73]

Whereas with a collection of physical media much of the appeal is possessing an item that someone else does not, with file-sharing the attraction is discovering something new and then sharing an identical copy with anyone else who might be interested, either on an interpersonal level or through a file-sharing service. Technology and its use by music fans is ever-evolving, and artists, record companies, and the law need to catch up if the music industry wants to survive relatively unscathed. Physical music formats will always have their market niches — just as the World Wide Web has not meant the death of paper books, MP3s do not imply the complete death of physical collectible media like CDs and records, though it does signify a notable change in the market for these items.

Notes

1. DSL, which stands for Digital Subscriber Line, allows for digital data transmission over a telephone line. Speeds range from 128 kbps to 24,000 kbps. Use of DSL requires a special DSL modem. The other popular means of at-home broadband access is cable Internet service, which connects a user's computer to Internet service over the same line as their cable television.

2. 56.6 kbps is the theoretical maximum data transfer speed of a traditional telephone line.

3. George Plasketes, "Romancing the Record: The Vinyl De-Evolution and Subcultural Evolution," *Journal of Popular Culture* 26.1 (1992):119.

4. Ibid., 119.
5. Ibid, 115.
6. Philip Auslander, "Looking at Records," *The Drama Review* 45.1: 79.
7. Lee Marshall, "The Effects of Piracy Upon the Music Industry: A Case Study of Bootlegging," *Media, Culture & Society* 26.2 (2004): 177.
8. Hence, a "peer-to-peer," or p2p, connection, though Napster also used a central server to maintain lists of connected machines and their files, which later services chose to avoid.
9. An MP3, short for MPEG-1/2 Audio Layer 3, is a digital audio file. The MP3 algorithm is special because it was designed to compress the digital data required to reproduce audio while sounding to the common ear relatively identical to the original, uncompressed audio by removing the sound data that the average listener cannot hear. Mp3s are compatible with all operating systems and most versions of music playing software.
10. A regular dial-up connection using a telephone line has a maximum transfer speed of 56.6 kbps. On a peer-to-peer network, this seems to usually translate to a transfer speed of about 2 kbps or less per song. As there are 1000 kilobytes in 1 megabyte, a 5 MB file would take approximately 2500 seconds, or 42 minutes, to transfer. A 10 song album, then, would take 420 minutes, or 7 hours, to transfer — assuming that no one needed to disconnect from the service to do anything as unproductive as making a phone call. With a high speed connection, the transfer speed on a P2P network usually rises to anywhere from 6 to 25 kbps or more, in turn lowering transfer speed for a large single song to anywhere from 14 minutes to 3 minutes or even fewer.
11. Jonathan Sterne, "The Mp3 as Cultural Artifact," *New Media & Society* 8 (2006): 832.
12. Ibid., 830.
13. Ibid., 837.
14. Plasketes, "Romancing the Record," 111.
15. Tom McCourt, "Collecting Music in the Digital Realm," *Popular Music and Society* 28.2 (2005): 249.
16. Jack Bishop, "Who are the Pirates? The Politics of Piracy, Poverty, and Greed in a Globalized Music Market," *Popular Music and Society* 27.1 (2004): 102.
17. Steve Jones and Amanda Lenhart, "Music Downloading and Listening: Findings from the Pew Internet and American Life Project," *Popular Music and Society* 27.2 (2004): 194.
18. Laura Robinson and David Halle, "Digitization, the Internet, and the Arts: eBay, Napster, SAG, and e-Books," *Qualitative Sociology* 25.3 (2002): 378.
19. Briefly, United States copyright law states that the copyright owner has the exclusive right to reproduce, create derivative works based on, distribute copies of, perform, or display the copyrighted work, in this case, a song. Any song recorded in or after 1978 will remain copyrighted until 70 years after the death of its creator. Songs recorded between 1923 and 1978 were originally copyrighted for only twenty-eight years, but additional legislation gave copyright holders the option to renew their copyrights by an additional sixty-seven years, so most of these works are likely to still be protected by copyright. Only recordings from 1922 or earlier are automatically in the public domain, and this is how things will be until 2018, when copyright on items from 1923 will finally expire, barring additional changes to copyright law.
20. The case was partially settled that following September, with Napster agreeing to pay $26 million in settlement damages to music creators and copyright holders and, in order to pay these fees, soon attempting to convert their free service to one that was subscription-based. The prototype was never made publicly available. In 2002, Napster announced that its assets would be acquired by Bertelsmann AG, a German media firm, and the company filed for Chapter 11 bankruptcy protection. Later that year, a bankruptcy judge blocked the sale, forcing Napster to instead liquidate its assets under Chapter 7 of U.S. bankruptcy laws. Roxio, Inc., bought the Napster assets with the intention of basing on those assets a new, fee-based and legal music downloading service: Napster 2.0. That service was launched in October 2003. As of 2005, users could either pay a monthly subscription of $9.95 for unlimited access to its collections (plus another $5 a month for the ability to download the songs to a computer or portable MP3 player) or 99 cents a song without a subscription.

21. As would be expected, Audiogalaxy soon met the same fate as Napster. The company was sued by the RIAA on May 24, 2002, and immediately blocked sending of all copyrighted songs. Several weeks later, Audiogalaxy reached an out-of-court settlement that would allow them to install a "filter-in" system requiring consent from the songwriter, music publisher, and/or record company for use and sharing of the work. Later in 2002, the company licensed and rebranded Listen.com's fee-based Rhapsody audio streaming (meaning that one could listen to music on their computer but not download it) system and terminated its p2p system.

22. Grokster is most famous for the 2005 Supreme Court ruling in MGM v. Grokster where the court held that p2p companies could in fact be sued and held liable for inducing acts of copyright infringement (on the part of their software's users) if they market those kinds of acts as a use of their software.

23. Needless to say, Kazaa spawned a whole new round of lawsuits. A free downloadable software financed by embedded spyware (software that tracks a computer user's internet surfing habits and reports back to a third party) and adware (software that runs advertising on a user's machine), on the surface, Kazaa was otherwise very much like the original Napster, using an almost identical file-transfer interface. Like its predecessors, Kazaa's developer, Consumer Empowerment, was taken to court to curb its use in the sharing of copyrighted material, in this case in the Netherlands by Buma/Stemra, the Dutch music publishing organization. The owners in turn sold Kazaa to Sharman Networks, a company headquartered in Australia but incorporated in Vanuatu. In 2005, the Federal Court of Australia found Sharman, while not guilty of copyright infringement itself, had encouraged its users to illegally trade copyrighted songs. Kazaa settled out of court with Universal Music, Sony BMG, EMI, and Warner Music for $100 million and has since become a legal download site supported by third-party advertising. The lawsuits surrounding Kazaa also saw the advent of a new tactic on the part of the record companies. Individual users also found themselves served with lawsuits. In September 2003, the RIAA filed suit in civil court against private individuals who had used Kazaa to share large numbers of files, including among them a twelve-year-old and a retired school teacher.

24. Marshall, "Effects of Piracy," 163.

25. Ibid., 164.

26. According to RIAA numbers, in 2000, 942.5 million CD units were shipped. In 2001, the number dropped more to 881.9 million units. The trend continued in 2002 (803.3 million units) and 2003 (745.9 million units). There was a slight rise for 2004 (766.9 million units), but a dramatic decrease in 2005 (705.4 million units). U.S. Bureau of the Census, *Statistical Abstract of the United States 2007*, 126th ed. (Washington: Government Printing Office, 2007): Table 1123.

27. The average American disposable income (calculated as personal income minus personal tax and nontax payments) grew by only approximately $1000 a year, from $25,471 in 2000 to $29,404 in 2004. It grew only to $30,509 in 2005. These numbers do not take into account inflation or rising costs of living. U.S. Bureau of the Census, *Statistical Abstract*, Table 661.

28. The RIAA started collecting data on sales of downloadable music in 2004. Legal downloads increased from 139.4 million songs/4.6 million albums in 2004 to 366.9 million songs/13.6 million albums in 2005. U.S. Bureau of the Census, *Statistical Abstract*, Table 1123.

29. Sterne, "Mp3 as Cultural Artifact," 830.

30. While, in addition to their own copyright laws, many countries have copyright relations with the United States, many others—for example, Ethiopia, Iran, and Vanuatu, do not, or the relationship is unclear.

31. Jones and Lenhart, "Music Downloading and Listening," 191. For comparison, slightly over half, 53 percent, of surveyed internet users at the time agreed. Only 35 percent of the general population (internet users and non-users alike) surveyed believed that file sharing was, in fact, stealing. Ibid., 192.

Jones and Lenhart also note that "All surveys mentioned in this study showed that the great majority of respondents believed that making a copy of prerecorded music for one's personal use, whether the original was obtained through purchase or by other means, was considered acceptable. ...it can be reported at least from anecdotal evidence that most subjects seem to confuse fair use with the personal exception in copyright law that allows one to make copies for private, noncommercial use of copyrighted materials one has legitimately obtained." Ibid., 195.

32. Sterne, "Mp3 as Cultural Artifact," 828.

33. Jones and Lenhart, "Music Downloading and Listening," 189–191.

34. Mary Madden and Lee Rainie, "Pew Internet Project Data Memo: Music and Video Downloading Moves Beyond P2P," Pew Internet & American Life Project, March 2005, http://www.pewinternet.org/PPF/r/153/report_display.asp (accessed February 5, 2006): 7.

35. Chris Gaither, "Dozens in State Face RIAA Suits Recording Industry Runs Risk of Raising Anger of Consumers," *The Boston Globe*, September 10, 2003: C1, in LexisNexis Academic Universe (accessed February 19 2006).

36. Scott Morrison, "Song Pirates Forced to Face the Music," *Financial Times*, September 13, 2003: 8, in LexisNexis Academic Universe (accessed February 19 2006).

37. Marcella Bombardieri, "Students Tune Out Industry Lawsuits," *The Boston Globe*, September 14, 2003: A1, in LexisNexis Academic Universe (accessed February 19, 2006).

38. Gaither, "Dozens in State Face RIAA Suits," C1.

39. Peter Shinkle, "Music Downloader Takes on Recording Industry," *St. Louis Post Dispatch*, April 21, 2005: A1, in LexisNexis Academic Universe (accessed February 19, 2006).

40. Marshall, "Effects of Piracy," 173.

41. McCourt, "Collecting Music in the Digital Realm," 251.

42. Sterne, "Mp3 as Cultural Artifact," 836.

43. Interview with downloader, March 2006.

44. Bishop, "Who are the Pirates?," 105–106.

45. Ibid., 104.

46. Martin Dujmovic and Lisa Mellegard, *How the Mp3-format Affects Music Habits* (Göteborg: Department of Informatics, 2002), http://www.handels.gu.se/epc/archive/00001584/ (accessed February 5, 2006): 21.

47. Sterne, "Mp3 as Cultural Artifact," 831.

48. Marshall, "Effects of Piracy," 164.

49. McCourt, "Collecting Music in the Digital Realm," 250.

50. Ibid., 249.

51. Ibid., 251.

52. Dujmovic and Mellegard, *How the Mp3-format Affects*, 25.

53. One such device, the Apple iPhone, was released in 2007 with much fanfare.

54. McCourt, "Collecting Music in the Digital Realm," 250.

55. William D. McIntosh and Brandon Schmeichel, "Collectors and Collecting: A Social Psychological Perspective," *Leisure Sciences* 26 (2004): 86.

56. Ibid., 86.

57. Ibid., 89.

58. McCourt, "Collecting Music in the Digital Realm," 251.

59. Ibid., 251.

60. Ibid., 252.

61. Markus Giesler and Mali Pohlmann, "The Anthropology of File Sharing: Consuming Napster as a Gift," *Advances in Consumer Research* 30 (2003): 273.

62. Ibid., 274–275.

63. Ibid., 274.

64. McIntosh and Schmeichel, "Collectors and Collecting," 92.

65. In February 2004, 58 percent of current downloaders had at one point downloaded music from a p2p site, but only 31 percent claimed to be current p2p users. (The other 27 percent said that they had in the past.) In January 2005, only 41 percent of current music downloaders "admit to trying peer-to-peer networks," and only about half of them, 21 percent, claim to be current p2p downloaders. Of those who have stopped downloading music, the largest percentage, 28 percent, report that the main reason they have stopped downloading music is "because they were afraid to get in trouble or heard about the RIAA lawsuits." Others stopped because of viruses, pop-up ads, or other computer problems that they attributed to their downloading (15 percent), they decided that downloading was wrong (10 percent), they found other ways to get their music (7 percent), they found downloading too

time-consuming (7 percent), or that they just lost interest (5 percent). Madden and Rainie, "Pew Internet Project Data Memo," 8–9.

66. Interviews with downloaders, March 2006.
67. Madden and Rainie, "Pew Internet Project Data Memo," 2.
68. Interviews with downloaders, March 2006.
69. Robinson and Halle, "Digitization, the Internet, and the Arts," 380.
70. Interview with downloader, March 2006.
71. Jones and Lenhart, "Music Downloading and Listening," 192.
72. Ibid., 193.
73. Interview with downloader, March 2006.

9

Trading Online Objects on Friendster.com

Cyber Collecting as Socialization

CARSON METZGER

Despite the apparent immateriality of the Internet, cyberspace abounds with opportunities for the collector. I embody practices of collecting as I point and click at online objects—accumulating bookmarks, exchanging links with friends, browsing virtual family-photo-albums. As a collector of letters, I know emails as online "objects of memory."[1] Having reached the space limit in numerous email accounts, I feel offline frustration when the account operators dispose of my saved mail. My hard drive is a landfill where downloaded songs and videos, television shows, and photos—forgotten Internet-detritus—clutter my computer and slow its operations. The Internet is a space where thumbnails, links, and files are accumulated, exchanged, and displayed for others; a space for socializing over and through these online objects; a space for collecting.

This convergence of cyber collecting and social interaction has become increasingly apparent over the last five years in the proliferation and use of online dating and social networking sites like Friendster and MySpace; sites where socialization proceeds through acts of collecting. Online dating and socializing remain daunting endeavors to many who fear the truism that Internet encounters differ from offline interactions due to the anonymity of the cyber medium. This general state of anonymity enables users to fabricate identities. Journalist Jennifer Egan states the truism as such, "The defining fact of online dating is that it begins outside any context — historical, temporal, physical" in contrast to "real" dating where people, upon first meeting, share the contexts of space, time, and materiality.[2] Presumably, these shared contexts of offline dating reduce one's ability to fake an identity to strangers, ensuring a more authentic expression of self.

Rather than assuming this categorical distinction between online and offline socialization — between real and represented identities — I see both the landscape of the Internet, and much of my behavior in cyberspace, as paralleling my offline American-environment and behavior. Our cyber contexts reflect customary "real world" activities and interests. Where offline socializing routinely proceeds through things people have in common — movies, books, video games, food, collections — Internet interaction, in spite of its seeming immateriality, is no exception. In the case of the social networking site Friendster.com, the practices of fabricating and collecting thumbnail identities — online objects — are activities that forge social community.

CEO John Abrams' Vision

Matchmaking and social networking websites abound on the Internet. As journalist Phillip Harper notes, "If you haven't heard of social networking, stay tuned because it's the Next Big Thing. New Economy Magazine Business 2.0 named it 'technology of the year' for 2003, and venture capitalists have started throwing money at social networking startups with a zeal not seen since the first generation of dot-coms came down the pike."[3] Many of these sites, like eHarmony, Yahoo! Personals, and Match.com, offer a forum for "traditional" dating where single men and women post profiles in the interest of a romantic encounter. More recently, innovators have broadened the idea of the dating site by offering cyber spaces through which people can network and make friends. Such sites provide users with a space to post a personal profile, a search engine for finding people, and a mailbox for e-communication. Friendster.com is an example of such a site. A free, privately owned service, Friendster encourages users (I will call them friendsters) to seek both romance and friendship.

Why Friendster.com? Why not MySpace? In the four years that have passed since the inception of this essay, the "new" technology of online social networking has become the "Next Big Thing," as evidenced in Fox News Corporations purchase of MySpace.com in 2005.[4] Despite the popular currency of MySpace and other sites like Facebook, Tribe, and Hi5, many consider Friendster the progenitor of the current online social networking fad.[5] When former CEO John Abrams launched Friendster in March 2003, his novel vision garnered immediate success: by September of 2003 — the month that Tom Anderson and Chris DeWolfe went public with MySpace — 1.5 million friendsters had already joined Abrams' site, posting personal profiles and collecting and communicating with a database of online friends.

Although the number paled in comparison to the 12 million date-seeking Match.com users, Friendster seemingly served a different market and a different purpose. Egan describes the site as such: "Wired New Yorkers under 30 seem to be universally mesmerized by Friendster, which functions as much as a social cross-referencing system as a dating site: a way of keeping track of, and learning more about, people they have already met in real-world contexts."[6] From its inception, then, Friendster has bridged the gap between the older matchmaking sites and the current fad of online social communities—serving both dating ends and as a database that allows people to learn about and keep up with others they may "have already met." Yet with some 36 million reported users in 2006,[7] Friendster now receives only a fraction of the traffic of MySpace with its 99 million members.[8] What happened to Abrams' trailblazing creation, the site that had the "the initial edge among arbiters of cool"?[9]

I first learned of MySpace through community-chatter posted on Friendster. Users frustrated by lagging page loads and slow upload speeds were slowly migrating over to MySpace. These technical glitches certainly had some effect on Friendster's waning popularity.[10] Yet the erosion of interest in the site was seemingly based on a poor business decision as well. Shortly after founding the company, Abrams turned down a Google offer to buy and mainstream his creation; he chose, instead, to fund his site with venture capital. Melissa Gilbert, a former colleague and a self-proclaimed first investor in Friendster, claims the investors who threw their money behind Abrams were disconnected from the world of online social networking—out-of-touch with the needs and desires of their young clientele. In the summer of 2004 the out-of-touch investors on Friendster's board demoted Abrams, replacing him with a new CEO; Abrams remained on as chairman until 2005.[11] During his tenure as CEO and chairman, tensions developed between his vision of the site and the unruly practices of a group of users known as the Friendster Revolution. I will return to this conflict—a conflict bound up in practices of fabricating, circulating, and collecting online objects—after discussing some of the particularities of the site.

The database of Friendster.com is a network of interconnected-user profiles. Logging onto the site, one is met with a personal home page. Here, friendsters post a scanned photograph of themselves. This photograph appears as a thumbnail to other users and serves as a doorway to the user profile. Friendsters navigate the network by clicking on thumbnail representations of their "friends" and the "friends" of others, jumping from one user profile to another.

The profiles reveal the identity of the user through a number of pre-determined categories including: "Gender," "interested in meeting people for" (i.e., dating, relationship, friends, etc.), "status" (i.e. married, single, etc.), and "date of birth." Optional categories include "hometown," "occupation," "location," "interests," "favorite music," "books," "movies," "about me," and "describe who you want to meet."

Profiles are governed by Friendster's Terms of Service agreement which states, "Your profile must describe you, an individual person. Examples of inappropriate profiles include, but are not limited to, profiles that purport to represent an animal, place, inanimate object, fictional character, or real individual who is not you."[12] This agreement is an attempt to insure that friendsters, in the words of digital copyright attorney Martin Schwimmer, "'say who [they] really are.'"[13]

Journalist Lessley Anderson describes the importance of the Terms of Service in relation to former CEO John Abrams' notion of the site: "He envisioned a matchmaking site that worked more like real life, in which friends introduce you to available people."[14] In other words, Abrams' concern with a site that was "more like real life" reflects his desire to overcome the aforementioned truism of online anonymity. Anderson addresses this condition:

> When it began, the Internet offered a world of new opportunities for anonymous communication and self-representation. Here was a unique medium that revealed nothing about you — not the way you looked, the sound of your voice, or even your handwriting. The possibilities for self-invention were nearly limitless — and, some would say, highly liberating. Online, you have far more control over how people perceive you, free from stereotypes about race, gender, income, and age.[15]

The very communication technology that makes Internet socialization possible is also seemingly responsible for facilitating "self-invention"; the anonymity enabled by Internet technologies lends itself to creative, if not false self-representation. Anderson, having interviewed Abrams, cites the former CEO's opposition to "limitless" parameters of "self-invention." She states, "The people behind Friendster want to make their site as unlike the Internet as possible" by ensuring, via the Terms of Service, that Friendster profiles characterize a "real individual," and by allowing users to "flag" rogue profiles that violate the agreement for review by the Friendster corporate office.[16]

This goal of a less-anonymous Internet led former Friendster COO Kent Lindstrom to describe a vision of the site as such: "'The idea is how you would really meet someone at a beach party.'" He continues, "'We want people to feel comfortable, for people's behavior to be what's normally socially acceptable.'"[17]

The Friendster Revolution

Yet some friendsters took exception to the Abrams/Lindstrom vision of "what's normally socially acceptable." Loosely organized under the banner of the "Friendster Revolution," these critics — known as Fakesters — attempted to develop alternatives to the "earnest," "boring" beach-party metaphor: alternatives centered on acts of creating, circulating, and collecting intentionally fake profiles, thereby subverting the Friendster.com Terms of Service agreement. Through email correspondence on Yahoo Groups, Fakesters plotted "invasions" of the site—fabricating illegal profiles and "embedding" their false identities as friends amongst other friendster profiles—and publicized their revolutionary philosophies.

Even the most casual friendster will notice that, in spite of Abrams' vision of thumbnails that reflect "real individual[s]," Fakester profiles of famous people, places, objects, and ideas proliferate. Embedded amongst the real friends of real people, users will find thumbnails of fake places like "Detroit"; states of being like "True Love"; the idea of "Evil"; Faked people like "Osama" who declares, in the "About Me" section of his profile, "really i'm not all that bad! i'm very misunderstood"; and fake things like the children's toy "Speak n' Spell," which, known for its robotic voice, lists "all of Stephen Hawking's books on tape" as an interest.

Through "Speak n' Spell," users can connect to eighty other "friends," including "metal detector," "robot," and "parking meter." These illegal profiles act as social hubs, allowing users to collect and exchange both real friends and fake profiles with strangers. The Fakesters have created a blackmarket for socialization where people connect over thumbnails of common interest, like a Reese's Peanut Butter Cup.

Such Fakester hubs were a problem for Abrams: his idea of friends connecting via friends was suddenly being thwarted by strangers contacting strangers via their mutual interest in a place—"Detroit"—a thing—"Speak n' Spell"—or a faked person—"Osama." "'The whole point of Friendster,'" says Abrams, "'is that you're connected to somebody through mutual friends, not by virtue of the fact that you both like Reese's Peanut Butter Cups.'"[18] He reacted by deleting numerous fake profiles—an action that angered many Friendster users. Consequently, a handful of friendsters organized in opposition to the deletion of their profiles, articulating revolutionary philosophies justifying the Fakester mission.

One dissident known to members of the Friendster Revolution as both "K-J" and the "Mad Quotester" articulates the mission as such, encouraging users to "Make Fake ... spread infamy [and] insurrection" by proliferating false profiles throughout the Friendster.com network.[19] Such were the bottom-line requirements of being a Fakester: creating fake profiles and embedding them in the profiles of others by befriending as many friendsters as possible.

Given Abrams' policy of deletion, many Fakesters began creating, circulating, and collecting fake identities as quickly as possible in anticipation of the swift erasure of their profiles. As Anderson notes, "Fakesters ... create problems by adding friends indiscriminately in contests to see who can collect the most [thereby] strain-[ing] Friendster's already overloaded servers."[20] Herein begins the tension that separates the beach-party vision of social interaction from an alternative vision; a vision that acknowledges the creation, collection, exchange, and display of thumbnail identities—online objects—as the capillaries through which online social interaction proceeds.

K-J explores the act of collecting thumbnails in her personal faking-philosophy. She begins with a criticism of the beach party vision:

> friendster was conceived to simply connect those who felt a certain lack in their social connectivity. that is, it was once a dating thing. i find that the people who attempted to use friendster to this end (that is, in earnest) A) are boring and B) give up and abandon their profile after a short while or C) [sic] very young which embarrasses me.[21]

K-J describes Abrams' vision as having passed ("it was once a dating thing") and offers her own method of using the site to counter those "boring" people who use Friendster as it was intended; a method centered on the creation and collection of fake profiles:

> [W]hich brings me to the second possible objective one may have on friendster. This one would explain my existence ... [T]hanks to the advent of fakesters, the friendster universe has provided [us with] the opportunity to reduce all of humanity to collectible baseball cards ... [T]he objective of friendster is to accumulate 500 of the coolest profiles possible and establish yourself as some kind of friendster cult celebrity.[22]

Here, K-J addresses the idea of online objects by suggesting that a particular Internet space — the "friendster universe" — allows her to "reduce humanity to collectible baseball cards." In other words, in contrast to the beach-party vision where friends connect through mutual friends, cyber networking on Friendster.com can alternatively be conceived of as an act of connecting through online objects; an act of trading and collecting thumbnails (friends) like "baseball cards." While Abrams wants these thumbnails to characterize the identities of "real individual[s]," K-J treats the thumbnails as objects of interest in-and-of-themselves; as objects worthy of a collector's objective: "to accumulate 500 of the coolest profiles possible." K-J's vision of the Friendster enterprise highlights the objectification intrinsic to the profiling process. When friendsters create profiles — when they represent themselves as online individuals — they also objectify themselves as thumbnails; a Fakester like K-J indulges in the online objects that are both produced by cyber socialization and facilitators of further online interaction.

Lessley Anderson furthers this metaphor of Friendster.com thumbnails as objects to be collected, "Thumbnail versions of your friends' photos appear on your profile page like a collection of trading cards."[23] Anderson's statement reminds us that thumbnails are "versions of ... photos." In other words, offline objects (photos) translate into online objects (thumbnails) that help organize space and activities on Friendster.com. Anderson then suggests, much like K-J, that these online objects can be collected like "trading cards": thumbnails are the collectibles of Friendster.com. The act of "inviting friends" — a primary social activity on the site — becomes a process of adding thumbnails to one's collection. A friendster named Jade materializes this metaphor by representing herself with a scanned, Garbage Pail Kids-trading-card, "Jay Decay," as her thumbnail.

The Form of the Site: Beach Party or Collector's Convention

While the creators of Friendster might not have intended it to be a medium for collecting, the formal design of the site itself contributes to this notion of the thumbnail as a collectible. Pages contain links to "See More People," "Add ... Friends," and "Meet People." Insofar as online "People" are thumbnails, and given the metaphor of thumbnails as collectibles, such links encourage users to browse others' collections ("See More People"), to increase the size of one's collection ("Add ... Friends"), and to forge relationships through these online objects ("Meet People"). Collections can be tailored through the "Edit Friends" command that allows users to "Add/Delete Friends."

Friendsters socialize, in part, by mutually exchanging each other's thumbnails. The dating and networking functions of the site are facilitated by the displaying and browsing of thumbnails on the "Friends" page. Each profile has its own "Friends" page, accessible through the "view friends" icon. This icon leads to a full-screen spread of up to fifty friends, neatly boxed by a solid line, like trading cards arranged in a display case.

The size of a user's collection of thumbnails—the number of friends/objects a user has—dominates the text of the personal profile page. The site monitors these numbers closely, updating them when you add or lose a friend as well as tallying the total number of people a user is connected to: "You are connected to [x number of] people in your Personal Network, through [x number of] friends." This numerical indication allows friendsters to monitor both the number of friends they have in their own collection, as well as the total number of people they are connected to through the collections of others (I might have a collection of fifty friendsters, yet I could be connected to one-million people through my friends' collections of friendsters). The constant tally adds a dynamism, if not a competitive edge to the personal profile page that allows users to measure the size of their collection against that of others.

Rather than viewing the number of friends as a popularity contest based on the "real individual[s]" one knows, K-J takes pleasure in accumulating fake profiles:

> my little gimmick is ... having the most Britney Spears of all the 6 million people who use this thing—its not genius or anything but in my own humble little way i have a certain specialness that some people seem to enjoy and i am happy to share.[24]

K-J's "gimmick" involves collecting Britney Spears thumbnails. She takes pride—"a certain specialness"—in her collection of these thumbnails; a collection that allows her to connect and socialize with others over a common whimsical-interest in particular online objects—representations of Britney Spears. This recognition of online objects, rather than "real individual[s]," as the medium through which online socialization occurs raises questions about identity.

Revolutionary Fakester Roy Batty, author of the Manifesto, "Fake People as Real Outlaws," "believes that the concept of identity is quite elastic," claiming, "'Identity is provisional,'" while advising friendsters to "'NEVER STOP LYING ABOUT YOUR IDENTITY!'"[25] Another Fakester suggests, "'At least we're more real about being fake [than traditional friendsters],'"[26] accentuating the "cliché that everybody bends the truth in a personal ad."[27] Such Fakester philosophizing intimates that confusion over the realness of identities lies more in the act of representation itself—"Identity is provisional"—and in the conventional social networking form of the profile—the "personal ad"—than in some essential quality of the Internet.

The actions and words of Fakesters like Roy Batty and K-J suggest an alternative vision of Friendster.com; a vision wherein thumbnails are online objects rather than real representations of real people; a vision that indulges the ambiguity of representing identity rather than resisting it; a vision wherein users derive pleasure from the act of producing, distributing, and collecting these playful and subversive identities—these online objects. With the site's emphasis on the size of one's collection of friends and the boxed manner in which these friends are displayed, with its options for browsing, editing, and trading thumbnails, and with its requirement that users profile their "real" qualities like the vital statistics on the back of a baseball card, the very form of Friendster.com supports the Fakester vision: the site feels more like a collector-card convention than a beach party.

Conclusions

While our experience with the Internet might seem new and different, we engage in practices and metaphors from our offline lives to navigate and understand online space. Many of our offline lives are enriched, if not complicated, by both our collections and the socialization that occurs through these collections. The Internet offers similar possibilities for complication and enrichment. Of course online objects seemingly lack the materiality of offline objects. Yet I offer, through this paper, that objects need not be "material"—containing mass and exhibiting physicality—to be collected or to shape social interaction. This distinction might explain, in part, the tension between Abrams and the Fakesters.

Where Abrams and Lindstrom attempt to combat the truism of Internet anonymity through a beach party vision of the site, K-J and the Fakesters play with the uncertainties of identity produced through the very practices required by social-networking sites—representation through profiles. While both Abrams and the Friendster Revolution appear to share the same aim —the creation of a space for socializing—Abrams, by enforcing the Terms of Service, rejects the notion that people often want to connect "by virtue of the fact that [they] both like Reese's Peanut Butter Cups." In doing so, he founds his vision of the site on the assumption that profiles should be true representations of people; he does not value the relevance, much less the reality, of online objects as vessels of socialization on Friendster.com.

In contrast, Fakesters like K-J assume online objects as vehicles of Internet socialization. They value connecting over objects of common interest—be they Reese's Peanut Butter Cups, baseball cards, or Britney Spears thumbnails. Furthermore, much in the way that objects physically mediate our offline communication—the paper of a hand-written letter, the receiver of a cell-phone—thumbnails and profiles mediate interactions on Friendster.com. In the Fakester vision, cyber-interaction itself—"Meet People," "Add ... Friends"—is a practice of socializing through objects as we point and click on thumbnails and links.

The Fakesters thus provide insight into the manner in which objects, collections, and practices of collecting stake out and organize the space within which we interact on the Internet. In the privately owned, publicly trafficked environment of cyberspace, users are not always encouraged to influence site content. Yet the Fakester creation and collection of fake profiles reveals an attempt at a bottom-up organizing of Friendster.com space. The Friendster revolutionaries embedded themselves in public collections to tailor the look and feel of a privately owned site.[28]

This look and feel is evident when I casually browse the site. I notice that many "friends" pages are filled with hybrid collections of both real and fake profiles. I am connected to people who use the site for dating, "social-cross referencing," and as a collector's convention for the displaying and trading of fake profiles. While the Friendster Revolution was loosely bound by tenants of resistance, many users, like myself, seemingly create fake profiles without revolutionary intent: I have both a real profile, and a fake one of the dead artist Egon Schiele. I made mine for personal amusement and for the amusement of the six people who have linked up to Egon's profile, becoming his "friends." K-J self-consciously notes the enthusiasm many "real" friendsters have for Fakesters, "Friendster members mostly like the Fakesters ... From the steady onrush of Realster friend invitations, testimonials, messages and such that [K-J] gets to her various profiles, she knows this to be true."[29] Tweaking identities, being someone else, speaking for an inanimate object: these are playful activities that facilitate the socializing and collecting aspects of Friendster.com. Like K-J, I enjoy using online space creatively as I would use space in my offline life.

Perhaps the fluid dynamic of offline/online, real/fake, material/cyber is best-stated by "Eight-Track Cartridge," the offline, analog object, reconceived as an online spokesthing for the Revolution ideology:

> I am an Eight Track Cartridge. I assert my right to be an inanimate object on Friendster and on the internet at large. We started as an expression of self perhaps truer than any soi-disant representation, but we ended as a Revolution when our creativity was ruthlessly squelched by Friendster. Why shouldn't we peacefully coexist there? What makes the relationships we have formed any less real and important than those of a typical, square dating service? In solidarity with Fakesters everywhere — Eight Track.[30]

Objects with rights, thumbnails that speak, eight-tracks that sing the self: as online and offline collectors, we mediate between the animate and the inanimate, people and objects, real and fake, seeking an "expression of self" and the forging of relationships through the production, accumulation, exchange, and display of objects. As online actors and collectors, we seek cyberspaces that allow for the materialization of our own personal aesthetic. Amidst generic banner-advertisements and links dictated by site designers and financially interested parties, our online lives offer similar choices to those we encounter in our offline-lives: opportunities for collecting, creativity, resistance, and socialization over and through objects. And perhaps, some day, the peaceful coexistence of both real and fake.

Has MySpace already enabled this coexistence of real and fake? As tensions between the Revolution and site administrators ran high in the summer of 2004, I recall a number of Fakesters advocating a shift from Friendster to MySpace. MySpace's general lack of concern with policing fake identities, and the site's allowance of personalized html code to stylize home pages seemed to validate the oppressiveness of the Friendster.com Terms of Service. In granting broader options for the creative expression of identity, MySpace seemed hip to the fact that any effort to be oneself on a social networking site is necessarily a representation.

When I reluctantly joined MySpace after a year on Friendster.com, I was met by many playful identities, including the Friendster-inspired profile "Fakester Revolution." Pure Evil draws a direct connection between the Fakester migration away from Frienster.com and MySpace's subsequent success:

> I'm PURE EVIL ... I brought Friendster TO IT'S KNEES with organized action, action that helped mold this valuable communication tool called Myspace that YOU'RE USING NOW ... Ask TOM [Anderson] about when he INVITED my band of Friendster Fakester warriors to come live here ... IT'S ALL DOCUMENTED.[31]

Here, Pure Evil suggests that Tom Anderson, co-founder and now President of MySpace, actually courted the dispossessed "Friendster Fakester warriors." Whether or not this diaspora of fake identities was directly responsible for MySpace's rise and Friendster's decline, Pure Evil's comments intimate that Abrams, too, in his desire to court "real" users and thwart Fakesters, was out-of-touch with his clientele. Since 2004, many Fakesters have continued to thrive, faking and socializing in the less-prohibitive MySpace environment. I am more apt to use MySpace. While I still have a personal profile on Friendster, I rarely log in. Pure Evil maintains a page on Friendster.com as well; yet he seemingly does so out of spite for John Abrams and what the site could have been: "A toast to you, Jon [sic] Abrams, you had a great idea but not the vision ... to make it realize it's potential ... [T]he ol' ZEITGEIST is fickle, my "friend," and you have been passed on."[32] While Friendster's dominance might be a thing of the past, the site's legacy remains present in what has become the routine practice of socialization through the fabrication and collection of ambiguous Internet identities; identities embodied in online objects— in the profiles and thumbnails through which we remake ourselves to make friends with each other.

NOTES

1. The phrase "objects of memory" comes from the essay Barbara Kirschenblatt-Gimblett, "Objects of Memory: Material Culture as Life Review," in *Folk Groups and Folklore Genres*, Elliott Oring, ed. (Logan: Utah State University Press, 1986).

2. Jennifer Egan, "Love in the Time of No Time," *New York Times Magazine*, November 23, 2003, 68.

3. Phillip Harper, "Is Friendster the 'Next Big Thing'?," *Microsoft Network*, http://mobilemomentum.msn.com/article.aspx?aid=4 (accessed March 27, 2004). Note that New Economy Magazine Business 2.0 recently went out of print; for specifics, see http:://www.nytimes.com/ 2007/09/05/ business/media/ 05mag.html.

4. Richard Siklos, "News Corporation Buys An Internet Company," *New York Times*, July 19, 2005, http://www.lexis-nexis.com.

5. Gary Rivlin, "How Friendster Lost a Chance for a Jackpot," *International Herald Tribune*, October 16, 2006, http://www.lexis-nexis.com.

6. Egan, "Love in the Time of No Time," 71.

7. Chok Suat Ling, "Friendster Mania Lights Up Cyberworld," *The Strait Times*, March 18, 2007, http://www.lexis-nexis.com.

8. Celeste Altus, "Friendster Looks to Big Sky as its Eyes Rebound," *PR Week*, August 14, 2006, http://www.lexis-nexis.com.

9. Swati Pandey, "From Fakery to Comfort in MySpace," *Los Angeles Times*, November 26, 2006, http://www.lexis-nexis.com.

10. Vauhini Vara, "Friendster Founder Takes Another Crack at Social Networking," *Globe and Mail*, March 16, 2007, http://www.lexis-nexis.com.

11. Ben Fritz, "Sassa trades H'w'd for dot-com gig," *Daily Variety*, June 3, 2004, http://www.lexis-nexis.com. Since leaving in 2005, Abrams has founded a new networking site, Socializr Inc. Abrams' replacement was Scott Sassa, who had worked with NBC, helping to launch several of the Turner corporations cable ventures. Sassa served until May 2005, when he was replaced by Taek Kwon, see David Shabelman, "Networking Companies Feel Pressure," *Daily Deal*, May 30, 2005, http://www.lexis-nexis.com. While Kwon has a personal profile on Friendster, his name no longer occurs in news publications in association with the

title CEO. The site itself lists a member of Abrams' original team, former COO Kent Lindstrom as current company president, http://www.friendster.com/info/index.php (accessed Nov 25, 2007); see also Abbey Klaassen, "Making Friends With the Social Networks," *Advertising Age*, June 11, 2007, http://www.lexis-nexis.com.

12. "Content Posted on the Site," Terms of Service, http://www.friendster.com/info/tos.jsp (accessed on March 19, 2004). Note that this information and this discussion of the site layout are based upon the rules and content that existed in 2004. Friendster has updated its Terms of Service, at http://www.friendster.com/info/tos.php (accessed November 23, 2007). The quoted text remains in the agreement, but the site has broadened its rules to allow for groups, organizations, places, and famous individuals to represent themselves by registering their identity as a "Fan Profile." The look of the site has undergone numerous changes as well.

13. Lessley Anderson, "Attack of the Smartasses," *SF Weekly*, August 30, 2003, http://www.lexis-nexis.com/.

14. Ibid.

15. Ibid.

16. Ibid.

17. Ibid.

18. Ibid.

19. K-J, email to Yahoo Groups mailing list, December 5, 2003, FriendsterRevolution@yahoogroups.com.

20. Anderson, "Attack of the Smartasses." Note that one of the potential perks of MySpace in 2004 was the ability to send out an indiscriminate number of requests for new friends. At the time, Friendster restricted users, allowing only ten friend requests at a time, presumably as a means of limiting traffic, and thereby increasing the speed of the site.

21. K-J, email to Yahoo Groups mailing list, March 10, 2004, FriendsterRevolution@yahoogroups.com.

22. Ibid.

23. Ibid.

24. K-J, email to Yahoo Groups mailing list, February 28, 2004, FriendsterRevolution@yahoogroups.com.

25. Anderson, "Attack of the Smartasses."

26. Ibid.

27. Ibid.

28. I use the past tense here — "used public collections" — as the Revolution seems to be inactive, in part, due to the popularity and leniency of MySpace as I explain at the end of the paper.

29. Ibid.

30. Fakester Revolution, Our Dedicated Team, http://fakesters.netfirms.com/team.htm.

31. Pure Evil, email to "Pure Evil's Fight Club," November 4, 2004, http://forum.myspace.com/ index.cfm?fuseaction=messageboard.viewThread&entryID=369070&categoryID=0&IsSticky=0&groupID=100043617&Mytoken=A0A68A65-2756-4E75-A8937AAAD4411F6F8453 (accessed on November 21, 2007).

32. Pure Evil, http://profiles.friendster.com/219209 (accessed on November 21, 2007).

10

Tales from the Thrift

Thrift-shopping Enthusiasts Tell Their Stories Online

ALISON FRANKS

> The essence of collecting is not only that one collects "objects," but that in collecting objects, one also acquires memories and stories. Collections, as they are used, are built on talk. They are objects of narrative, and not only vision.[1]

These rich words by Gary Alan Fine, in his book about the outsider-art market *Everyday Genius* highlight an aspect of collecting well-served by the Internet and the kinds of postings, dialogs, and conversations it supports. Well-represented on the Internet is a special class of storytelling collector, the habitual thrift store shopper. I love reading these stories, but I do not collect them; thus, what I am telling here is a story about collectors telling stories on the Internet, rather than telling of an Internet collection.

People who frequent thrift stores on a regular basis are a particular class of collector: they may have very specific collections of things like old typewriters, teapots, or tourist scarves; on the other hand they may exhibit the relish and zeal of specialized collectors while they gather up practical items—clothes, shoes, dishes, towels—for use in everyday life. I myself was drawn into the thrift store initially by the need for a bargain but also by the thrill of the hunt and by the serendipity involved. Who knows what I will find—and when! I actively collect 1940s–1950s print tablecloths, silver jewelry, and Japanese jackets, and through the years I have had a lot of success adding to these collections from the thrift store. I feel just as gleeful and victorious as a formal collector of specific treasures would, though, and just as ready to praise the occasion, when I find a pair of shoes, or a replacement for a broken wine glass—things for my everyday life.

In 1995 I finished a master's thesis entitled "Drawing from the Discard

Pile: Frequent Thrift Store Shoppers as a Folk Group"[2] in which I characterized ardent thrift shoppers as a folk group with shared expressive behaviors that cut across cultural categories of gender, income-level, age, and ethnicity. The word "thrifting" has entered the mainstream vocabulary now, and it is by feeding this keyword into the Google search engine that I find the richest trove of stories, mostly told—and illustrated with posted snapshots—by thrifters in their teens and twenties, for whom posting on the Internet is as natural as breathing. In keeping with our Internet theme, I bring you the definition of thrifting from the online user-created and user-edited encyclopedia, Wikipedia:

> **Thrifting** refers to the act of shopping at a thrift store, flea market, garage sale, or charity shop, usually with the intent of finding interesting items at a cheap price.
>
> A larger *philosophy* permeates the act of thrifting which celebrates the recycling of formerly owned items, finding new use and new love for vintage material goods which had been thrown out, and the thrill of imagining what the former life of the item was like.[3]

In my own research I only looked at shoppers in thrift stores, rather than in those other venues described in the definition (a charity shop, though, is what small thrift stores benefiting specific charities are called in Britain).

At the time that I was doing my research, sometime in 1994, the Internet had just the beginnings of a thrifter-posting culture (and I was too inexperienced with the medium to do much with what postings there were). Now, as I write these words in 2007, the crush of online thrifting lore and stories is overwhelming; by the time these words appear in print there will be more sites added, and some of the ones now existing will have faded away. The Internet, I believe, has a lot in common with the thrift store. Things are here today and gone tomorrow, but there is always more. There is a constant influx of new material on the Internet, like the thrift store claim of "over 1,000 new items put out daily." The items in both places range from gems to trash; the visitors come from all walks of life and all levels of knowledge and expertise. In both venues, one browses.

I'm still a green and clumsy Internet user. Nonetheless, every so often I go online and Google-search both "thrift + stores + shopping" (these keywords keep away the kind of thrift associated with savings and banking) and "thrifting" (this one occasionally brings up sites that have something to do with metallurgy). Sometimes I do this search because I am giving a talk or writing something; mostly I do it for entertainment (being of the thrifting persuasion myself) and for the thrill of seeing that my master's-thesis characterization of the thrifting culture is alive, well, burgeoning, and thriving on the Internet. There it all is: in both print media made digital and in online ("born-digital," as is the term) newsletters for the elderly, for mothers, and for those on a budget; in cyberzines, those small underground magazines created online; on websites;

in blogs, forums, and online community postings. I will sometimes print a piece out and physically archive it in my filing cabinet of materials in print, but when I am simply enjoying the genre I let these postings be ephemeral without trying to capture them. Indeed, things come and go on the Internet every day. I am sure there are wonderful stories, tips, and listings hidden away from most of us in locked sites and in live chat room conversations, too.

Although an enthusiastic thrift store shopper since my teens, I don't post my own thrifting tales on the Internet. I've put in too many years before the advent of the personal computer and its use as a communication tool, and I feel no great urge to toss a pebble of my own into the stream of online storytelling for an unknown audience. I suppose I am a bit of a lurker then, as they say in the cyber-parlance, since I am not posting stories myself or commenting on the offerings of others, but there is nothing sinister in my silent enjoyment of these other thrift-troubadours— it is only for the pleasure of the tale.

Why do thrifters tell stories? It seems as though they can't help themselves. If they didn't see stories in things (the "thrill of imagining what the former life of the item was like" mentioned in the Wikipedia quote above), they might not be thrifting at all, and it is a joy to share that perceived story. Also, reaching out through storytelling helps relieve the tension that exists between thrift shoppers, a tension between community feeling and the "me first!" desire for the best goods. Not all stories are about favorite finds; some of them involve very generous tips and useful information. There is also an element of boasting. Katrina Ramser, writing as Fashion Whore for the online version of the zine Nervy Girl, remarked, "Nowadays, you can bump into anyone at a thrift store. Once about shame and lashing out at society, thrift store shopping is now about bragging rights."[4] So in these tales we have sharing, bragging, and the pure and simple deliciousness of reliving the beloved past-time by telling about it afterwards.

As I conducted my participant-observation and interviewing research for my thesis, I heard thrifting story after thrifting story, related with glee. If it wasn't a story about the narrator herself, it was a story about an aunt or the man down the street. The stories were mostly about favorite finds— one's own or those of someone else — but some of them were about favorite stores, specific expeditions, or about thrift store people. Stories about thrifting while traveling are a whole genre in themselves. Some of the favorite-finds stories are urban legends, of the *objet d'art* genre: "once this man found a junky-looking watercolor in the Salvation Army, for $1.00, and it was worth $10,000" (quotation marks mine). The urban legend classification doesn't mean a story isn't true — all of us know *true* ones, and these tales are the juicy parts of things like the Antiques Road Show program on PBS. As I indicated earlier, at the time of my Master's research the thrifting stories, the tip-trading and other conversations were mostly through the oral tradition — in-store conversations, talk at parties, talk at work, and so on. Some of this made its way into magazine and newspaper pieces, and in the 1990s through the present, into print (as opposed to cyber) zines, and other self-published print venues. Now, the same people who clip articles for me send me addresses for the Internet.

The cult of thrifting is more popular and acceptable today than it was in the early 1990s, when it was definitely healthy. During my research, I concluded that most people who walk through the thrift store door can use the savings offered, at least at the beginning of their shopping history. Not only have we experienced downsizing, outsourcing, and all those other things that affect people's work situation, but even those destined for prosperous careers must get through long years of medical, law, or other professional schools or graduate training. Most important to the proliferation of thrifting, though, is the abundance of used goods due to the never-ending supply of goods produced and goods discarded by our consumer society. It used to be that thrift stores were considered shopping venues for the poor. In the present economic climate, the truly destitute can't afford to shop anywhere, and low-income people have the choice of the discount department stores for budget shopping. Thrift stores are available for people of all income levels who are happy to comb through secondhand goods.

The constant quest for new styles and trends leads to the validation of vintage and retro chic as well as the watching of "street style" for new fashion concepts. Young "street-style" setters run one step ahead of the co-opting fashion industry, and what better place to dig for new "looks" than the big pile of discards donated to the thrift stores. Now, too, with the unbridled excitement generated by eBay and other online auction sites, and the accompanying impression that anything under the sun is desired, purchased, and collected by somebody, we have an onslaught of hopeful vendors visiting the thrifts, too. (These pickers are not as likely to tell stories as their ultimate customers are, however.)

After the part about a larger philosophy that "permeates the act of thrifting," which I quoted above, the Wikipedia entry on thrifting goes on to say, "A zine called 'Thrift Score,' published in the 1990s by Ms. Al Hoff, celebrated this lifestyle."[5] I am so pleased Wikipeda mentions Al (and provides that "Ms." as a clue to her gender), because she really is the impetus for the style of storytelling proliferating on the Internet today: personal thrifting tales complete with cultural commentary, history of material culture, uses, and even laundering tips for thrifted items. Having a chance to go thrifting with Al and her husband back in 1996 was a highpoint in my own thrifting autobiography. She is no longer chronicling thrifting,[6] but as of this writing she still has some of her zines[7] for sale via her website,[8] although the sample excerpt page is not there any longer.

Perhaps the most prevalent stories on the Internet today are the ones told in the Al Hoff spirit—and photo documented with digital cameras and cell phones by predominantly young thrifters for whom Internet posting is a routine part of life. The stories tend to be short (longer narratives, with full accounts of a trip to the store or expostulations on popular culture, are more commonly found in the online journals, zines and newsletters), and of course the pictures are worth, well, many words. In fact, the snapshots are so key to the communication that the postings move into another favorite concern of collector-thrifters, that of display. The Internet makes a great knick-knack shelf or open closet.

These illustrated, short thrifting tales are the ones easily found on Google under the keyword "thrifting" and are part of the blogging phenomenon. My more learned and tech-savvy colleagues know just what the software innovations are that led to blogs; all I know is that it is easy for people to post on these individually owned online journals, much easier than maintaining the websites established with an earlier software and still used today. There are easy mechanisms for posting reader-response to the blogger as well, with each discussion "threaded" to the remarks that the response references, so the postings related to the same topic can all be read together. There are various host sites for blogging, under which individuals can open their own blogs and get help with the project. The site Blogger.com, owned by Google, reports that it was launched in 1999[9]; the burgeoning of blogs accompanies the turn to the twenty-first century. These host sites, such as Blogger, LiveJournal, and others, may host communities, forums, and other mechanisms for people to share and discuss a particular topic. Livejournal.com defines a community as follows: "A community is basically a journal run by a member of LiveJournal for people with common interests. Communities are free to use and create ... anyone can have them, and they're easy to set up, too!"[10]

I sometimes check into the Livejournal community "the thrift store ate my wallet!," which has been designed with a set of user's rules that keep it to topic on the sharing of items found at thrift stores, yard sales, rummage and estate sales, and consignment stores. There are strict instructions to insure that visual images are clear enough and will open readily for most computer users. Here is the description of "the thrift store ate my wallet!"

> User: thriftwhore (121965)
> Where it doesn't take a lot of money
> To look this cheap.
> Name: the thrift store ate my wallet!
> About: are you a thrift whore?
> can't pass up a thrift store without dropping in?
> like to brag about your latest treasure/find/score/loot?
> Do it here. Post about your latest thrift store adventure. Post pictures of your latest conquest.[11]

On September 23, 2007, the story-telling is going forward, as it does every day on thriftwhore. A community member, with the user-name of "tteen angst," is posting for the first time (the heading for her post is "poppin my thriftwhore cherry"). Her headshot photo shows a charming young woman in a set of bunny ears. She tells us:

> My name is Allie.
> I collect owls. My nickname is Owlie, actually. Haha
> Owl mirror. Bought it last summer from Goodwill so I have no idea how much it was. Probably like, $8-$12.

The mirror is a large wooden oval with carved branches in its frame and a couple of owls carved near the bottom. Allie and her camera make a nice reflected image in the glass. Although Allie shows us many more thrifted owl figurines (and a few other things, too, like china deer figurines) the mirror attracts the attention of most of the responding posters, starting with the user known as ifeelgoodlost, who says, "um, owl mirror? Genius!" The easy format inspires people to make those little encouraging comments, and Allie sends brief responses to most of her posters. Mightbemisery chimes in with

> i have that 3rd owl figurine.
> it's a salt shaker, right?
> we can team up and have a set.

Allie tells her:

> i don't think mine is, but maybe i can poke some holes in it? Hahaha

Owl-fanciers—and just lately there are so many of them!—continue to post to Allie all day: mango_sama speaks for that group with:

> man, I just went to thrifting yesterday and there was owl stuff EVERYWHERE—like at least five different necklaces and a YARN TAPESTRY. I think I need to go back and get some of them. D: [The upper-case D and colon combination makes a little sad-face icon.]

One of Alley's owls was missing an eye, and she responded as thrifters so often do and rushed in to rescue him. Some people opt for an elaborate restoration, but she merely made him a little black felt eye-patch. Several of her respondents were charmed by this.[12]

Although the owl mirror and a few other treasures shown, for instance the owl earring-holder, serve Allie in her daily life, she is presenting herself here as a formal collector of thrifted owls (and we see that she is a collector who uses her finds, rather than one who keeps the collection in a special closet or other filing system). The narratives are short (and photo documented), and not all comments are profound, but there is an opportunity for support here and indeed for community. Not all posters on this site are as young as Allie, but many appear to be teens or very young adults.

The use of snapshots with the thrifting stories—with any online stories, I would imagine—has really taken off in the last several years, with the mastery of digital cameras and especially with the use of cameras in cell phones. The photo posting and sharing website, Flickr, hosts a community called Thriftstores, with a continuing stream of photos offered for public viewing. A visitor to this site can also choose to access all public photos on Flickr that are tagged with keywords related to thrift shopping. Such a community site is an opportunity for doing what the members of thriftwhore are doing, but with even less narrative (maybe a line or so). The photo is the thing. Rather than offering photos of favorite finds—booty brought home and laid on the bed or table—the most prolific photographers have chosen vignette shots taken at the store. In fact, a great many of them are evocative shots of the store façade. Because of this, they come across much more as stories, rather than collection display, than do the postings on thriftwhore. They take us along on the expedition, rather than showing us the specimens brought back home.[13] The blog "Jesus, Family and Scrapbooking" has a special archive spot for people's postings of thrifting photos,[14] although no photos have been posted since February of 2006.

As I've prowled the thrift stores since my research in the early 1990s, I've felt that the cell phone has been the personal electronic device changing the climate of thrifting, whereas the computer, with the Internet, has enhanced the experience that I chronicled in my thesis by providing a vast storytelling arena. It used to be that people talked to one another, stranger to stranger, while shopping in the informal world of the thrift store. (I admit that they still do, but I think there is less of it now). So often these days, each shopper is talking to someone not present, and not a stranger, while perusing the aisles of the store. Instead of getting help from strangers as to whether or not a shirt might fit a husband not present or whether a certain color would be good on a redheaded sister, the shopper calls the relevant party and gets a firsthand opinion.

Not even ten years ago, I was amazed to see someone getting a cell phone call in the thrift store, of all places! Now half the ears in the store are engaged, and we are all groping at our bags and pockets as we hear the tinkling of little ditties all around us. (I admit to a little frisson of wonder when I myself receive a call while in the dressing room.) While reading about Blogger.com, though, I discovered that some of those thrift store photos are coming into blogs live, from cell phones. Using a feature called Blogger Mobile, people can, by sending a message to an Internet address, send photos (and text, too) right to a blog while, one might say, they are out in the field.[15] I imagine some of the snapshots I admire on blogs and community groups have been posted that very way.

Returning to the topic of online thrifting-tale sources, if Al Hoff was the thrifting story-woman of the 1990s, that title should, in the 2000s, go to Thriftgoddess, aka Kristi Siegel, who, in gracious response to my questions, writes the following about her Thriftgoddess website:

> I run a Web site, Thriftgoddess.com, which basically champions the fine art of thrift shopping (and we really believe that it IS an art....)We also encourage our readers to be crafty as well as thrifty, and to make the best of what they have in an economy that pretty much kicks you in the seat of the pants!

She goes on to give some personal history:

> I got into thrifting basically for selfish reasons: I'm a history and pop culture buff, and what better place to get a first-person view of American pop culture than a thrift shop? All those bits of history held together with equal parts of glamor and tackiness ... it really is quite the rush to see it and know that you can possess it for mere dollars and sense.

And, even in an e-mail with me, an unknown fan, she starts a story , illustrating some of my favorite points from my Masters thesis: that thrifting crosses gender lines, and that thrifters shop for a network of people other than just themselves.

> Last week I was in my local and favorite thrift shop, just milling around, and it was amazing to see the number of people shopping for Christmas. I mean, people were literally loading up their "granny carts" to the top with sweaters, books, toys ... and it wasn't just women, either. There were a fair number of male shoppers represented in the store, too. Everyone, regardless of gender, deserves a chance at a good bargain. I made out well, too. I personally managed to knock about four people off my Christmas list for about $7.

She sums up her motivation for launching the website Thriftgoddess:

> Having a Web site about thrifting helps to affirm that there is a legitimate community of bargain shoppers. It isn't just little old ladies on a pension. Thrifting has turned into this larger-than-life sub-culture, that, amazingly, crosses gender and class boundaries. It's creative living at its best. It really makes you think.[16]

Indeed her above comments affirm my research and my personal views. All this Internet participation celebrates a larger-than-life culture, with much to make us think. Thriftgoddess sends an e-mailed newsletter to the subscribers, filled with postings (such as "thrifting Colorado Springs" and "Dress for less ... Inside the Indianapolis thrifting scene"), and links and news about the things Kristi and her associates market with an online store. Thriftgoddess also links to Kristi's thrifting blog, her thrifting tips, a photo blog, and to other thrifters' postings as well.[17]

Let me indulge in a bit of a smirk here as we look at the popular-culture icons of womanhood represented in the names of thrift-story sites just discussed. Although there are indeed men posting on thriftwhore and thriftgoddess, we have these female-archetype labels, the "thrift whore," and the "thrift goddess," and then we have, presumably, a family-centered mother represented by the blog Jesus Family and Scrapbooking. Someone other than me may analyze this, but for me, not at least mentioning it is like ignoring a small but trumpeting elephant on these pages.

Market research has made the big thrift store companies very aware of their regular customers' proclivity for storytelling. Two of the biggest thrift store chains in North America have even gotten into the act of providing their customers with story-posting possibilities. Savers and Thrifttown are both for-profit stores that partner with local nonprofits. The nonprofits collect the donations and sell them to the stores; the stores provide the shopping venue and do the merchandising. Savers (some of their stores are called Value Village, but not all stores with that name are theirs) provides a place for customer stories as part of their Fun Stuff page on their website. "Send us photos and stories of your best Savers finds," they encourage.[18] Posted shopping stories are usually accompanied by a snapshot.

Thrifttown posts stories on their customer comments spot, along with the less story-like comments about the store, but they also have a feature called Get Used. Opening this reveals a series of photos to click. A store representative, Ashley, shows cushions made from felted and cut sweaters, lampshades decorated with felt flowers, and cleaned and restored vintage kitchen and furniture items. Interspersed with these homey offerings are customer favorite finds, such as a lynx collar found by a thrifter at the San Francisco store for $6.50. Cleaned and freshened, the collar was valued at a thousand dollars. Ashley invites all thrifters to share their favorite finds with her. The best clothing find submitted by the end of September was to get a $25.00 gift certificate, and indeed winners (two of them) were just announced, one with a full-length cashmere coat and the other with a high-end bicycle jersey.[19]

I am especially intrigued by the personal website of Wendy Darling, who is also the operator for the web-design business Metrogirl.[20] Ms. Darling has created her website as though it were a thrift store, with corners to browse and a "shopkeeper" (Wendy herself) to "talk to" (clicking on the shopkeeper gives you much information about her). Book listings, interviews, poems and the like are found by clicking on the book corner, called "the stacks." There are links to online stores featuring used goods and collectibles.[21] She clearly perceives the same similarities between the Internet and the thrift store that I do.

Websites about specific kinds of collections sometimes have a thrifting article or two, in connection with the acquiring of desired items. An interesting example is CED Magic, a website about Capacitance Electronic Discs (CEDs), "a consumer video format on grooved vinyl discs that was marketed by RCA in the 1980s." There is a fine piece on thrift-shopping for vintage technology, by a seventeen-year veteran of thrifting, with photos of his electronic and electronic-media finds. Also posted is a series of thrift-store interior shots featuring each store's electronics shelf. The writer even has commentary on the nature of thrift stores in the current era.[22] I have come across a number of such thrift references on the Internet, from websites for collectors of vintage video games, collectible clothing, books, and more.

Some thrifting stories involve romance—meeting a like-minded soul in the store, or discovering thrifting as a mutual favorite activity. The aforementioned Al Hoff wrote a small book with quotes from newspaper personals ads, *If You Like Pina Coladas*,[23] inspired by her quest to see how many personals ads mentioned thrifting along with long walks on the beach and foreign films (it was mentioned many, many times!). One can meet fellow thrifters for "dating" online by going to hotornot.com, keyword "thrifting."[24] Free-lance writer Amy Halloran has written a whole guide to thrift store meeting-and-dating on the Big To-Do, a dating-tips section of the website Breakupgirl.net (Breakupgirl.com is a different site). She entitles it Vintage Look: Thrifting Toward Romance, or The Joys of Second-Hand Booty. She mentions a man who became "more than a friend" when they got together after separate thrifting expeditions and compared their loot. "Nostalgia is a great breeding ground for companionship," she writes. "Saying 'I had that when I was a kid!' could be a quick way to round out a morning with a cup of coffee at the nearest diner." "Used goods are a great route to being a great couple," she remarks. Halloran gives plenty of tips on the art of thrifting (and yard-saling and fleamarketing) along with her tips for meeting Mr. Right while doing it.[25]

I expect there are many people like me who are more apt to tell thrifting tales in face to face encounters, and the website meetup.com, that helps a wide base of interest groups organize face to face get-togethers throughout the United States and beyond, does indeed have a thrift-shopping category. As of last viewing,[26] there were 4,756 members of thrift shopping groups throughout the United States, 4,066 people waiting to join new groups, and a total of nine groups in nine cities (and one county group). A map on that same statistics page shows that most of these groups are clustered in the Eastern third of the country, with the next-largest cluster along the West Coast. Meet-up's advice for starting thrifters meet-ups now suggests "customizing" the groups, which seems to mean choosing a specific focus (for instance, several are clothing swaps, others are specifically concerned with flea markets).

I am one of eighteen people—and a diverse lot we do seem to be—listed as being interested in joining a group in Albuquerque, New Mexico. So far, no one has come forward to lead a group into being. This seems to be the case in the other communities encompassing the 4,066 people waiting. I expect there are others like me who might prefer to head off to the thrift store rather than spend the time needed to organize a group and to meet in a coffee shop or like location.

I enjoy the circular progression this endeavor represents, though, of moving from oral and print storytelling to online storytelling — without seeing the listeners, unless one counts their little thumbnail headshots— to using the Internet to find people who would like to share stories face to face once again. However, some groups seem interested in moving in the other direction: the New York group in particular has a photo album for posting thrift store shots online[27] and profile pages for members, wherein they can introduce themselves, talk about their favorite stores, and give answers to other thrift-related questions. There's a place for a personal snapshot and even links to profiled friends.[28] Thus they seem to be an online community as well as people who meet up face to face.

Since I first perused the thrift-shoppers meet-up websites in 2005, more groups have followed New York's example, with the members manifesting a strong online presence (profiles, some with headshots, thrift-story postings) as well as meeting regularly in person. The lists of people waiting for thrift-shopper meet-ups to start in their communities sometimes have headshots next to their names, and some include a little testimonial as to why they would like a meet-up group.[29] Will the in-person meet-ups ultimately fade away, replaced by yet another posting site for stories and photos, all by people living and shopping in the same city?

At this moment in time on the Internet, thrifter-collectors are telling their tales and displaying their trophies with gusto. Pinning down today's online thrifting stories is like pinning down one particular date of the month and day of the week in the thrift store. Tomorrow, next week, next month, or next year, it will be different. I think I see a slide away from thick verbal narrative and toward more visual imagery (mostly snapshots), whether as collection display or as the evocation of a shopping experience. But there still remain plenty of stories-in-words on the Internet. Not only are there well-developed blog entries and feature articles in online journals, but stories told in print media, such as those in newspapers and print journals, are made available on the Internet as well.

I am still not moved to post my own stories on this great Internet bulletin board of show-and-tell, but if I did, and if I had to "customize," as they say on the meet-up site for thrifters, maybe I'd tell only tales of senior discount days at the thrifts— what went into my basket at Savers on Wednesdays, when those over sixty get 30 percent off. (The cheery little PA announcements about senior day make all of us who've had a few birthdays sound like deserving and honor-worthy World War II veterans.) Perhaps I'd score big in the "better clothing" department on Monday at Thrift Town, the day clothing is 30 percent off for seniors. Maybe I'd put the purchases of a younger person into my cart, so that I could help out by buying with my discount and settling with her later. The check-out line of smug-looking sixty-to-ninety-year-olds on a Savers

Wednesday would be a nice cell phone photo. Don't look for this any time soon, but the stories are there to tell and the Internet awaits.

Notes

1. Gary Alan Fine, *Everyday Genius* (Chicago: University of Chicago Press, 2004), 187.
2. Alison Franks, "Drawing from the Discard Pile: Frequent Thrift Store Shoppers as a Folk Group" (master's thesis, University of New Mexico, 1995).
3. Wikipedia, s.v. "Thrifting," http://en.wikipedia.org/wiki/Thrifting (accessed August 21, 2007).
4. "Fashion Whore," Nervy Girl zine, http://www.nervygirlzine.com/200312/columns/fashion-whore.html (accessed February 26, 2004; site now discontinued).
5. Wikipedia, s.v. "Thrifting," http://en.wikipedia.org/w/index.php?title=Thrifting&oldid=124620175 (accessed September 13, 2007; entry has since been updated).
6. Al Hoff, *Thrift Score* (New York: HarperCollins, 1997).
7. Al Hoff, *Thrift Score, the Zine About Thrifting*, issues 1–14, 1994–1999.
8. Al Hoff World, http://www.tinyrat.com (accessed September 12, 2007).
9. Blogger, http://www.blogger.com (accessed September 13, 2007).
10. LiveJournal "Community Center," http://www.livejournal.com/community (accessed September 12, 2007).
11. "thriftwhore — Community Info," LiveJournal, http://community.livejournal.com/thriftwhore/profile (accessed September 12, 2007).
12. tteenangstt, "Poppin [sic] My Thriftwhore Cherry," thriftwore LiveJournal Community, http://community.livejournal.com/thriftwhore/3666101.html#cutid1 (accessed September 24, 2007).
13. "Thrift Stores— and Where to Find Them," Flickr, http://www.flickr.com/groups/thriftstores/pool/ (accessed September 28, 2007).
14. Jesus, Family and Scrapbooking blog, http://scrapalicio.us/index.ph ex.p?s=thrift ing (accessed September 28, 2007).
15. Blogger on the Go, http://www.blogger.com/mobile-start.g (accessed September 12, 2007).
16. Kristi Siegel, e-mail message to author, December 22, 2005.
17. Thriftgoddess, http://www.thriftgoddess.info/ (accessed September 18, 2007).
18. "Fun Stuff," Savers.com, http://www.savers.com/funstuff/stories.php (accessed September 28, 2007).
19. Thrift Town, http://www.thrifttown.com/ (accessed October 3, 2007).
20. Metro Girl, http://www.metrogirl.com/index2.htm (accessed September 27, 2007).
21. "The Shopkeeper: A Closer Look at Wendy Darling," The Thrift Shop, http://www.abraxis.com/wdarling/wendy.html (accessed September 27, 2007).
22. "Thrift Store Experiences," CED Magic, http://www.cedmagic.com/misc/thrift-store/thrift-store.html (accessed October 1, 2007).
23. Al Hoff, *If You Like Pina Coladas: The Humor and Weirdness of Personal Ads* (Kansas City: Andrews Mcmeel, 1999).
24. "Meet Thrifting People at HOT or NOT," HOT or NOT, http://meetme.hotornot.com/keyword/thrifting (accessed October 2, 2007).
25. Amy Halloran, "Vintage Look: Thrifting Toward Romance," Breakupgirl.net, http://www.breakupgirl.net/todo/000329.html (accessed October 3, 2007).
26. "Thrift Shoppers Meetups on the Map," Meetup.com, http://thriftshoppers.meetup.com/about/ (accessed October 3, 2007).
27. "Photo Album: Thrift Finds," Meetup.com, http://thriftshoppers.meetup.com/87/photos/?photoAlbumId=60970&photoId=269285 (accessed October 3, 2007).
28. "The New York Thrift Shoppers Meetup Group," Meetup.com, http://thriftshoppers.meetup.com/87/members (accessed October 3, 2007).
29. "Thrift Shoppers Meetups," Meetup.com, http://thriftshoppers.meetup.com/cities/us/nm/albuquerque/ (accessed October 5, 2007).

11

The Venus of Willendorf Project

Brenda Oelbaum

I've collected a lot of things in my life—1930s pottery mixing bowls and tea pots, Fenton glass shoes for my sister-in-law, and sterling silver napkin rings with my family monograms and those of our friends for gifting. But one collection that started rather unintentionally didn't really bring the same joy as the items listed above, or provide the thrill of hours spent at antique malls, collectible shows, and yard sales. It would be from this bizarre collection that the Venus of Willendorf Project would evolve, greatly facilitated by the Internet.

This superfluous collection started with the collecting of pounds, pounds of fat, a most frightening thing to collect for a preteen girl in this society. But the collection of pounds was only the precursor to the collection to which I refer. It was the collection of diet books that found its way to my bookcase as a result of my attempts to turn myself into someone else that has haunted me to this day. Every few years I would come to my senses and throw them all out, take them to a used book store for resale, or donate them to charity, determined not to waste another moment of my life on the hopeless pursuit of thinness. And then somehow, years later I was doing it again, unloading shelves and shelves of diet books. If I had thought of this project years ago, I would have had a massive lead on this current creation of mine. I believe I have purged myself of diet books at least four times in my life (the same number of times in a year I often gained and lost 50 lbs.). Shocking and an incredible waste!

Disordered eating, chronic dieting, binging, and overweight have really been a dominant part of my life. Whether I was waiting to be a certain number on the scale before doing something or I was wasting my life hiding and stuffing my feelings, issues of diet and weight loss have dominated my existence, as evidenced by the ever-growing number of diet books that would find themselves on my bookshelves year after year. They never worked once I tired of the gimmick or unique way of eating. I would go back to my old ways and gain the weight back and then some. In fact I am pretty darn sure they made me the truly fat person I am today. After years of dieting, I developed some very bad habits, and some crazy food rules, all of which contributed to making it very difficult to eat in a natural, healthy manner. I was so busy following some nonsensical food rules I had found in diet books or fashion magazines that I was no longer able to recognize my own body's natural cues of hunger and fullness. I ate so much of certain foods that to this day I can't even look at them in the market. Unfortunately many of these foods were so-called healthy foods, fruits for example, pineapples to be exact; I can't stand the smell of ripe pineapple to this day because of the months I spent on Judy Mazel's *Beverly Hills Diet*.[1]

If you are not aware of this infamous diet, the first week was basically a week of eating nothing but fruit: pineapple, papayas, mangos, watermelon and grapes. On the watermelon day my stool, if I might be so crude, was bright red. It has taken me nearly 35 years to be able to eat a simple handful of grapes. You see, grapes, like watermelon, were only to be eaten alone, and if you started a day with grapes you could eat nothing else because the food would get trapped and ferment in your stomach and slow down digestion. The only way I can describe my experience on the Beverly Hills Diet was training for bulimia: eat all the pineapple you want in one day and it just shoots out of you like a goose.

My favorite form of dieting was fasting; I could go for weeks eating nearly nothing. This created the habit of skipping meals, and would often end in a series of binges. I know there are papers published in medical journals that both dispute and support my findings, but I don't much care what they have to say. This is my experience and until you've walked a mile in my shoes you can't tell me otherwise. It was from this painful life experience that the Venus of Willendorf Project arose.

The formation of the Feminist Art Project at Rutgers University in the summer of 2005 allowed me to revisit a more intimate and personal kind of art. For years I had thought my art trite — who cares about me, my angst and my depression? The art that really excites people is political, historic, and universal. Unless you are Frieda Kahlo you are not going to get away with painting nothing but self-portraits, and so I stopped doing art about me and started doing art that was political.

While attending the twenty-fifth anniversary of ArtTable in the spring of 2005 I met a wonderful artist and curator named Carol Cole, and she was the first person to tell me about a project called "A Year of Feminism in Art" and that if I was interested in curating shows myself, I should think about projects related to this theme. I was then introduced to one of the founding women of the program at Rutgers, Ferris Olin. At the time she was trying to make contacts across the country to create WAAND, The Women Artists Archives National Directory at Rutgers. As it turned out, Olin was one of the major players in the "Year of Feminism in Art" or what I soon was to learn was The Feminist Art Project (TFAP). As I sent her information I received from the Michigan area, Olin came to invite me to be the Michigan regional representative for the project as a whole.[2]

It was only after Olin formally invited me to become the Michigan coordinator for The Feminist Art Project that I began to look at the work I was doing and remembered the old feminist axiom that "the personal is political," and I decided to reconsider my earlier decision to stop making art about my own life experience. The Venus of Willendorf installation is both political and personal. Every day the increasing government involvement in monitoring our food intake and dietary choices makes it so. The most recent event is Mississippi House Bill No. 282, introduced by Representatives Mayhall, Read, and Shows.[3] Basically the bill would allow food establishments the right to refuse service to any person who could be considered obese. I'm sorry, but have you been to your local fast-food restaurant lately and seen the people who are serving the food? I don't think that any teenager in a paper hat getting paid minimum wage should be given the power to deny service to anyone, let alone the right to pass judgment on the person on the other side of the counter. Even the vice president of PETA, Bruce Friedrich, speaking for the more than 1.8 million members and supporters of the organization, had to chime in regarding this bill.[4] In a letter dated February 5, 2008, Friedrich suggested the bill be changed to have the restaurants serve the fat folk only vegan food. Yeah, right! Vegan KFC! The writers of this bill claim that they knew it would never pass, and it didn't; but they hoped it would bring attention to the "obesity crisis," like it needs more.

Then there was the Cupcake Crackdown. Parents in the state of Texas lobbied to get a "Safe Cupcake Amendment" added to the state's nutritional policy to ensure that they could continue to bring the frosted treats to school celebrations. In reaction to the federal law requiring every school system in the National School Lunch and School Breakfast programs to write a "wellness policy" by July 2006, some schools had gone so far as to ban sweets like cupcakes from being brought to the schools for events such as birthdays.

After losing 100 pounds because of a diagnosis of diabetes, then-governor of Arkansas, Mike Huckabee, pushed for a law requiring schools to measure students each year and report to their parents whether or not pupils were overweight or at risk of becoming overweight. By February of 2007 seven states were on board with these Obesity Report Cards: kids in kindergarten, children as young as five years of age, are being paraded into school nurses' offices for regular weigh-ins. It's not enough that we do this to ourselves. Now it is legislated and pushed on our babies. Though I applaud Mr. Huckabee on his personal health success, he is not representative of the majority of people who diet and regain the weight. Nor do I believe humiliating young children and creating a fear of fat at such a young age is useful. Studies have shown that when mothers worry about their children's weight the children are at higher risk of becoming overweight.[5] Dr. Donna Spruijt-Metz, of the University of Southern California in Alhambra, points out:

> When mother interferes with the child's ability to regulate his or her own energy intake, kids might lose their ability to self-regulate. In other words, they stop functioning on inner cues like "I feel full" or "I feel hungry" and start operating on social cues like "time to pork out on chips because mom isn't watching" or "there is no way I am going to eat this just because mom wants me to."[6]

Former U.S. Surgeon General Richard Carmona declared: "As we look to the future and where childhood obesity will be in 20 years ... it is every bit as threatening to us as is the terrorist threat we face today. It is the threat from within."[7] Declaring war on the obesity epidemic! [It's hard to keep track of all our "wars."] The government should keep its eyes on its own plate; it should be managing the country. As with the abortion issue, it should not be telling us what to do with our bodies. This is obscene and guaranteed to make matters worse. My own personal experience has now become a political issue because of the government's decision to legislate against fat, and so begins the Venus of Willendorf Project.

The Venus of Willendorf, c 24000–22000 B.C.E., Oolitic limestone 4⅜ inches (11.1 cm) high, in the collection of the Naturhistorisches Museum, Vienna (photograph from the public online use image bank of *Wikipedia*, "Venus of Willendorf," http://commons.wikimedia.org/wiki/Category:Venus_of_Willendorf, accessed March 11, 2008).

The Venus of Willendorf Project will be a large installation consisting of one large and several smaller works of art. The centerpiece of the installation will consist of a seven-foot tall, approximately five-foot round papier-mâché statue of the Venus of Willendorf said to be the oldest naturalistic representation of a human being. In 1908 the Austrian archaeologist Josef Szombathy found the Venus of Willendorf about 90 feet (30 meters) above the Danube River, near the town of Willendorf in Austria. Thought to have been made between 24,000 and 22,000 B.C.E., it has been called a Paleolithic Venus. Similar naked female figurines, usually less than 4 inches (10 cm) in height, and made of stone or ivory, have been found on many sites. While breasts, buttocks, and stomachs are voluminous, hands, feet, and faces are neglected or not represented at all. Although conventional archaeologists often associate them with fertility rites, they are fat, not pregnant.

Because of her great age and exaggerated female form the Venus of Willendorf quickly became an icon of prehistoric art and replaced other examples of Paleolithic art in introductory art history textbooks. Because she was both female and nude, she fitted perfectly into the patriarchal paradigm of the history of art and, because she was also the earliest known representation of the human body, she became a prototype, "acquiring a sort of Ur-Eve identity that focused suitably, from a patriarchal point of view, on the fascinating reality of the female body."[8]

In the 1960s her image was adopted by the feminist art movement as an icon of female power, for her presence was physical evidence that perhaps there had been a time when women were revered as gods, or a society that was matriarchal as opposed to patriarchal. Her large, voluptuous form was also appealing, as it added credence to feminists' arguments against institutionalized beauty standards such as those espoused by the Miss America Pageant. Her image can still be found in jewelry and emblazoned on T-shirts, chocolates and fridge magnets. She has been and continues to be used to promote size acceptance, fertility, and the earth mother. Sadly, as I did research on the Venus of Willendorf, I found that the use of her image has changed and now includes a more sinister message: not only is her image not employed to empower women, but more and more it has become a vehicle for selling the ideas of an increasingly fat-phobic society. Christopher L. C. E. Witcombe, in his 2000 essay "Women in Prehistory: The Venus of Willendorf" has even suggested that the name Venus was used in mock irony as, "Venus, of course, was the Classical goddess of sexual love and beauty," hinting that the "Woman" of Willendorf (as she has now come to be called) was the opposite of that.[9]

Actually, the third, and truest, catalyst for my project in this incarnation was a very short-lived commercial for some diet system. The commercial was so unbelievably wrong that it probably didn't air for more than a week or two and was pulled so quickly that I didn't get a chance to see it more than once or twice, so I don't know the name of the company and, after trying for some time to find the culprit, it seems no one would fess up to it. I mean it was blasphemous. It was a TV spot, with a man's voice-over that droned on about the dangers of obesity while a picture of the Venus of Willendorf rotated on the screen. The voice asked viewers if they really wanted to look like her. Some ad man (it could only have been a man) had appropriated one of the most powerful symbols in women's history as a means of selling self-hatred and promoting patriarchal body-loathing ideals.

Regardless of how modern society views the Venus of Willendorf, she is by far the most realistic representation of my physical body that I have seen in the public domain, far more realistic than the images one sees in fashion magazines or in film and television. Nor is she headless, the way the media likes to depict fat people on the street and in society.[10] I intend to reclaim her as an honest depiction of what dieting and weight obsession does to the human body by making her the centerpiece of The Venus of Willendorf Project.

I am collecting discarded diet books to use as the sole source for the papier-mâché from which my Venus will be constructed. However, not all the books I have collected are suitable for the medium of papier-mâché. High-gloss paper, often used in the printing of cookbooks, for instance, does not take the glue very well, so books of this nature will be used to create a landscape or environment that will surround the central Venus figure. Smaller figures of the Venus will also be included in the installation. Each one will represent a particular diet, and each Venus will be made from copies of one particular book or author; for example, there will be an Atkins Venus and a Dr. Phil Venus and perhaps a Venus of Powter or the Stop the Insanity Venus. The weight of each Venus will depend on how many of each author's books I have been able to collect.

One benefit of working with papier-mâché is that it is lightweight. But with each subsequent layer it becomes stronger and does increase in weight. This works as a physical metaphor for what happened to me with each subsequent diet: I gained more and more weight. With each diet book I add, the Venus, too, will gain weight. Over the years some diets have been more popular than others, and there are more books promoting them, which have then ended up on the used book market. It is the smaller Venus sculptures made from one single author or title that I would like the viewer to be able to weigh — literally — to see which one was the "best." Would it be the one that weighed the least, as people would still be holding on to them? Or would it be the one that weighed the most, as so many were published and sold? Personally I grew tired of weighing my success as a person on a bathroom scale. Perhaps we should be weighing the diet industry and all the misinformation it sends our way, and my installation will allow the viewer to do just that.

I will encourage visitors to the exhibition to feel the difference in the weights of each of the individual sculptures either simply by physically picking up the sculpture or by actually placing the piece on a scale. The central Venus figure will be compiled of a multitude of different books, titles and authors including at least one copy of each book used to make the smaller pieces. There will be a separate inventory for this central piece as well as an inventory for each of the smaller ones. I am compiling a complete inventory of all the books I incorporate into each statue and a bibliography that will catalog the books that are used in the project as a whole. I feel that this is the most historically responsible way to destroy the books physically without destroying the record of their existence. The evidence of all the books that were required to complete the creation of this installation allows the viewers truly to understand the enormity of the problem: since "overweight" and "obesity" have become an issue to be resolved.

"Venus of Willendorf Armature" side view of central figure for the installation (©Brenda Oelbaum, 2007-2008; photograph by Daphne Doer).

We are taught from childhood on to hate our bodies when there is nothing "wrong" with them. I can't even empty my bladder in the morning while listening to the radio without hearing at least three ads for some new diet product. "Eat all you want and still lose weight. We couldn't say it on TV if it wasn't true!!! Go to eatallyouwantandstilllose weight.com," Green Tea, Hoodia, it's never ending. The Problem has gotten worse. I wonder, perhaps, if the so-called cure, and the multi-billion dollar industry that has been created to resolve this "problem," is actually the cause. (Perhaps instead of suing fast-food chains we should start suing diet doctors and authors of diet books.) Diets make people fat.[11] The diet industry and all its money is actually feeding its own face. By making us feel dissatisfied with our bodies and obsess about our size, the diet industry is actually making the problem worse, working to their advantage, capitalizing on our despair.

We have been hearing for a while now that diets don't work, even from the diet authors themselves,[12] so when are we going to stop buying their crap? Perhaps when people can visually experience the volume of the issue by standing at the center of this installation, they will be able to feel the weight and the pressure in both a physical and intellectual way. Imagine yourself in a room that is filled with diet books up the walls cluttering the floors in mounds and mounds and in the center of the gallery there is this giant iconic Venus larger than life, while interspersed amid the landscape of diet books there are the smaller Venus sculptures, leaning, resting, propped throughout the installation. My collection of diet books has not made a dent in the multi-billion dollar industry that continues to publish and promote diet after diet. "How's that working for you?" to quote Phil McGraw, TV pop psychologist and star of the *Dr. Phil Show.* Dr. Phil McGraw likes to use this phrase when his guests continue to do things that aren't working for them, and he and his son have both put out their own diet books, so in a sense he represents the diet industry. Is it working for us??? Hell NO!

Although papier-mâché is relatively cheap, the books from which I am acquiring the paper are not. That is why the Internet has proved to be the perfect place to get my books. I can trade unwanted books for the diet books on www.bookmooch.com.[13] Although friends and family may not have diet books to donate they often have libraries full of books that they have finished reading and give those to me so that I can list them as books I am willing to send to other people. With each book that I send out I receive a point I can then use to mooch or "collect" a diet book from someone else.

Some of the books I have found are so priceless or unique that I have decided to treat them in rather a different manner. Some I have conserved in frames, maintaining their legibility with a humorous disclaimer that reads "In Emergency, Break Glass." Of all the elements of this installation, this best represents my personal relationship with dieting. Eating disorders don't just go away. They are with you forever, hanging there in the back of your mind, and can be triggered by the smallest of internal or external stimuli. An invitation to a party, an upcoming school reunion, a family function, meeting an old friend, a picture in a magazine, my own reflection in a shop window can all trigger obsessive thoughts of negative body image and food restriction, which in the past led to drastic and dangerous steps in an attempt to recapture a slender body from an earlier time.

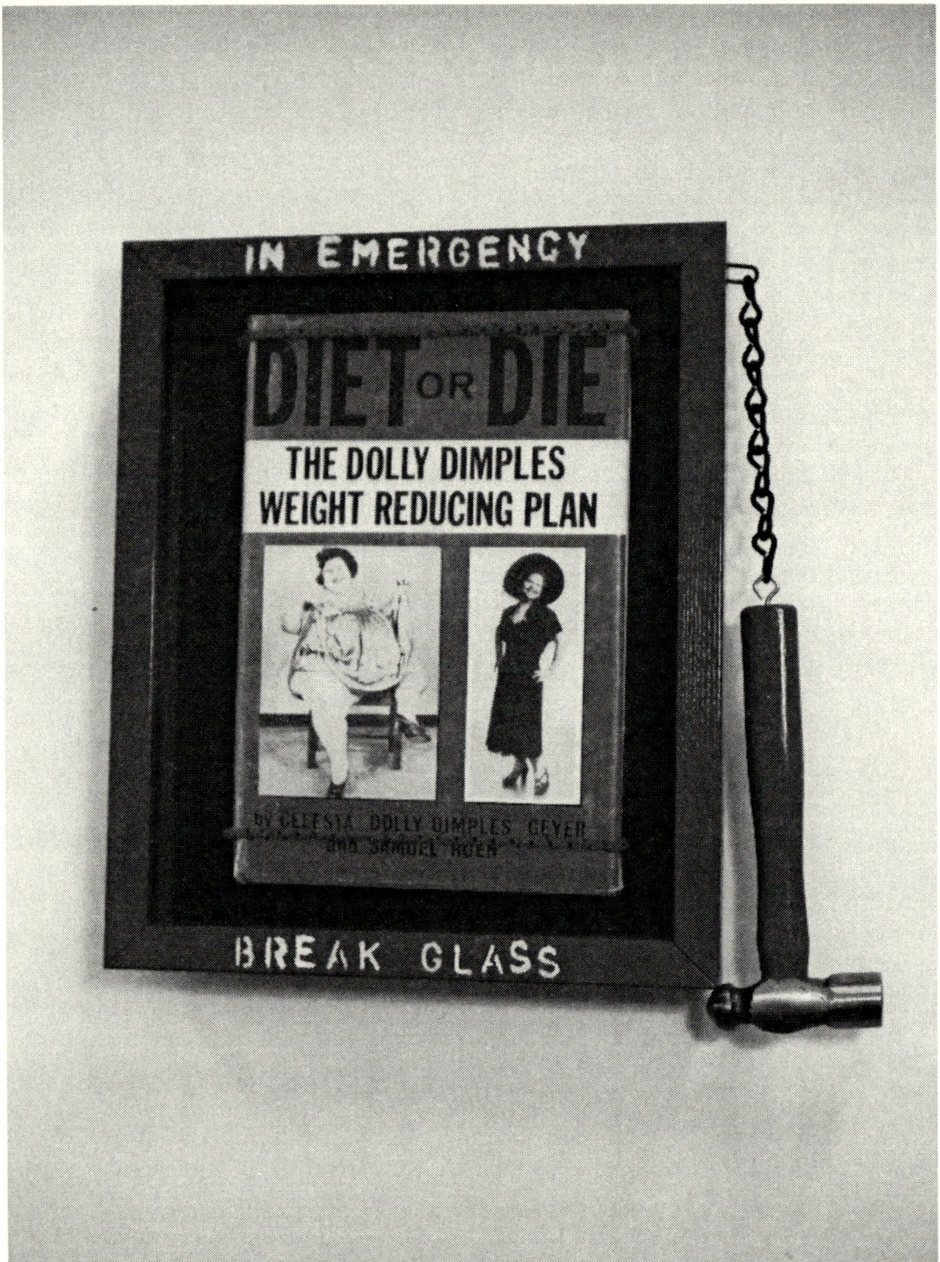

"In Emergency Break Glass: Diet or Die," Brenda Oelbaum, 2007, mixed media assemblage 10 inches high and 8 inches wide (©Brenda Oelbaum, 2007-2008; photograph by Daphne Doer).

For the most part making diet books into papier-mâché seemed like the best treatment for the books. I wanted them destroyed and virtually unreadable except for the evidence that they had once been diet books. I will leave the sculpture unpainted so that people can read some of the type on the outer layers of the finished piece. There is a long history of papier-mâché being used in art, and as a medium it has extra-special significance for this piece. *Papier-mâché* is a French term that means "chewed paper." Not only does that metaphorically describe how I devoured these books in my earlier years, but it reminds me of a crazy diet tip I once read online, probably on some Pro-Ana (Pro-Anorexia) or Pro-Mia (Pro-Bulimia) Web site, about models chewing and swallowing facial tissue and cotton balls as a way to fill themselves up so they couldn't consume more food calories. I wonder how many calories there are in seven cotton balls? The fact that papier-mâché has been used in political art in Italy for centuries is also significant.

The Internet is an intoxicating place. I can be lost for hours searching for inspiration and imagery for my art there. For the Venus Project, however, I decided to use the computer not for ideas and images but as a means of acquiring my materials. It's not my only source; I still go to garage and yard sales and scour used bookstores and recycle centers, but the Internet has proved to be the best source. Not only have I been able to find large numbers of books for the project, but at the same time I am spreading the word about my project worldwide. People as far away as India have contributed to the piece. It has become a community project not unlike Judy Chicago's Dinner Party. (Contributions by many supporting artisans helped make Judy Chicago's famous installation, *The Dinner Party*, possible. Created during the years 1974–1979, *The Dinner Party* now has a permanent home at the Brooklyn Museum of Art.) By contributing books to the project people are taking part in the installation's creation. Not only is the Internet a great way to get advanced PR, but the people I make contact with are constantly giving me feedback. Good or bad, their responses inspire me to go on.

When I first decided to use diet books as my medium I went immediately to the Web, posting my call for unwanted diet books on different message boards.

> Starving Artist Seeks Diet Books [emoticon]: Hi any and every one ... I am an artist who is looking for any unwanted diet books to use in an installation piece I am working on ... they can be in any condition hard cover or soft cover ... repeats are great ... the more the merrier ... I will gladly pay for the shipping. I hope to hear from some of you soon.

I've posted on Craigslist and iVillage without much success.[14] With Craigslist I tried to think of cities that might be more body conscious than others, so I posted in LA and New York. But I don't think I even got a nibble. Either they are all still dieting, or Craigslist isn't really that effective. For example, I have a friend who posted a beautiful entertainment center on Craigslist and got one response. Perhaps it is better for setting up illicit affairs and secret rendezvous.

And deciding which category would get the most relevant responses proved difficult. Diet/Health or Items Wanted? Even when placing an ad in the local newspaper classifieds I found it hard to figure out what section would get me the biggest response. In iVillage I posted on the non-diet approach group, diet groups, and the most obscure of all was the "free yourself of clutter group." Actually I did get several books from another artist on the anti-clutter, small spaces list, but I got the following warning from the non-diet approach group.

> Dear iVillager:
>
> We are very proud of our iVillage community areas, and we attempt to ensure that our members will have a safe and pleasant experience at iVillage. It has come to our attention that you have posted an inappropriate message on our message boards. When you joined iVillage, you agreed to abide by iVillage's Terms of Service.
>
> The Terms of Service state that you cannot use iVillage to promote chain letters, junk mail, "spamming," solicitations (commercial or noncommercial) or bulk communications of any kind, so please consider this a friendly reminder to refrain from any further spamming. Your post has been removed and we ask that you refrain from making this type of announcement in the future, as any future posts of this nature will result in a permanent violation record on your membership. Using iVillage for any commercial purpose or to obtain direct financial gain is prohibited and future posts of this nature will be considered violations. If you accrue three Terms of Service violations, your membership will be revoked, although we reserve the right to revoke your membership immediately should circumstances warrant it.
>
> We appreciate your cooperation in our efforts to protect our community areas.
>
> Sincerely yours,[15]

As you can imagine, I lost it! How could they remove my request for books and then send me e-mail that touted green tea as the new diet miracle or numbers of herbal weight-loss gimmicks? It was maddening! I don't take too kindly to rejection and protested their treatment of my posting. Then they responded to my response and the exchange went on and on without any willingness on the part of iVillage to reconsider their position.

Not all the contributors have been terribly invested in the project. I guess the best response has been from the Fat Acceptance community, but for the most part the feedback has been positive. One of the best exchanges came from a HAES (Health at Every Size)[16] researcher Linda Bacon, PhD, and author of *Health at Every Size: The Surprising Truth About Your Weight*. She had invited study participants to purge their diet books and clothes that didn't fit as a ritualistic release of the vestiges of their dysfunctional dieting lives. Though she had quickly found homes for the unwanted clothes, she felt torn by the thought of releasing the diet books back onto the market for resale. She felt that they were bad for everyone, not just her clients and friends, so she held onto them, tucked away in a box until she read my call for materials. I think she was relieved to have found a place for them at long last where they could do no harm and, perhaps, a little good. I was most grateful for her contribution. (I still need to figure out how to work those Jenny Craig coach-training videotapes into this project.)

I had one girl who expressed concern about literacy, yet her argument was kind of funny. What if the only book in the house for a person to read was a diet book? Would I really destroy that book, too? Well, yes I would, and then I would replace it with something worth reading, something truly educational, something positive like Laura Fraser's *Losing It: America's Obsession with Weight and the Industry That Feeds on It.* Several people were concerned that I would be destroying books that might actually be helpful for someone, but I have tried to focus my fury on books that are intended for "slimming" and not those that are strictly for heart health, blood pressure, or lowering cholesterol, you know, "genuine" health concerns. This is getting harder, however, as everyone is claiming their diet improves health and reduces the need for medication.

Some people offered cheers for the project ("I shall help you rid the world of diet books gladly!"; "Thank you for destroying this book!"; "I Love this Idea!!"), while others expressed heartfelt relief to get rid of a particular diet book: "I'm so happy to be sending it to someone that isn't going to go and try it. I went there. Dumbest thing I ever did." Some of my correspondents would alert me to diet books in their inventory that I might want, and others told me they deliberately got books from me because they liked the idea of supporting my project. One man shared about how sick his wife had become following one particular diet and how happy he was to be sending the book to its final resting place:

> Thanks for mooching from me! I'd love to donate this book for your art piece; it did nothing but make my wife's blood sugar crash and send her into a deep depression. It should get out within the week, Enjoy!

Yet, even though I'd been clear about the intent of The Venus of Willendorf Project, others passed on diet tips or the titles of diet books they had found useful.

> Oh! And thought I'd pass this along ... best "diet" in the world [emoticon] Eat lot's of HONEY! It boosts the metabolism and tastes great! Can also boost energy, sometimes.

One woman, because she was "just curious," had to ask which diet books I'd found particularly helpful. One individual even sent me a long list of all the diet books he'd found "useful," and challenged the point of my project:

"Don't Eat: Artist Brenda Oelbaum in Straitjacket with Diet Book Collection," October 2007 (©Brenda Oelbaum, 2007-2008; photograph by Daphne Doer).

> While I think what you're doing is cool and unique as an art form, I'm not sure I agree 100 percent with your "cause." Not all diets are Evil, and not all diets don't work. They're only Evil IF they don't work! I've lost 70 pounds using some of the better books! So just try not to mix any legitimate health/nutrition books into the shuffle. This one didn't work, so burn away! ;-)

His impulse to lecture me, and the patronizing tone of his message upset me.[17]

My ad hasn't really changed too much over the course of the project. I thought I was quite witty when early on I thought of the "Starving Artist Seeks Diet Books" caption, so that has always been my byline. As I have become more knowledgeable about fat politics, NAAFA (National Association to Advance Fat Acceptance), HAES (Health at Every Size), and Fat Studies (something that came directly from this project, I might add), I started to use the phrase "Health at Any Size." It was on Web sites like these, NAAFA and the Fat Studies Listserv, that I posted my next call for books. Of course most of these people had long purged themselves of diet books, but the community and support I have found there is priceless. I had the pleasure of sharing breakfast with Marilyn Wann, the author of *FAT SO!,* while she was speaking at the University of Michigan, at which time she invited me to join her Listserv and post my call for books. It was from one of the women on this Listserv that I was introduced to Bookmooch.com. I know from my communications with others online that there are other sites that do similar things, but I knew I could only manage one account and I must say it has been wonderful. Bookmooch.com has been my best source for books and my all-around favorite site.

When I think about how many diet books I have already amassed for the project it is truly astounding. I have not even scratched the surface and my studio is already filled to the ceiling with books. I can't imagine what all the diet books in the world would look like. One often reads about the multi-billion dollar diet industry, but what does that mean? To see it in paper, pages and pages of books, titles, the amount of natural resources that are used in the publishing of this nonsense and self-hatred-provoking drivel, it's unbelievable. To experience a room filled with it — to feel its weight and power — might really change how one thinks about dieting in the future and the personal waste. People will reconsider their choices when faced with the deluge of Diet books that come out at the beginning of the New Year each year. They will start looking at themselves less harshly and come to accept that we all come in different colors, shapes and sizes and they will embrace their differences as many women artists have come to do in this 4th wave of feminism.

This is a very personal project for me. Writing this essay and organizing my thoughts about this installation has taken me to an emotional depth that one finds mainly in the work of other women artists. I have no intention of neutralizing the subject; I want to be identified as revealing my femaleness and my fatness. For women artists that started the feminist art movement in the

Portrait of artist Brenda Oelbaum with diet book collection, October 2007 (©Brenda Oelbaum, 2007-2008; photograph by Daphne Doer).

1960s and 1970s expressing one's female aesthetic, one's feminist sensibility was considered a trap, in that it would hold the artist back and lead to marginalization. Their determination and hard work have created an environment where it is no longer necessary to "paint like a man" in order to achieve recognition. In fact, many male artists have taken to using some of the most intrinsically female modes to employ in their own art works.

My hope is that my project will lead to the knowledge that diets don't work, that we are being fed a load of bunk in regard to the "war on obesity," and that it is no longer necessary for women to maintain an androgynously slender figure, like sexless hangers for unwearable fashions, in order to qualify as beautiful, worthwhile, valuable human beings. If I now have the freedom to make art like a woman, I should now have the freedom to have hips and a belly and breasts that sag like a woman. I am the Venus!

Notes

1. My mother likes to tell people that the reason I moved out of the house in 1981, at the age of 20, was because I wanted to live like a slob, not pick up after myself. The real reason, however, was so that I could do what I wanted to do with food. Judy Mazel's book came out that year, and I remember very clearly her diet being the first thing I did when I had my own apartment. If I wanted to eat nothing but fruit for weeks, that would be all that was in the house. I was doing the shopping and I could restrict the groceries to the diet of the day; whether I was binging or fasting I was safe alone in my own little world.

2. Little did they know in 2005 that the activities of the 2006–2007 Feminist Art Project would grow to its current importance. The TFAP calendar now goes as far into the future as 2013. Post-feminism? I think not!

3. House Bill No. 282, 2008 Regular Session, http://billstatus.ls.state.ms.us/documents/2008/pdf/HB/0200-0299/HB0282IN.pdf (accessed March 11, 2008). For news about the bill, try a Yahoo! search for the keywords Mississippi house bill no. 282, http://search.yahoo.com/search?ei=utf-8&fr=ieas-dns-tb&p=mississippi+house+bill+no.282 (accessed March 11, 2008).

4. Bruce Friedrich to W.T. Mayhall, Jr., February 5, 2008, http://blog.peta.org/archives/Letter_to_Mississippi_rep_PDF.pdf (accessed March 11, 2008).

5. William C. Heird, "Parental Feeding Behavior and Children's Fat Mass, *American Journal of Clinical Nutrition 75* (2002): 451–452, http://www.ajcn.org/cgi/content/full/75/3/451 (accessed March 11, 2008). Comment on Donna Spruijt-Metz, et al., "Relation Between Mothers' Child-Feeding Practices and Children's Adiposity," *American Journal of Clinical Nutrition 75* (2002): 581–586, http://www.ajcn.org/cgi/content/full/75/3/581 (accessed March 11, 2008).

6. Charnicia E. Huggins, "Mom's Worry Over Kid's Weight Ups Child's Fat Risk," Reuters Health (February 27, 2002). Source: *American Journal of Clinical Nutrition 75* (March 2002): 451–452, 581–586. The writer's sources can be found online at: http://www.ajcn.org/cgi/search?ck=nck&andorexactfulltext=and&resourcetype=1&disp_type=&sortspec=relevance&author1=&fulltext=diet percent2C+children percent2C+mothers&pubdate_year=2002&volume=75&firstpage=451 (accessed March 20, 2008) and http://www.ajcn.org/cgi/content/full/75/3/581?maxtoshow=&HITS=10&hits=10&RESULTFORMAT=&fulltext=diet percent2C+children percent2C+mothers&andorexactfulltext=and&searchid=1&FIRST INDEX=0&sortspec=relevance&volume=75&firstpage=581&resourcetype=HWCIT (accessed March 20, 2008).

7. TIME/ABC News Summit on Obesity, June 2–4, 2004, http://www.time.com/time/2004/obesity/ (accessed March 11, 2008).

8. Wikipedia, "Venus of Willendorf," http://commons.wikimedia.org/wiki/Category:

Venus_of_Willendorf (accessed March 11, 2008). The Venus of Willendorf was carved from oolitic limestone, is 4⅜" (11.1 cm) high, and can be seen in the Naturhistorisches Museum in Vienna, Austria.

9. Christopher L. C. E. Witcombe, "Women in Prehistory: The Venus of Willendorf," *Images of Women in Ancient Art* (2000, revised 2003). Available online: http://witcombe.sbc.edu/willendorf/willendorfdiscovery.html (accessed October 21, 2007).

10. Charlotte Cooper, "Headless Fatties" image collection, "Images Collected by Charlotte Cooper." Available online: http://charlottecooper.net/docs/fat/headless_fatties.htm (accessed March 11, 2008). If you've watched any news segment about fat people, ever, you've undoubtedly seen the video that accompanies such news segments: the parade of headless fatties, fat people in public, shown from the neck down, voiceless, stripped of their humanity — most likely without their permission. Showing people's bodies without their heads implies that it's shameful to be fat, that we ought to be ashamed to show our faces in public. COFRA, the Coalition for Fat Rights Activists, has started a video project called Dare to Show Your Face which invites people to upload a video of themselves that shows who they really are in their real lives— with their heads attached.

11. Alison Field, ScD, Brigham and Women's Hospital researcher, says: "At a time when we need solutions to encourage healthy eating habits, it is troubling to see that dieting, which is often characterized by short-term and not necessarily healthy changes in eating, is so common.... Our study found that dieting was counterproductive —children who dieted gained more, and not less, weight than non-dieters." "Dieting May Actually Promote Weight Gain in Children; Study Finds About 30 Percent of Girls and 16 Percent of Boys Diet, but Habit May Hold Little Hope for Long-term Success." Available online: http://www.hms.harvard.edu/news/pressreleases/bwh/1003childdiet.html (accessed March 11, 2008).

University of Minnesota researchers analyzed the results of surveys conducted among teenagers from 1999 to 2004 to understand the perplexing finding that has been reported in several longitudinal studies, whereby dieting predicts greater weight gain over time in adolescents. Researchers led by Professor Dianne Neumark-Sztainer concluded that dieting might lead to weight gain in part because of the long-term adoption of behavioral patterns that are counterproductive to weight management, e.g., binge eating, decreased physical activity and a trend toward decreased breakfast consumption and decreased fruit and vegetable intake. "Dieting May Cause Weight Gain in Teenagers." Available online: http://www.earthtimes.org/articles/show/40693.html (accessed March 11, 2008).

12. Bob Schwartz, *Diets Don't Work: Stop Dieting Become Naturally Thin Live a Diet-Free Life*, 3rd ed. (Houston, TX: Breakthru, 1996).

13. BookMooch, http://www.bookmooch.com (accessed March 11, 2008), was conceived and designed, written and administered by John Buckman. It is a community for exchanging used books. When you first join you can earn points by putting books into an inventory, books that you are finished reading and are willing to send to someone should they request one from you. Every time you send someone a book from your inventory you receive a point which you can then use to acquire a book that you are interested in getting from someone else's inventory on BookMooch. It's totally free to be a member, and the only cost you incur is the cost of sending the books to people who mooch them from you. I quickly learned about media mail as the most cost-effective way of shipping the books within the United States.

I was first introduced to BookMooch by a woman on the fat studies listserv. She said she did not have any diet books to send me herself but that she was a member of BookMooch and, if I joined, she would donate points to me for my project that would enable me to mooch books from people who did have diet books in their accounts available for mooching. BookMooch has truly been an invaluable resource; not only can I locate books for the project at a reasonable price, but I am also able to keep track of all the people who contribute to the project. When all is said and done I will let the contributors know about the outcome of the project — where it is on display and when — and, of course, give them all the proper credit at the end of the day by including them in the list of contributors in the final installation.

14. Craigslist, http://www.craigslist.org (accessed March 11, 2008); iVillage, http://www.ivillage.com/ (accessed March 11, 2008).

15. [iVillage Community Staff], ["Board Spam"], iVillage Anti-Diet Approach forum, posted [October 10, 2006] http://messageboards.ivillage.com/n/mb/message.asp?webtag=iv-

fbantidiet&msg=5715.1&ctx=0 Starving Artist Seeks Diet Books (October 9, 2006). I think it's nuts that they would remove my call, and still have the nerve to remove my posting. After the above incident I had iVillage e-mail go directly to my spam box, so I have no idea how many of these special e-mails I missed, but come on!

16. Health at Every Size is an approach to wellness that supports people of all sizes in making nourishing and satisfying choices. HAES encourages people to respect and enjoy their natural drives for food, pleasure, and other needs, and to shift the focus away from weight, dieting and controlling one's appetite. Web site: http://www.lindabacon.org/LindaBaconHAES.html. (March 20, 2008).

17. One thing that became terribly clear while I was communicating with different folks online was how easy it was to get overly involved with the people you meet there. I have often in conversation said I "spoke" with someone when really I only communicated with them online. The Internet has a way of creating instant intimacy where there really is none. I can see how children and teens can get into trouble chatting online.

12

Grandmom's Collection

ELANA C. HURWITZ

In 1995 I co-founded one of the first Web design studios in western Massachusetts. The name I created for my new company became Blue Orb Design.[1] I found inspiration for this name in one of my favorite James Taylor songs, "There We Are," from 1977. I thought "Blue Orb Design"—design for planet earth—would be appropriate, because the Web would be creating a global community. At that time, the World Wide Web was radically different, both visually and technically, from the way it is now. Artists like myself were creating links on our web pages to other small companies and to our friends and associates to show mutual support. Sometimes a party or social gathering would present an opportunity to meet someone with similar interest and suggest a link. This is how I came to suggest to Rich Newman, of a band called TagYerIt in Amherst, Massachusetts, that I add a link on my website to his website.[2] What I also learned in talking with him and his partner Flo, was that Flo had a unique collection she began in 1977 or 1978. They said they were planning to publish it on their web site.[3]

Rich explains the publishing of their special collection on the Web:

> Flo & I started collecting toilet paper in the mid 1970s. It was a combination of two events. We were actively looking to collect something that had no value and no cost. This was partly a reaction to our breaking away from our "collection fever." At the same time a friend was traveling to Europe and asked us what we wanted them to bring back for us. Toilet paper seemed the perfect item, since it wouldn't cost our friends anything and wouldn't take up any space in their luggage. When the internet came along, it seemed the perfect venue to share our private insanity.[4]

Flo collected T.P., mostly autographed T.P. like the piece from Madonna.[5] Rich put a picture of this specimen, along with the rest of Flo's collection, on their website and entitled it the "Whole World Toilet Paper Museum." "How inspiring!" I thought, and suggested to Webmaster Rich that I contribute a copy of my Grandmom's 1959 scrapbook page, a collection of toilet paper samples from a European trip, to their museum. I scanned each T.P. sample in Grandmom's scrapbook and sent the images of the T.P. and some snapshots of Grandmom and Grandpop on their trip to Rich via email. Rich then added a

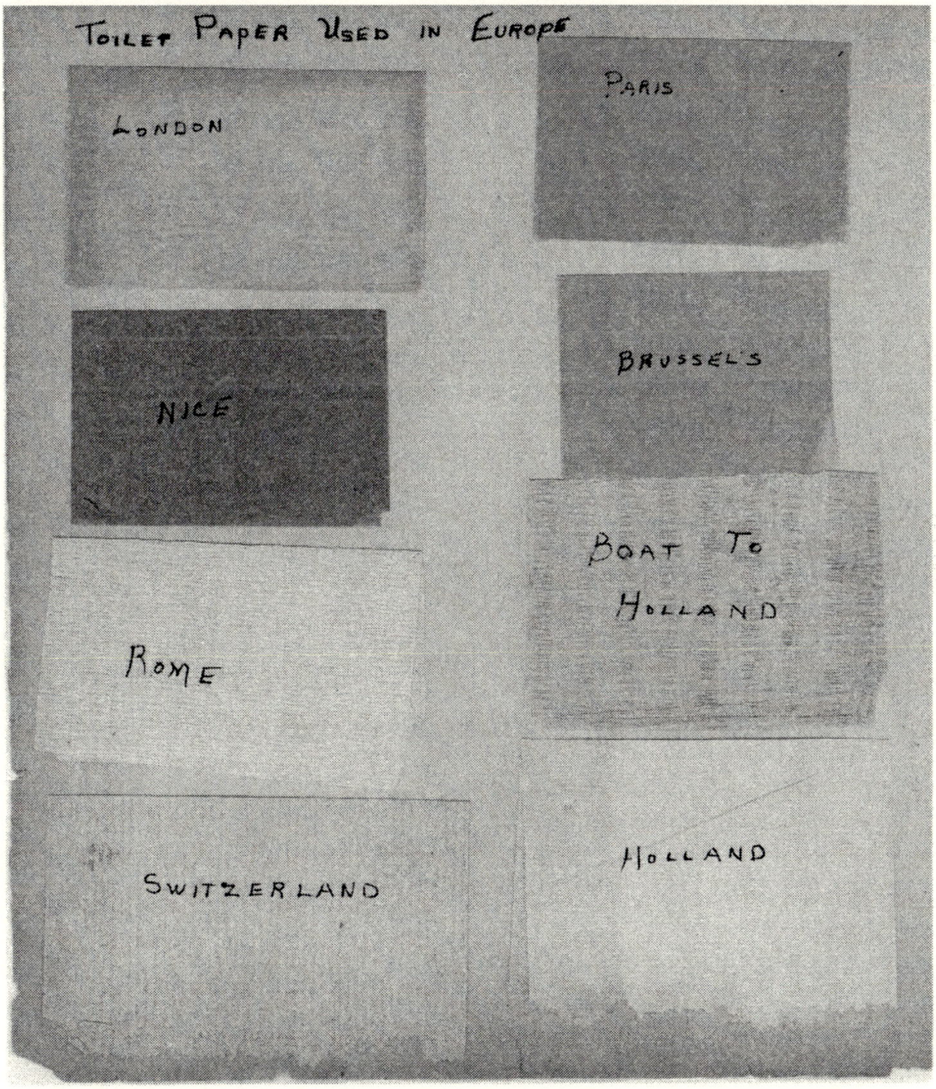

Grandmom's 1959 scrapbook page, "Toilet Paper Used in Europe" (©Elana Hurwitz 1995-2008, collection of Elana Hurwitz).

page to his online museum, just for Grandmom's collection, entitled "A 1959 Collection."[6]

My Grandmom was very dedicated to her job at the Academy of Natural Sciences in downtown Philadelphia. We'd often hear her stories about the Academy. She admired and respected her boss, Dr. "Jim" Böhlke, and working in his department may have had a great influence upon her. She told of his adventures traveling to other continents to collect rare specimens for the "fish department," as she called it. Ichthyology was the official scientific name. From the early 1950s to his death in 1982, Dr. Böhlke published over 120 papers on diverse groups of fishes (characids, gobiids, blennioids, dactyloscopids, ophidioids, siluroids, and anguilloids) and many works of considerable breadth and impact, such as The Fishes of the Bahamas, according to the Academy's website.[7]

Certainly, going to work every day at a place where a museum of dioramas depicting natural scenes was just downstairs for the public to view must have given my Grandmom a great deal of inspiration. There are thirty-seven dioramas in the Academy, the majority of which were created in the 1920s and 1930s. Their website comments: "The dioramas played a major role in the celebration of Americans in their natural heritage and increased their awareness and appreciation of the loss of wilderness. The rise of the Conservation Movement and the popularity of dioramas went hand-in-hand."[8] Grandmom seemed to enjoy cataloging and organizing things even at home. Strange little items, like a tiny set of plastic false teeth no larger than a gumball, even had a place in the wooden sewing basket next to her chair in the living room. She assembled her curious collection of toilet paper in her scrapbook with the title: "Toilet Paper Used In Europe."

Rich comments:

> The world, it seems, works in mysterious ways, and over time we've met several others who've had a similar interest. So it came as a wonderful surprise to us when a friend of ours (Elana) presented us with the photos of her grandmother's collection to put up in our virtual museum. Without ever having met her grandmother, we can only assume that she has a wonderful view of the world, combining a humorous glint in a practical, frugal manner. Maybe it's an illusion, but at times like this it feels good to find a like-minded soul who shares the personal inside jokes.[9]

Pretty soon, this new addition to the Whole World Toilet Paper Museum became one of the most visited pages on TagYerIt's site. In the spring of 2001, the "1959 Collection" page got an average of 402 hits a month.[10] Since then, their website has grown in size, with many popular pages. In 2005, Rich said Grandma's European page had been visited 2217 times.[11] He reports that in September of 2007, the W.W.T.P. Museum front page had 656 hits, with Grandmom's page getting 136, and in October, 2007 the W.W.T.P. Museum front page got 753 hits, with Grandmom's page getting 188.[12]

Page from Grandmom's 1959 scrapbook, souvenirs of her 1959 European tour (photograph ©Elana Hurwitz 1995-2008, collection of Elana Hurwitz).

In the summer of 1959, Grandmom and Grandpop went on an "Eleven Country Grand Tour" vacation run by Caravan Tours out of Chicago, Illinois. They went to Germany, Switzerland, Italy, France, and Holland, to name a few. Her scrapbook pages had the typical items one would expect to see: tickets and programs from shows; sugar cube wrappers; luggage tags and airplane menus; and color picture post cards of scenic attractions. She even had a type-written memo from the travel agency listing everyone on the tour along with their hometowns.

The scrapbook page that stands out as unique is the one she dedicated to her collection of toilet paper. On this page she assembled a collection of sample pieces of T.P. On each piece, she wrote the location from which she had gathered it—"Paris," "Switzerland," "Boat to Holland." It seems to me that the labeling style she used was very similar to the labeling style used for the specimens at the Academy.

At home, Grandmom's toilet paper had to be "Soft-Weve." To her, having the linen closet shelves well stocked was a serious matter. Located just outside the bathroom in the upstairs hall, this closet was neatly organized, to almost picture-perfect. What a contrast to the incredibly huge crack in the opposite wall! Over the years, the shiny, saddle-brown plaster wall had shifted and settled so much that there came to be a canyon-like crevice that arched vertically six feet up the wall. You really couldn't miss it, even in the typical darkness of the hallway. It seemed like Frankenstein might suddenly appear, or you might get sucked into some strange other world as you approached the top stair.

In her narrow linen closet that was somewhat inconspicuous in the dimly lit upstairs hall, Grandmom stored her neatly ironed and folded bed sheets, various sized towels, and, on several shelves, her toilet paper. She had T.P. in colors like blue, peach, yellow, and tan. All of them looked pleasing in the bathroom with its beautiful wall mural of swans on a willow-hung pond, a very realistic and detailed landscape painting over the tub. She never wanted to run out of T.P. Even when teased about what seemed to us as an endless supply, she would modestly smile and acknowledge being the "butt" of our jokes; make all the fun you want, but she knew better.

In the 1920s, when she was a little girl, Grandmom, her sister, two brothers, and her parents lived in a three-room apartment above a grocery store in South Philadelphia. Her parents ran the store. When the produce came in, the oranges were wrapped in a stiff waxy paper which the family would save to use for toilet paper. This was the story she'd tell us in explaining why she now hoarded T.P. The days of enduring scratchy paper were over when products like her beloved Soft-Weve(TM) came to the market. It seems that her childhood toilet paper experiences may have influenced her motivation in collecting the various samples from Europe during her trip with Grandpop in 1959.

Grandmom was the "Matriarchal Craftswoman" of our family. Her children and grandchildren have always recognized her love of the arts and sciences and have followed her example. She knit numerous sweaters for everyone she knew who had babies. She designed and sewed baby doll clothes and even Barbie doll clothes for my sister and me. In the late 1960s, she created clothes for a collection of one hundred dolls she and her colleagues at the Academy donated to the Pennhurst State School and Hospital in Spring City, PA. The newspaper article featured a photograph of her with a pile of dolls, taken in the Academy library.[13] This began a tradition for following years, when she also included her handmade cloth tote bags and mittens, as well as crayons and coloring books, along with the one-hundred dolls for the children.

Grandmom was a pioneer in her day. She had an appreciation for modern design. She chose Danish modern furniture for her home, unlike her friends who had colonial and ornate furnishings. They thought her taste was eccentric and odd. Grandmom only had a high school diploma from the late 1920s, yet she had a vision that was, I believe, ahead of her time. She collected her European T.P. specimens the same year that Alaska and Hawaii were admitted as the 49th and 50th states in the United States of America. It seems appropriate that placing her "Toilet Paper Used in Europe" scrapbook page on the World Wide Web will continue her visionary trend.

Having experience and education in photography, printing, and graphic design gave me the ability to produce images for the Web as close as possible to the real thing. As I prepared the 1959 T.P. samples for the website, I intended to give each an authentic look and feel, working within the limitations and standards of Web design at the time (1995). As I scanned the scrapbook T.P. samples, I was able to adjust the images in Photoshop (version 4) to increase their contrast or correct their color. Images had to be 72 dpi for the Web — a low resolution — and small file size. Also, keeping with the standards of email at that time, attachments were typically kept small since everyone only had dial-up connections. Large files were unheard of because they would take much too long to download as well as to upload. Small images were also preferred for loading quickly in the browser of a web page, in order to retain the attention of the user.

The layout of a web page is neither as simple nor as structured as it may seem. In 1995, our choices were quite limited in the colors we could use for text and backgrounds, as well as styles of type (fonts). Designing a layout for a page on the Web was not like designing for a printed page. The designer had a lot less control over exact placement, sizing and spacing of the elements on the web page. Web design, being much more fluid, was nothing like working with traditional paste-up and mechanical art. HTML, the code language written to create a web page that would be read and viewed in a browser, had limitations and so did the browser programs themselves. Eventually, browser programs and code evolved and began to open up many more possibilities for designers and users of the Web.

Creating a Web presence for Grandmom's T.P. scrapbook page takes her collection to a new level, one she would have never imagined — an electronic digital catalog, a world-wide connection that she would never believe! The Web creates a great environment for people to delve into strange ideas and curious information. Surfing the Web provides a "stream of consciousness" style of interacting with information that gives the user the ability to jump around, bounce back, and then go off in any direction. Now that there are powerful search engines, the World Wide Web has become, to many people with an insatiable curiosity, their own private world encyclopedia. Most Internet-savvy people with home computers tend to explore, as a private endeavor and at any time of day or night, a multitude of topics that interest them. The convenience of being able to tap into a resource as huge as the Web makes it quite exciting, if not inspirational.

Surfing along and gathering "bookmarks" is to me a form of collecting. What could be more appropriate than sharing the T.P. collection my Grandmom had in her personal 1950s scrapbook, making it available to anyone in the world who might relate, empathize, or be inspired, amused or educated. In a medium where the exchange of information is so far-reaching, there are bound to be other vintage T.P. collectors out there. It is interesting to me to see how the Web has become a venue for the personal to become public. When we share our own intimate worlds, we participate in a process of moving towards being a global community. We can acknowledge our similarities in being human.

Many things in our "hard copy" world have duplicated themselves on the Web, becoming the "virtual," although some of our actual human experiences may never become so. As a designer I have examined numerous printed materials. We are still utilizing magazines, books and newspapers in our daily lives. People continue to want the experience of physically holding and interacting with these items. Signs and billboards remain a part of our society. Though not everything has become electronic or digital, there does seem to be a trend toward its being inevitable.

An interesting thing about Grandmom's toilet paper collection is that T.P. is one of those ordinary items we see and use everyday, but without much thought. Funny how so much of the Web, and the elements that make it available, have now become ordinary and used without much thought by many of us. Flo's collection of T.P. takes great care to go to a global level of connecting to the actual lives of people. She does this by asking others to interact. This is a theme of the World Wide Web. Some people participate in her collection by gathering and sending her autographed toilet paper. I admire the uniqueness of Flo's collection. She has taken the concept of autographs, which normally we'd expect to see on traditional types of printed materials and photographs, to a presentation on a truly unusual substrate. The likes of Harrison Ford, Ram Dass, and Leon Russell have made their autographed contributions.[14]

Rich and Flo recently added a major collection to the Whole World Toilet Paper Museum, as explained on their site:

> On April First 2005 (no fooling), The Whole World Toilet Paper Museum was gifted the collection of the late Hugo G. Rodeck. Dr. Rodeck had been a Curator and Director at the University of Colorado Museum.[15] Despite his amazing cre-

> dentials, there is limited documentation on each piece. It appears that he traveled in his years leading up to his retirement. For the most part, these pieces were collected in the 1960s and 1970s. His usual method of collection was to store the folded sample(s) in the hotel envelope where he stayed. He preserved these mementos in a "Flings" Shoebox. They were shipped with some "current" issue T.P. used for packing.[16]

The connection between Dr. Rodeck,[17] and the collecting he did while traveling, as well as his working at a Museum of Natural History, seems curiously reminiscent of my Grandmom's collection and her job at the Academy. Now they have become united in a "museum" on the World Wide Web!

I find the similarities in the processes of design and scientific research to be remarkable. Both seem to require one to search and observe, to organize, to catalog, and to have a sense of curiosity. Discovering a design solution can begin with defining the problem, questioning the norm, looking for something different, challenging our expectations. It seems to me similar techniques may have been employed by the researchers at the Academy during their trips around the world conducting research, making discoveries in the sciences, and bringing back unique additions to the museum's collection.

In Grandmom's scrapbook, she brought something otherwise experienced privately to the public realm. What some might think was a taboo topic she presented in a documentary-like, scientific way. Her collection has given me an understanding of who she was, her personal power of observation, and her ability to appreciate the simple everyday surroundings of life. Taking her collection to the display and presentation stage made it an authentic collection or "collectible." In my view, her scrapbook page on the Web has the same effect as the dioramas on display downstairs at the Academy of Natural Sciences where she worked. There, natural things are suspended in time for the viewer to experience. The viewer can observe things one might otherwise not notice or think about. As described on the Academy's website: "The diorama — a distinctive fusion of art and science — has provided a window onto wilderness for generations of museum visitors."[18] The World Wide Web has become similar to the diorama. Its fluid interactive fusion of art with the science of technology provides a window on the world for the designers as well as the viewers.

Discovering and enjoying Grandmom's scrapbook page today, I recognize the historical value in questioning the taboo, taking risks that embrace one's personal interests, and documenting those interests. Now I also understand that some of what seemed to us all to be Grandmom's "hoarding," was really truly collecting.

Notes

1. Elana Hurwitz, Blue Orb Design: Handcrafted Websites, http://www.BlueOrbDesign.com (accessed November 20, 2007).

2. Elana Hurwitz, Blue Orb Design's "Gallery of Artists Index" and links page, http://www.BlueOrbDesign.com/gal2.html (accessed November 21, 2007).

3. Rich and Flo Newman, Original Intro to The Whole World Toilet Paper Museum and Society (archives), http://www.tagyerit.com/tp/old_intro_page.htm (accessed November 18, 2007). The current W.W.T.P. Museum Intro page is available at The Whole World Toilet Paper Museum, http://www.tagyerit.com/tp/index.html (accessed November 18, 2007).

4. Rich Newman, e-mail message to author, June 15, 2005.

5. Rich and Flo Newman, "Toilet Paper — Celebrity Examples from the Whole World Toilet Paper Museum," http://www.tagyerit.com/tp_celebs_1.php (accessed November 21, 2007).

6. Grandmom's 1959 Scrapbook Page is available at "The Whole World Toilet Paper Scrap Book: A 1959 Collection," http://www.tagyerit.com/1959tp.htm (accessed November 21, 2007).

7. More information on former curator and collection manager James E. Böhlke and the Department of Ichthyology at the Academy of Natural Sciences, Philadelphia, PA, is available on their site. "History of the Ichthyology Department," Academy of Natural Sciences, http://www.ansp.org/research/biodiv/ichthyology/history.php (accessed November 20, 2007).

8. "Dioramas," Academy of Natural Sciences, http://www.ansp.org/museum/dioramas.php (accessed November 17, 2007). "In 1948, long before water pollution and environmental degradation became topics of public concern, the Academy established the Environmental Research Division. This marked the beginning of a broadened research orientation for the Academy, which included applied research in aquatic ecosystems as well as the traditional systematics research — discovering and cataloguing organisms." See "History of the Academy," Academy of Natural Sciences, http://www.ansp.org/about/history.php (accessed November 17, 2007).

9. Rich Newman, e-mail message to author, June 15, 2005.

10. Flo and Rich Newman, birthday card to author, October, 2001.

11. Rich Newman, e-mail message to author, June 15, 2005.

12. "I think you could safely say that over the year more than a thousand people have enjoyed seeing your grandmother's souvenirs." Rich Newman, email message to author, November 20, 2007.

13. Harriet Eldredge, "Dolls for Dolls: Santa Didn't Forget," *The Bulletin: Philadelphia's Family Newspaper*, undated clipping.

14. Newman, "Celebrity Examples from the WWTPM."

15. University of Colorado Museum of Natural History, http://cumuseum.colorado.edu/ (accessed November 17, 2007). The museum's collections number more than four million objects in anthropology/archaeology, botany, entomology, paleontology/osteology, and zoology.

16. Rich and Flo Newman, "TagYerit & The WWTP Museum Presents: The Hugo G. Rodeck Collection," http://www.tagyerit.com/tp/rodeck/ (accessed November 17, 2007).

17. According to his obituary, "Rodeck was appointed director of the CU Museum in 1939 and held the position until his retirement in 1971. His association with the museum began in 1929 when he worked as a graduate assistant before being named curator in 1933, a position he held until 1939 ... He also served as the first secretary and treasurer of the International Council of Museums." "Former CU Museum Director Hugo Rodeck Dead At 102," University of Colorado at Boulder, October 1, 2004, http://www.colorado.edu/news/releases/2004/294.html (accessed November 17, 2007).

18. "Dioramas."

13

Being Collected

Selling Art on the Internet

HAROLD SMITH

To me, being collected is to the process of art what death is to life. It is the final part of the process and yet the beginning of the process. It actually splits the process of art-making into two processes. One is guided by the artist in the creation, exhibition, and distribution of the art. The other is guided by the art itself as it is acquired, enjoyed and displayed. Like human death, it can be a painful process depending on the level of attachment to the art. But it can also be a joyful process, as the artist can feel affirmed and validated in his artistry.

I look forward to being collected, and I regret being collected, too. There is a feeling of release and completion when a piece I feel is a true expression of my thinking has been acquired. There is also a feeling of regret and detachment as that piece is picked up or mailed off. Sometimes, I sit and think about pieces that I once made and long to see them once again. On the other hand, I know that if these pieces would be piling up in my backroom, I would feel as if my art is not valued or cherished. I would feel unaffirmed and unvalidated.

I hate being collected. I love it too. Being collected has helped to affirm me as an artist. It has humiliated me too. Sometimes, I feel like a village elder or town crier as a result of being collected. I feel as if my voice is carrying something of worth and meaning, that my message is worthy enough for other people to stop their lives and seek out my message. I feel, at times, like my art is akin to standing on a street corner handing out leaflets. There is a feeling of importance when someone stops, talks for a minute, and ASKS for a leaflet.

Other times, I feel like a whore. Maybe it's because I do most of my painting on the floor, on my creaky, arthritic knees. I'm selling my intimate self for money. I'm opening myself up emotionally for that check or money order, knowing that others look over my art. Sometimes, it is invigorating to know that someone wants to acquire a physical manifestation of my innermost feelings. Other times, it is demeaning to know that I have given this away for money. It is a choice, yet it is addicting. Just as death is a necessary stage of human existence, being collected is a necessary stage of being an artist. Without being collected, the artist is incomplete. The artist who is uncollected is a truncated creator, not an artist. The removal of the collection stage is akin to being castrated; it does not allow the artist to complete the normal cycle of art.

I feel that being collected has complicated my art. Sometimes, as a result of knowing my art is being collected and will be collected, I struggle with artistic honesty and purity. Being collected creates questions like "Does this piece really reflect me, or does it reflect what I want my collectors to think of me?" and "Is this piece painted as a result of what I feel, or as a result of what I feel my collectors expect?"

***Jibber Jabber (race relations in America)*, Harold Smith, 16" × 20", oil on canvas (collection of Dr. Susan Koppelman, Tucson, Arizona; offered on eBay September 22, 2001; photograph by Jeffrey Kessler).**

There is also sometimes a struggle of wondering how current pieces and trends will be viewed in the context of past works. Are the progressions too fast? Are the styles too contradictory to what I have done before? Am I "holding back" out of fear of disappointing collectors?

Being collected can create rules for the artist where there shouldn't be any rules. Some pieces may be pure and honest, but are just not marketable. They are not collectable. A blank canvas may reflect how I feel about something, but what collector will buy a blank canvas? So I don't exhibit the blank canvas. Now I'm no longer honest. I have failed to offer a piece that reflects what I think. Being collected has created a rule. The taste of my patrons used to influence my creating more than it does now. It probably still does, but not as overtly. I used to call it "chasing the cat" because it seemed I was trying to make pieces my patron liked but could never quite get a grip on what they really liked. As time went on, I became more confident in just letting it flow from me.

It hasn't been easy. Money doesn't grow on trees and neither do art supplies.

***The Funeral Procession*, Harold Smith, 16" × 20", acrylic and oil on canvas pad (collection of Patrick and Michelle Hinkebein, St. Louis, Missouri; offered on eBay August 18, 2001).**

Without being collected, the artistic process can wither and die for lack of funds. So, I've tried to balance the financial and economic need to be collected with the emotional and social need to create works that I believe in. It's a fine wire — a very fine wire. It's just like the line between genius and insanity. Sometimes I can cross from one over to the other and know it. I will readily admit that all of my works have not been "honest." Some works I made to get a resale from a collector. I regret that and may even regret openly admitting that. But, in retrospect, that is part of the downside of being collected.

There's a collector who is willing to pay $2000 to $3000 for a piece that is not in your usual style and a piece that you don't "feel." What do you do? Turn down the $2000 so you can say you always created according to the style that is natural for you? Or do you make the piece, get the money and move on? If you have made it, then are you still an artist? Or, have you become a decorator or an illustrator?

Collection is a relatively new concept to me, but art is not. I have always

***Sunday Morning*, Harold Smith, 16" × 20", acrylic on canvas panel (collection of Dr. Susan Koppelman, Tucson, Arizona; offered on eBay September 27, 2001; photograph by Jeffrey Kessler).**

created art. I have some drawings from when I was six years old. These will never be for sale (not by me, anyway). In high school, I never took an art class but I used to doodle while sitting in boring lectures. The same went for college, grad school, staff meetings, workshops, and all the other trappings of professional life. They provided opportunities for me to draw, to sketch. From 1993 to 1997, I took care of my father, who had Alzheimer's and later cancer. Sitting at home evening after evening provided time, plenty of time, to fill sketch book after sketch book. Never imagining that one day I would be collected, I usually tossed them out after they were full.

After my father passed in 1999, I stopped for about a year. Then, one day I discovered that the local public library (Kansas City, Kansas) would allow me to show works there. I had my first show in May of 2000 and sold about ten works.

In March 2001, I had another show, "Red, White & Black," at the Kansas City, Kansas Public Library. The artwork included mixed media pieces such as a flag shaped like a penis entering the mouth of Clarence Thomas and a flag cut to resemble a fist wrapped around the neck of a black man. This brought a lot of criticism and controversy that made both the local and national news. In July, 2001 I was interviewed by Meana Kasi of *VERGE Magazine*[1] about this. The show was scheduled to travel to San Francisco in November 2001, a few months after 9/11. People were on edge, and the San Francisco show was canceled. I was disappointed on the surface, but inside I was relieved. I was not sure I wanted that kind of exposure.

After the show in 2000, I began to offer my works for sale. But even then, I didn't consider it being collected. I only realized I was being collected after buyers began to call and ask if I had new works for them to purchase. I got a digital camera in 2001 and began offering some works on the Internet. That added a whole new dimension. I do my photos with an inexpensive Minolta camera. I use Photoimpact from Corel, which came with a scanner I bought ten years ago, for my online photo editing and other jobs.

For artists, the development of the Internet and the affordability of digital cameras possibly have heralded the biggest passing of the guard since the Abstract Expressionism movement of the 1940s switched the center of the art world from Paris to New York. Today, if you want to see and buy from emerging artists, you don't have to look for obscure galleries and studios in the dilapidated section of your city — you just look on eBay. eBay has provided a venue for these artists to easily sell their wares to the public. Individuals can browse hundreds of artists simply by typing keywords. The other day I typed in "abstract art" and over 40,000 lovely pieces of art came up on over 1000 pages. In the first few pages, I counted over thirty different artists. Art-selling on eBay has literally exploded, despite the fact that the traditionalists still try to brush it off as a "technofad."

As an artist who has sold on eBay, I see great upsides for the buyers. Buyers felt more confident purchasing through eBay than directly from me. If I didn't send their work or if it did not meet the description I placed online, they could apply for a full refund and place remarks on my feedback profile to represent this. They have a level of buyer protection. At the same time, because art pieces are listed on nifty little lines, one below the other, buyers can compare my work with the work of other artists on their computer screens.

From a seller's perspective, the fact that eBay is a worldwide phenomenon means that people who would otherwise not see my work could see it. I've sold work to buyers all over the United States, as well as Canada, Bermuda, Puerto Rico, Israel, Belgium, France, England and Japan. In a traditional brick-and-mortar gallery, this would be impossible.

Prices are another issue. The growing accessibility of eBay combined with the large number of talented artists out there has produced a market with a lot of truly amazing work being sold at incredibly low prices. There are a number of sellers who start their pieces at one cent and sell most pieces for under ten dollars. The pieces they are selling are anywhere from 18" × 24" to 36" × 48". If someone is looking for an inexpensive piece to finish a room, this is the place.

***Shotgun Houses*, Harold Smith, 18" × 34", acrylic on paper (collection of the artist).**

At the same time, there are a lot of "knock off" sellers. These sellers market copies of the most popular works selling on eBay. They are the eBay equivalent of the guys on the street corner selling illegally copied CDs. Most of these sellers are located in Asia or South America and it appears they are running art "sweat shops." Their artists are shown a picture and told to make several copies of it. For collectors who are simply looking for a piece to match their sofa, this is great. For an artist who is at least trying to recoup supply expenses, it's not so good. Interestingly, these "knock off" sellers have very high feedback ratings, which means their many clients are satisfied.

Also, the anonymous nature of the Internet makes it easier for other artists to engage in not-so-nice competitive practices. I've seen artists create bogus accounts and then place ridiculously high bids, sometimes over thousands of dollars, on the auctions of other artists. When the auction ends, the person with the bogus account simply vanishes or refuses to pay, leaving the seller having to go through the tedious process of filing a complaint and waiting up to sixty days to be reimbursed for their seller fees.

Sometimes it gets even more personal than that. Several years ago, I sold several pieces of art (at pretty good prices) to patrons of a competing artist. For the next two to three years, this artist would post detrimental comments about me in various message boards. He even made several pieces of art mocking me and created a webpage designed to embarrass me. I've seen this happen to other artists, too. It's amazing what people find the courage to do when they are hiding behind a computer screen and an ISP connection.

One of the beautiful things about selling online is that it allows a person to develop a fan base easily. I've had several patrons who have collected more than one of my pieces. Sometimes they place me on their e-mail lists and send me opportunities to show other places and sometimes they let me know how things are going in their personal lives. One of my collectors lived in the Ninth Ward of New Orleans and lost everything when it flooded. He relocated to North Carolina and I sent him some pieces to replace those which he lost.

Here's one of the weird things. My most well-received and popular pieces take me about ten to fifteen minutes to paint while those that take a few hours never seem to sell very well. Maybe it's something more primal and authentic about just "whipping it out" that makes it more appealing. That's one good thing about art online — you can get a feel for how a piece is received within days of listing rather than within months as it would take with a gallery. This brings me to something I told a struggling artist. "When you are hot, everything sells regardless of the price ... when you are slumping, nothing sells regardless of how low the price is."

Another advantage to selling online is that the rapid pace of creating, listing, selling, and then creating more allows an artist to move through stages seamlessly. One friend pointed out that I have gone through grief about my father's passing to anti-racist rage to representations of some of the "normal" daily activities of African Americans to the moving works about father/son relationships to the works exploring black men bonding in leisure time activities to the early jazz paintings to the increasingly abstract jazz paintings. I've tried to allow my art to reflect what was on my mind at the time, which creates conflict with the tastes of patrons. Sometimes I have tried to synthesize what's on my mind with what the patrons like but most times I try to choose one over the other.

I've tried advertising on other websites besides eBay. I also ran a $600 ad in the magazine *ArtNews* and saw absolutely no increase of traffic on my website. I ran a $600 ad on the website All About Jazz[2] and have seen an increase of web traffic but no increase in sales.

I have mixed feelings about my experiences on eBay, but overall, they were good. I don't get a lot for my art. Of course, that is disappointing. I wish I got thousands of dollars for each piece. But I've finally come to peace with that fact and with the reality that selling my art on eBay allowed me to create as prolifically as I wanted and still get a little spending money out of it. Since I am not a professionally trained artist, the fact that eBay has so many buyers with various tastes allowed me to experiment with new styles and media and to sell the products instead of tossing them into the trash.

On eBay, I've seen some artists develop cult-like followings. They have message boards dedicated to themselves and their art. This is why a lot of the big artists like Lemya El Sophia[3] and The Raw Artist[4] keep blogs going. They have a fan base and by keeping those fans "in the loop" they are preparing for future sales.

I've tried my own hand at working with fan base. I launched a sometimes-weekly newsletter that I sent out to my regular customers. Sometimes, I included previews of upcoming pieces. My mailing list was over five hundred people. I suspected 70 percent or more of my mails were going into bulk folders and another 10 percent were probably never read or deleted. I sent out a verification e-mail and found that really only two or three people actually were bothering to look at the newsletter. Most were either deleting it or just ignoring it. So, I stopped it. It just didn't work for me.

I started on eBay in 1999, and it has changed dramatically. The sweat-shop sellers have poured in, and a lot of the artists who started when I did have left. Some have become so discouraged they have left art altogether. I remember one particularly gifted artist whose sales plummeted so badly that he sold all his art supplies and just gave up.

I had planned to stay on eBay. At one point, I was hoping eventually to become a fulltime artist, but unless Picasso rises from the grave and takes me by the hand, that's not going to happen. So, for me, the eBay sales were extra cash. Not a lot, but enough to buy a McDonald's value meal and maybe upgrade it a bit.

***Consumption VI*, Harold Smith, 36" × 48", acrylic on stretched canvas, collection of the artist).**

Now, in early 2008, it has been over two years since the original version of this essay was written. I haven't listed anything on eBay in months. Sales continued to slow down, and eventually it became a money drain. With the sweatshop paintings proliferating into the niche markets such as African American art, it became impossible to break even with a sale.

At the same time, I have been selling in a gallery on the East Coast and in a non-profit gift shop here in Kansas City. The proceeds from the gift shop help fund a domestic violence prevention program for young women, so I feel a lot of comfort in selling there. I am one of their most promoted artists and best sellers. It feels good.

It's easier too. No shipping, mailing, and hoping someone doesn't claim the item arrived damaged when they simply want a refund. That became an issue my last few months of active selling on eBay. Two separate buyers claimed items arrived damaged and demanded refunds but they did not want to file insurance claims. Go figure.

I've had a website of my own,[5] in various incarnations, since 1998. It has changed name several times. I just used Microsoft Office Frontpage to create it and tried to make it as simple as possible. I chose to put all my images on it. I have sold only a few paintings off this website — most of my sales were on eBay or are from galleries.

I miss the old days of eBay. When I look back, I don't think I appreciated it like I should have. I was basically getting a paid art education and my patrons were online. I was selling my projects and experiments and using the money to purchase more supplies and continue to find my path. It was fun. I miss the thrill of a painting sold, the ecstasy of a last minute flurry of bids, and the joy of seeing positive feedback.

Even the artists' communities are different. I've checked up on some of the artists I used to communicate with and some are long gone, their eBay stores shuttered and no activity on their account in years. One guy got killed in a motorcycle accident, another went to Iraq and is now a vegetable, courtesy of shrapnel in the brain. Many still talk about art but gave up selling long ago.

As I look back, there was something liberating in those days. Painting fast and listing it faster and keeping them coming freed me from thinking too much in the process. It made it hard to be contrived when I was listing two to three items per day and constantly running out of pieces. It made it easy to just let loose and let it fly and throw it up there.

When I look at some of the newer big selling artists on eBay, I see that freedom in their work. Some of their paintings look like they took thirty minutes at the most to do. Some would look down on that, I don't. I think the spontaneity and the rawness of their work comes out. I miss that. I need to come back to that more. Just grabbing the color that moves me in the moment and just putting it up there. Thinking less and just moving on impulse. Letting art be the outlet for stress, and not the source, is how it should be.

It was a beautiful time, now that I look back on it. I enjoy selling in the galleries and doing the local shows. But, nothing replaces the thrill and high of those days.

When I first wrote this essay, I said "On the other hand, I know that if these pieces would be piling up in my backroom, I would feel as if my art is not valued or cherished. I would feel unaffirmed and unvalidated." Ten feet away, in a guest room, is a stack of paintings that are large and lush. But, for some reason, I don't feel unaffirmed and unvalidated. I just feel ... tired.

We were the artists
Borne of bits and bytes and bandwidth
We were like a group of ragtag bohemians
In our own East Village
The message boards were our pubs and saloons
Hanging our work digitally as if from tenement balconies
We
Coddled together by the fires of mutual inspiration
Our brushes emblazoned in a flurry
Creating swirling typhoons of color and texture
Successful listings fueling our inspiration and drive
We were
Just being and expressing ourselves
With immediacy
Like holding our heads in the wind
And feeling the freedom
Then someone realized that it was a business
And the fire went out
And the typhoon died
We lowered our heads and picked up our brushes
And walked back home

Notes

1. Meana Kasi, "Interview with Harold Smith," *VERGE* (July 2001), http://www.vergemag.com/0701/featarts/featarts1.html (accessed January 31, 2008).
2. *All About Jazz*, http://www.allaboutjazz.com (accessed January 31, 2008).
3. Lemya El Sophia, http://www.elsophia.com (accessed January 31, 2008).
4. Michel Keck, *The Raw Artist*, http://www.therawartist.com (accessed January 31, 2008).
5. Harold Smith, *Harold Smith Art*, http://haroldsmithart.com (accessed January 31, 2008).

Bibliography

Bellemore, Marilyn. "Jazzin Up Art." *The Newport Times*, August 2, 2006, http://www.haroldsmithart.com/press.html (accessed January 31, 2008).

Kasi, Meana. "Interview with Harold Smith." *Verge* (July 2001), http://www.vergemag.com/0701/featarts/featarts1.html (accessed January 31, 2008).

Smith, Harold. *Harold Smith Art*. http://haroldsmithart.com (accessed January 31, 2008).

Stapley, Candace. "Intimate Images Explore Racism, Injustice." *Kansas City Star*, June 8, 2001, http://www.haroldsmithart.com/press.html (accessed January 31, 2008).

14

The Past Is Always on Sale

Revisiting Culture as Commodity: Internet Auctions and Judaica Collecting

EMILY ALICE KATZ

Contemporary America is a society of budding connoisseurs, patrolling distant destinations for the perfect souvenir and digging through family basements in search of a unique find. The interwoven strands of nostalgia, curiosity, business savvy, cultural and family pride, memorialization, and scholarly inquiry that shape and are shaped by this culture of collecting have found the ultimate partner in the Internet, that universe of information in which objects can be sold or swapped, connections can be made, and stories can be shared. For those who have discovered in the Internet the great collecting frontier, eBay is the supreme venue, its (largely) unchaperoned, endlessly shifting byways a kind of virtual world bazaar. Ubiquitous, accessible eBay has remade the contours of collecting, creating from an amorphous mass of estate-sale junkies and thrift shop sleuths an enormous community of trading mavens, thereby transforming a collective collecting habit into a full-fledged national pastime.

As a master's student in Jewish art and material culture, and then as curator at The Judaica Museum in Bronx, New York, I had learned to gauge the provenance of seder plates (used during the Passover meal to hold special foods symbolic of the Exodus story), to decipher the iconography of *parokhot* (curtains that hang at the front of the Torah ark to shield the Torah scrolls from view), and to tell an etrog (citron) box from a silver sugar casket. EBay was simply not part of my rarified universe. And yet, as I soon began to grasp, the encounter of Jewish fine and ceremonial art with online auctions and e-commerce seems destined to have an indelible effect upon the Judaica market and the individuals and institutions that are bound up with it. Spurred by the testimony of my director at the museum, an inveterate eBay addict, I became increasingly intrigued by the marriage of Judaica collecting and the Internet.

I conceived of the exhibition *Culture as Commodity: Internet Auctions and Judaica Collecting* as a hands-on exploration of just this phenomenon. The challenge: to purchase all the objects for display in the exhibition through online auctions, almost exclusively on eBay, over the summer and early fall of 2001 (the exhibition opened in November of that year). Aside from the fear that my efforts would come to naught — lose enough online auctions and there wouldn't be an exhibition at all — I was stirred with wonder and near incredulity at the tremendous diversity of available objects. Trained as a traditional Judaica curator, I now faced the task of creating a cabinet of curiosities wholesale, from the fantastic and somewhat dubious coffers of the World Wide Web. Armed with little more than a username and password (as well as a healthy dose of skepticism), I was ready to test my eBay mettle.

The connoisseurship of Judaica long predates the keyboard and mouse, of course; the formal history of Judaica collecting parallels that of the museological trend in Western culture generally, its roots firmly planted in the Enlightenment drive toward scientific classification and study, its direction guided by the imperatives of European nationalism. The collecting and display of Judaica for its aesthetic and historical value is a practice that emerged in the mid-eighteenth century when Court Jew Alexander David of Braunschweig (Germany) presented his private collection to the public as a kind of museum of Jewish art.[1] Jewish museums as such began appearing in Europe at the end of the nineteenth century. The first was established in Vienna in 1895. The emergence of the European Jewish museums—as well the establishment of the Bezalel Museum (precursor to the Israel Museum) in Jerusalem in 1906 — was part of a broader movement in Europe to establish great national museums. Such institutions would serve to legitimate national identity by means of material "proof" (often archaeological and anthropological in nature, and as such bearing the seal of scientific authority) of a nation's antiquity and worth, whether large and ascendant or small and oppressed.

Emancipated and/or acculturated European Jewish communities grappled similarly with the project of cementing a proud national identity — of shaping a diversity of experience into a cohesive cultural narrative through material artifacts. Such a project would serve an educative, unifying function within the community, and illustrate to the surrounding culture the equal worth of Jewish civilization. Tom Freudenheim points out that:

> For Jews, as for many other groups grappling with identity issues, the museum was a manifestation of self-definition.... The notion of the museum as a critical element of a fully developed societal structure (very much a European concept!) was as available for exploitation by Jews gaining a new sense of themselves as it was for other peoples. Nevertheless, the museum was not necessarily a first

> priority.... However, once the bourgeois model is in place and accepted—that is, self-examination and communal history as a leisure activity, education for social (rather than simply economic) gain, and collecting as a natural offshoot of these interests—Jews would obviously partake as well.[2]

The impetus for creating Jewish museums, for asserting Jewish presence by means of public visual media, arose from a mixture of "apologetics, nostalgia, patriotism, historical consciousness, and nationalism," in the words of one historian of Jewish material culture.[3]

Serious interest in Jewish art in a museum context blossomed in the nineteenth century and came to full fruition only after World War II. The last century has been characterized by a steady growth of Jewish museums of various stripes, often predicated on the substantial donations of great Judaica collectors such as Hadji Ephraim Benguiat (whose collections were loaned to the Smithsonian Institution in the last decade of the nineteenth century and were later purchased by the library of the Jewish Theological Seminary, in 1925) and Harry G. Friedman (who, at the time of his death in 1965, had donated or secured over 6,000 works for the Judaica, fine arts, and archaeology departments of The Jewish Museum in New York).[4] Great museums, from this perspective, were the legacies of great collectors. Whatever the intentions of the individual collectors, however, the collections themselves were interpreted and displayed according to the directives of curators and exhibitors, who might present objects as finely executed decorative art, as archaeological or anthropological evidence from the ancient world, or as tools for comprehending Judaism as a complex and unified religion (to name a few strategies).[5]

However, the increasing importance of Judaica collecting and Jewish museums in America parallel, and in fact are inextricable from, the rise of interest among nonprofessionals in Jewish material culture in the postwar period. As cultural historian Jenna Weissman Joselit has shown, the Jewish community has, since the early twentieth century, coalesced around the idea of the centrality of the home and family even as it differed, sometimes dramatically, on matters ideological, social, and political. Jewish women's groups initially fostered an appreciation of Jewish ritual objects to elevate the taste of the immigrant generation and, later, as a means of spiritualizing the home, thereby instilling religious sentiment and assuring loyalty to Judaism among future generations. Judaica was positioned as "a bona fide form of artistic expression," that conferred stylistic éclat to the home and encouraged positive attachment to Jewish heritage, even as it was divested of a viable sacramental existence.[6]

Synagogue gift shops rose to prominence in the postwar period as the synagogue itself became less a site of explicitly religious behavior and more a locus of social activity. Stocked with a spectrum of ceremonial objects for various holidays and appropriate gifts for life-cycle events such as bar and bat mitzvah and weddings, they provided "an ideal venue for explicitly Jewish consumer behavior," in which "Jewish women not only familiarized themselves with Jewish ceremonial lore and customs but educated others as well."[7] Jewish museums thus became central tools in the shaping of cultural pride and the fostering of continuity. Group trips to Jewish museums, sponsored by temple sisterhoods and similar organizations, often coincided with Jewish holidays to maximize the educational freight of the visit. More than just an intellectual or aesthetic encounter, museum-going was an enactment of the visitor's connection to her Jewish heritage, meant to establish a visceral bond between observer and object.

An increasingly museum-savvy American–Jewish audience, primed by the sisterhood gift shop to procure Judaica for the home, cultivated the connoisseurship of Judaica as an end in and of itself. Increasing affluence coupled with a vigorous interest in Jewish material culture spurred the emergence of the largely nonprofessional Judaica collector. Historian of Jewish civilization Cecil Roth noted over thirty years ago that the market for Judaica antiques had exploded in the postwar period as part of a "universal collecting fever," in which demand far outstripped supply (leading to a preponderance of fakes and forgeries in the market).[8] Indeed, Roth had earlier confessed his own predilection for the sport of Judaica collecting, saying (in 1957) that he "must own one of the most preposterous collections of miscellaneous Jewish junk to be found anywhere in the world today in private hands."[9] It is precisely the emergence of this acquisitive (and, Cecil Roth notwithstanding, largely untutored) milieu that led The Jewish Museum to establish its own design studio in 1956 in order to provide contemporary, high-end ceremonial art to an increasingly affluent audience seeking tasteful examples of their cultural and religious patrimony.

In the age of the Internet auction, this appreciation-cum-commodification of Jewish objects has only intensified as a cultural (and economic) phenomenon. Typing "Judaica"—as well as the misspellings "Judiaca" and "Judica," another trick gleaned from my intrepid museum director—into the eBay search engine on an average day produces hundreds upon hundreds of widely varying auction lots. (Jewish art and Judaica appear regularly on other online venues as well, from Christie's to Yahoo.) Exploring the eBay site for objects, one notices quickly that the concept of Judaica is subject to broad interpretation.

The term "Judaica" itself, in fact, was formally defined only in 1998 by Grace Cohen Grossman of the Skirball Center in Los Angeles, at the request of the American Association of Museums; collectors and museums were in the habit of creating their own guidelines for distinguishing the category. Her definition reads:

> The term "Judaica" is most broadly defined as the material culture of the Jewish people. First and foremost this includes the ceremonial objects for communal or domestic use. In addition, Judaica comprises historical artifacts relating to important Jewish personalities, momentous events and significant communal activities, as well as literature relating to Jews and Judaism.

"Many museums," the statement concludes, "also have acquired material of everyday life that expresses a uniquely Jewish identity."[10]

In large part, eBay practice itself dictated the use of this broadest conception of Judaica for the purposes of the exhibition. Alongside high-end ceremonial pieces and fine art, a dizzying range of Jewish objects has accumulated on eBay for the collecting public. Coins, posters and records, historical documents and ephemera, books, jewelry, and celebrity paraphernalia have, in a certain sense, reoriented collecting activity away from elite agendas. The primary objective, to my mind, was to let the public conception of what "counts" as Judaica (as manifested on popular auction sites like eBay) shape the content of the exhibition. For *Culture as Commodity*, then, I employed the most inclusive definition of Judaica possible. Sifting through auction listings I detected four basic categories that I could use for the purposes of the exhibition —ceremonial objects, books, works on paper, and material and popular culture.

This exhibition was, above all, an opportunity for educating the museum-going public about the value of artifacts of material and popular culture within the museum context, and to expand the conception, for visitors, of what counts as significant within the space of The Judaica Museum itself. Indeed, it presented the opportunity to tweak the concept of what belongs in a Judaica museum at all. The core collection and permanent exhibition of The Judaica Museum, for instance, comprise traditional ceremonial objects: silver Kiddush (sacramental wine) cups and spice boxes, ceramic Seder plates, embroidered Torah binders (bands traditionally used by Ashkenazi Jews to hold the two staves of the Torah scroll together), and so on. I found myself searching specifically for ephemera — letters, postcards, long-forgotten pamphlets and programs— and for paraphernalia related to Jewish celebrities, from baseball legend Hank Greenberg to comedian klezmer performer Mickey Katz. I wanted to secure a place for baseball cards, records, sheet music, and posters amidst the turreted spice boxes and mezuzot (parchment scrolls containing passages from Deuteronomy, encased in a protective cover and affixed to the doorposts of Jewish homes). As I wrote for the exhibition:

> Material culture encompasses the seemingly mundane artifacts of civilizations—furniture and buildings, clothing and toys, souvenirs and advertisements— while the study of material culture recognizes these objects' worth as repositories of social and cultural history. The body of relics from people's everyday existence is sometimes referred to as "low" or "folk" culture, whereas "high" culture usually describes the art, literature, and music that have been recognized by a society as extraordinary examples of human creativity. But often, it is an object's very "ordinariness" which grants us the most fascinating glimpse into the human experience. It is precisely these workaday objects that can clarify the substance and patterns of day-to-day life.

Bidding on objects, I was less concerned with how much particular objects were actually worth, according to the market, than with finding a diverse and interesting collection of objects and, of course, winning the auctions (while staying within the purchasing budget). In other words, I was collecting in a vacuum. One of the purposes of the exhibition was to provide our audience a glimpse of the values of the online Judaica-collecting community. To that end I decided to include on the label for each object a listing of the bidding information — the starting and ending prices and the number of bids offered. Visitors to the exhibition were thus confronted with the nitty-gritty details of acquisition and encouraged to ponder the vagaries of popular taste first-hand. The object in the exhibition which attracted the highest number of bids, for instance, was an engraved and hand-colored map of the Holy Land executed by Pieter van den Keere in 1676, which included such details as the locations of the tribes of Israel and the sites, year by year, of the wandering Israelites during their 40 years in the desert. The auction closed at 27 bids; the final price was $295.00. On the other hand, sheet music for the Al Jolson number "Carolina Mammy," published in 1922, went for the lowest price: $1.00 — and I was the only bidder. For me, the thrillingly vertiginous gap between (relatively) high-market and low-market objects was a subject of display in and of itself.

Displaying this information in the exhibition fostered a dissonance between the perception of museum-as-temple and the reality of museum-as-marketplace. Furthermore, it was a playful gesture, an attempt to elicit a personal reaction from our audience. Often enough, objects would spark reminiscences or anecdotes among visitors. I was more intrigued, however, to hear comments that would never have been uttered in the usual museum context — the suggestion that the museum paid too much for one item, for example, or an expression of surprise that another object was so inexpensive. What's more, rather than acquiring the items in the exhibition for our permanent collection, we had decided to sell the items to the public once the show completed its run. Visitors interested in a particular object were able to sign a waiting list, with the understanding that they would pay the price listed on the display label (this was not a for-profit venture). Anything left over, we decided, would be sold on (what else?) eBay.

So, what actually made it into the show, the reader might ask? Here, briefly, is a guided tour of some of the objects included in the exhibition, in light of the various problems and opportunities each presented from a collecting and curatorial perspective. The most expensive item bought for the exhibition, and one of the most traditional, was a cast brass Shabbat lamp. The seller, a man from Long Island, listed the item as "19th century huge shabbat lamp from Poland" and set the first bid at $1.00, later adding to the listing that the piece might be as early as the eighteenth century. The iconography and style — rampant lions amidst a scrolling openwork background; a double eagle crest flanked by a crown — were certainly characteristic of East European brass work. The object was clearly all of a piece, rather than a pastiche of various periods, as is often the case with Judaica, which has often been repaired and "updated" over the course of centuries. The question, from a standard curatorial perspective, revolved around the actual dating of the object. Brass Judaica lacks hallmarks, so the dating of this genre of object is fraught with ambiguities. Purchasing such an item basically sight unseen through an online auction is (needless to say) rather risky under "normal" collecting circumstances.

Nonetheless, the object had caught my attention, and I won the auction for $1,125.03, at 23 total bids. Afterwards, the seller mentioned that he had acquired the piece from an antique store in Hungary in 1981, and, upon returning to New York, had had it authenticated by "one of the curators" of the Jewish Museum. While his initial appraisal of mid-to-late nineteenth century was plausible, however, the piece was probably made even later. What's more, I spied another exactly like it sitting on a table outside of a hole-in-the-wall antique store on the Lower East Side of New York shortly after winning the auction. An acquaintance claims to have one just like it at home, which she bought at a flea market for a paltry sum. However dubious its provenance and authenticity, the Shabbat lamp was a wonderful object for the purposes of the exhibition. It was visually interesting and, perhaps more importantly, raised questions about origin and worth that I wanted the audience to contemplate.

A pair of tefillin bags that I procured for Culture as Commodity highlighted another problem with collecting through online auctions. The bags, meant to hold the phylacteries traditionally wound around a man's arm and forehead during prayer, were both of embroidered velvet. They were charming examples of their kind, in aged but good condition. Upon my request, however, the Florida-based seller was not able to provide any information about their provenance or subsequent history. In this case, the lack of information about provenance was less problematic than their lack of documented history; these tefillin bags had lost their specificity, their anthropological and historical resonance, and were therefore noteworthy in the museum context only as fine examples of a particular category of object. Surprisingly, these items garnered little attention; the starting bid was $12.99, and I acquired the pair for $15.99, at a total of six bids.

The objects I most enjoyed collecting for the exhibition (and that I found most fascinating) were those that fell under the "material and popular culture" rubric. These are the objects for which sites such as eBay are most useful (and popular) but which, excepting very rare celebrity paraphernalia and historical material, often sell for very reasonable amounts of money. Low-end ephemera and collectibles are still eBay's *raison-d'etre*. One such item that appeared in the exhibition was a *Harper's Weekly* cover dating from February 15, 1891, entitled "New York Rabbi." The cover art, an engraving by an artist named T.V.

Chominski, depicts a traditionally garbed, bearded rabbi praying in a darkened synagogue. In the artist's rendering, the particular (exemplified by the precise ethnographic detailing of the rabbi's accouterments) meets the universal (manifest in the unmistakable aura of nobility and intelligence in the rabbi's erect carriage and his tranquil, uplifted face); to my mind, it is a portrait of rabbi as a wise, exotic, if not quite noble savage. It was a fitting companion to its related article, found inside the issue, in which the author provided for his audience an informed discussion of the role of the rabbi in Jewish tradition. This object spoke eloquently of *Harper's* vision of itself as arbiter of learned, Liberal gentility in nineteenth century America. It added, as well, to the history of images of Judaism, Jews, and Jewishness in the American public sphere. As such, it was well worth the $8 I paid for the item. I was the only one to bid.

Another favorite purchase was a Hank Greenberg baseball card, dating from 1938, which I won (in the middle of the night) at $175.03, after a total of 11 bids. It was produced by The Goudey Gum Company of Boston, one of the first to manufacture baseball cards. Meanwhile, an illustrated Hebrew language version of *Uncle Tom's Cabin* for children, probably dating from the 1950s (there was no publication information), was a remnant of Israeli interest in Harriet Beecher Stowe's anti-slavery melodrama. A Hebrew translation for children was first published in Jerusalem in 1917 by writer Asher Barash; it was one of the first works of American literature to be translated into Hebrew.[11] I was very surprised at the lack of interest in this book online; the seller set the first bid at $20.00, and I won the item, one bid later, for $20.50. Although I've since forgotten where the various objects purchased for the exhibition finally found homes, I remember the fate of this book; the museum administrator, a devoted member of the staff for more than 15 years, intended to buy the book for her first grandchild—completing the circle from culture to commodity and back again.

There is no doubt that the advent of eBay and its ilk has diversified and democratized Judaica collecting. Internet auctions have expanded the collecting community just as they have, in the best-case scenario, broadened the parameters of Jewish cultural inquiry to allow for an increasingly nuanced canvas of Jewish life and cultural activity, past and present. But just as the Internet has radically democratized and diversified Judaica collecting, so has it complicated a thriving market already saturated with fakes and forgeries. With everything for sale to the highest bidder, essentially sight unseen, questions about the worth, authenticity and provenance of objects inevitably arise. As one eBay seller put it bluntly to me, eBay is a minefield for the ignorant. What's more, as bids increase and prices climb online, museum donations themselves may dwindle. Meanwhile, professional Jewish museums (like others) are likely to retain mixed opinions regarding the worth of popular culture in the museum context.

Jewish culture has, in the collecting context, become yet another salable good, to be auctioned off with impunity. The museum world acts as both complainant and accomplice in this seemingly inevitable conflation of commerce and culture, economics and edification. In our post-modern, globalized American society the commodification of culture is a fact — and a way — of life. In the *New York Times Magazine* in December 2001, Verlyn Klinkenborg considered the cultural significance of eBay, and wrote — in a kind of free-market gloss on Faulkner's maxim that "The past is never dead. It isn't even past,"— that eBay is a place where "the past is always present and, better yet, always for sale."[12] Perhaps in the end, whatever the earnest intentions of the museum professionals and informed connoisseurs, it is the small-time collector at home in front of the computer in her pajamas and slippers, who will have to make the final distinction, if there is in fact any to be made, between culture and commodity.

NOTES

1. The Court Jews (Hofjuden) acted as advisors in the princely courts in Central Europe, from roughly the late sixteenth century to the late eighteenth century. Drawing upon broad mercantilist networks and commercial expertise, such individuals served initially as suppliers of credit or cash, as tax collectors, and as army provisioners and became indispensable instruments of the absolutist state. By dint of their prestige and authority at court, such figures often acted as intermediaries between the Jewish community and the local rulers. While Court Jews accrued great wealth and renown and were among the first Jews to adopt the cultural norms of European elites, they were precariously positioned between the Jewish community and the royal court, and were often victims of court intrigues and popular vitriol. For patronage and collecting practices among the Court Jews, see Richard I. Cohen, *Jewish Icons: Art and Society in Modern Europe* (Berkeley: University of California Press, 1998) and Richard I. Cohen and Vivian B. Mann, *From Court Jews to the Rothschilds: Art, Patronage, and Power, 1600–1800* (New York: Jewish Museum, 1996). For more on Alexander of Braunschweig's collection, see Vivian B. Mann, ed. *Jewish Texts on the Visual Arts* (New York: Cambridge University Press, 2000), 86–89.

2. Tom Freudenheim, "The Obligations of the Chosen: Jewish Museums in a Politically Correct World," *European Judaism* 34:2 (Autumn 2001), 82.

3. Richard I. Cohen, "Self-Image Through Objects: Toward a Social History of Jewish Art Collecting and Jewish Museums," in *The Uses of Tradition: Jewish Continuity in the Modern Era*, ed. Jack Wertheimer (New York and Jerusalem: Jewish Theological Seminary of America, 1992): 242.

4. See Vivian B. Mann, ed. *Jewish Texts on the Visual Arts* (New York: Cambridge University Press, 2000).

5. See Barbara Kirshenblatt-Gimblett, "Exhibiting Jews," in *Destination Culture: Tourism, Museums, and Heritage* (Berkeley and Los Angeles: University of California Press, 1998), 79–128.

6. Jenna Weissman Joselit, *The Wonders of America: Reinventing Jewish Culture, 1880–1950* (New York: Hill and Wang, 1994), 151. See also Joellyn Wallen Zollman, "Shopping for a Future: A History of the American Synagogue Gift Shop." Ph.D. diss. Brandeis University, 2002.

7. Ibid., 159, 161.

8. Cecil Roth, "Caveat Emptor Judaeus," *Commentary* 43:3 (1967), 84–86.

9. Cecil Roth, "The Art and Craft of Jewish Collecting: Dealings in the Higher 'Junk,'" *Commentary* 23:6 (June 1957), 541–547.

10. Definition appears as footnote in "AAM Recommended Procedures for Providing

Information to the Public about Objects Transferred in Europe during the Nazi Era," http://www.aam-us.org/museumresources/prov/procedures.cfm (accessed February 10, 2008).

11. A discussion about *Uncle Tom's Cabin* in Yiddish and Hebrew translations can be found on the H-JUDAIC Digest (listserv), December 13, 14, 17, 18, and 24, 2001.

12. "The Way We Live Now," *New York Times Magazine*, December 23, 2001.

15

Online Museums, Exhibits, and Archives of American Disability History

PENNY L. RICHARDS

You can visit the world's finest museums—and their gift shops—at midnight, in your pajamas. You can explore a once-in-a-lifetime multimedia exhibit that was mounted briefly, years ago, in a faraway city. You can examine unique primary documents from private collections and restricted university archives, with a coffee at hand and a noisy toddler on your lap. (Have a comment or a question? The curator is often just a click away.)

You can even open your own museum, welcoming hundreds of visitors to share your passion for, say, vintage calculators, or the Connecticut highway system.[1] These are among the previously unattainable wonders realized by the internet. But the very accessibility of virtual exhibition is also its danger.

Beautiful visual or audio presentation may lend an undeserved air of reliability to incomplete or ill-informed content. Search engines make it possible to find specific exhibits, but offer no guidance as to quality, motivation, or timeliness. Excellent websites may disappear without warning while obsolete material remains available for years past its relevance. Frequent editorial changes may enhance or damage an online archive, but in either event it can still be tricky to cite virtual content.

Disability history is a subject well-suited to online exhibition for several reasons. The field draws from a diverse web of other disciplines for primary sources and means of analysis. Medicine, law, education, art, literature, popular culture, public policy, economics, technology, and even religion inform and are informed by the history of disability, meaning the field has no single "natural" home on campuses or in libraries. Online, however, a disability history exhibit can easily link visitors to materials from all these other disciplines. Adding to this advantage of gathering diverse materials in one virtual space, online environments invite the specialist non-professional to create displays.

For a field busily unearthing its hidden stories, especially for twentieth-century movements and cultural, legislative and technological changes, it is exciting to have activists and collectors sharing their memoirs, photos, and ephemera in such a visible and interactive setting. Disability history exhibits can also use technological tools—captions, videos, audio clips, alternative fonts, magnification and text-only versions—to make online materials accessible to visitors with various information access needs. Finally, online disability history content provides the public with narratives, timelines, and details that are useful in understanding current events, medical controversies, and legal rights, and sets disability in a context which should work toward challenging harmful stereotypes and misconceptions.

In this essay, I report on the content and format of online museums, exhibits, and archives dealing with American disability history, in light of their objectives, usefulness, reliability, and potential for future growth. Some are online extensions of bricks-and-mortar institutions with similar content; others are the more permanent online record of a temporary exhibit in a museum or gallery, while others are exclusively virtual entities. I focus on American sites, but many of the issues raised apply equally to sites in other national contexts; and Americans interested in disability history should certainly bear in mind the international dimensions of the subject. I do not include websites that offer only bibliographic or curricular materials, nor purely local-interest sites, nor commercial pages. A large and growing number of websites are dedicated to disability culture, disability activism, and disability studies. While many of these are excellent, they are also beyond the scope of this review, unless they include a significant historical component.[2] I conclude with ideas about future directions for online resources for American disability history.

General American Disability History Websites

If, as Douglas Baynton suggests, "disability is everywhere in history, once you begin looking for it,"[3] a general history of disability in America must encompass an enormous range of subjects and materials to tell the basic story. Disabled veterans, special education, Gallaudet University, disability rights activism, legal milestones, insane asylums, Helen Keller, Blind Lemon Jefferson, assistive technologies, prosthetics, immigration restrictions, eugenics, sideshows, adaptive sports ... the list could run for pages. How can a website take on this giant project and hope to succeed in presenting something informative, coherent, and responsible?

One site that shows great promise toward achieving this goal is the extraordinary Disability History Museum,[4] maintained by Straight Ahead Pictures, a non-profit production company whose projects focus on innovative and educational historical presentations that "foster community dialogue about contemporary social issues" (from their website[5]). Called "The Internet at its best" by a 2001 Boston Globe editorial,[6] the Disability History Museum is an impressive resource now, and further services are planned soon. Only the Library area is open at this writing; the Museum and Education wings are still under construction. But the Library itself is rich and diverse within its stated goal to be a robust study collection for American disability history, 1775–1990. The vast and growing collection is searchable in various ways, and includes materials in formats both expected (photographs, letters, short stories, interview transcripts, magazine articles) and unexpected (comic book pages, sheet music, children's inspirational materials). Some of these items are in private collections and, without the Disability History Museum, would remain almost totally unavailable to researchers or other interested visitors. Other items come from special collections libraries and industrial archives across the country, brought together and made accessible to a much wider audience than ever before possible. The Museum wing will offer exhibits and even a gift shop when it is launched; the Education wing intends to provide teacher resources such as course packets. A long list of academic and community advisors, funding sources, and partners are attached to this site, and the breadth and depth of this support shows in the site's design, mission, and content.

While the Disability History Museum's exhibits are not yet ready, curious visitors may find clues about the direction they will take from visiting another Straight Ahead Pictures project online, Beyond Affliction: The Disability History Project.[7] Straight Ahead's co-founder Laurie Block co-produced the "Beyond Affliction" series on American disability history that aired on National Public Radio in 1996. The four episodes of that series are available at the website (in RealAudio or transcript form), but there is much additional content here, too. The site is organized around five interlocking "themes" (Community, Education, Evidence, Charity, and Policy), and within each, four eras are summarized (1820–1870, 1870–1930, 1930–1970, 1970-present) with a short but cogent text summary and links to appropriate objects, including interviews with scholars, photographs, movie posters, audio clips and other formats (drawn from the archives at the Disability History Museum). This is an imaginative and thoughtfully organized exhibit that gathers a long and ranging history into a coherent narrative, invites the visitor to discover connections across eras and themes, and seems likely to whet many an appetite for further study.

Next to the extraordinary projects of Straight Ahead Pictures, other similar sounding sites attempting a general American disability history coverage appear less successful, but they are not without merit; and the reasons for their shortcomings are, perhaps, instructive. The Disability Social History Project[8] is built from, and welcomes, community participation, a format in keeping with the activism backgrounds of archivist Stephen Dias and designer Patricia Chadwick. The idea is that historical material concerning disability (from any place or time period) will be submitted by the public and incorporated into the site's content. There are elements of the site that show the promise of this approach: the exhibit "Disability Campaigns in the United States, 1930s-1960s," for example, displays lapel pins, stamps, stickers, and other ephemera associated with campaigns against polio, for disabled veterans' employment, toward various cures and in suppport of greater awareness. This fascinating collection of small objects is photographed well, and the display is organized to help visitors notice continuing themes and changing attitudes.

Too often, however, the community participation aspect of the Disability Social History Project leads instead to wildly uneven coverage. To detail a typical instance, the timeline of world disability history includes three dates in the BC period, then jumps to AD 1500, and is heavily weighted toward Deaf history and the history of prostheses. Blind history seemingly begins in 1809 with the birth of Louis Braille, and there is very little history of developmental disability or mental illness. Like many sites, the DSHP is evolving and should improve with time (and further contributions from a broader spectrum of the disability community); but the "bibliographies" page seems not to have been updated within the past years (latest entries are dated 2003), a troubling sign that frequent updates may not be forthcoming.

The Disability Social History Project described in this chapter aimed at being a "community history project." But this goal was somewhat stymied by the format of the website, which asked for submissions that would be incorporated into the site by a webmaster—somehow, later, perhaps much later. Community is constricted by such a bottleneck. A more promising format for a disability-focused "community history project" is Disapedia, a collaborative encyclopedia of disability resources created in May 2007 by Peter O'Connell.[9] The "Our History" section is still small but growing daily, and currently includes substantial entries on Ed Roberts, Braille, and ADAPT, among other topics. Disapedia is a "wiki," a collaborative website that is directly edited by a wide array of contributors. The ease with which community members can contribute to a wiki holds great promise for growth and dynamic content; admittedly, it also leaves open the questions of bias and reliability that haunt all wiki-built encyclopedias.

The wiki format has also been employed to educate schoolchildren: In April 2007, eighth graders at Harrison Middle School in Yarmouth, Maine, set up a wiki to gather and organize information about civil rights history, and several teams were set to create sections about the disability rights movement.[10] The students also mounted an actual exhibit at their school, for one night, to display their findings for a local walk-through audience. A new generation of scholars learning and sharing history with a new generation of technology—the online presence of disability history archives and exhibits is secure in a beautiful and constant flux.

A somewhat related project, the Disability History Dateline,[11] uses the timeline from the DSHP pages as a starting point. More points and details are being added, again with community input, but with more evident attention to citations and searchability.

The unconventionally named Museum of disABILITY History[12] is sponsored by People Inc., a western New York agency serving people with developmental disabilities. A bricks-and-mortar museum recently opened in Williamsville, New York, with the website serving as an outreach program and an opportunity to collect and display materials. There are three exhibits on the site. The first two, "The Birth of Newborn Screening" and "Idiocy in America: The Path to the Institution 1850–1920," despite their general titles, mainly cover New York state developments in medical history. The exhibits offer text with photo illustrations; the photographs are often striking and well-chosen, and succeed in clarifying certain passages of text (especially where technical descriptions of blood screening procedures are given). The emphasis is firmly on tracing the prevention and treatment of disability, rather than on lived experience. The third exhibit in the Museum of disABILITY History, with the grand title "Pantheon of disABILITY History: Changing the Face of disABILITY Culture," extends this emphasis on state authority and medical treatment.

This "Pantheon" includes no people with disabilities, no twentieth-century advocates central to the usual story of disability culture. Instead, the exhibit consists of short biographies (with portraits) of four reformers in the history of mental illness or mental retardation: Itard, Pinel, Dix, and Seguin. Throughout the site, upbeat text expresses confidence in medical progress as an unqualified good for people with disabilities. Visitors with more complicated approaches to the history of disability, aware of a past where people (especially those with developmental disabilities) have been marginalized, segregated, harmed, or killed in the name of medical necessity, will find this tone simplistic, patronizing, and even disturbing, given the supporting agency's mission.

The Museum of disABILITY History has undergone a major renovation, and now shows some much-needed improvements in presentation. The interactive version of the site creates the feeling of moving through the door of a real museum, toward an information desk, where the visitor can then choose to enter wings labeled Media, Medicine, and Society. Each of these choices leads to further display options, from sports to eugenics, cures to the Kennedys. Unfortunately, most of these second-tier options are currently dead-ends, and lead back to the front desk. Now that the presentation has been made friendly and creative, this Museum still needs content to be a useful addition to the realm of disability history online.

Is the general history of disability in America just too large and diverse to be the subject of an online museum? Not at all. The sites designed by Straight Ahead Pictures make a great case for the potential and value of such a broad archive and virtual space for exhibition. We still need community outreach to retrieve documents, photographs, and objects important to this history from the family scrapbooks, town hall attics, and antique shops, but there are signs that the internet is helping in this effort. Americans with disabilities have lived a rich and complex history, which deserves a frank and creative presentation. Sketchy and sanitized online versions of this narrative do more harm than good by perpetuating invisibility and harmful misconceptions to a wide audience.

Issue- and Era-Specific Sites

An alternative approach to creating online historical content about disability in America is to limit content to a specific era, issue, or even personality in this diverse history. Such sites may be no less extensive than those attempting a general coverage; and the level of detail may be more satisfying to the curious visitor. However, these sites risk missing the "big picture" when content is too narrowly presented to include larger social movements or cross-disability cultural infusions.

Two of the finest of the era-specific sites are from the Smithsonian's National Museum of American History. The Smithsonian's Disability Rights Movement exhibit[13] is a multimedia recreation of a groundbreaking 2000 exhibit curated by Katherine Ott and Harry Rubenstein. The website uses the content of kiosk displays from the original experience to guide online visitors through the objects and sections presented.

Although the exhibit is focused specifically on the disability rights movement in the U.S., in the latter half of the twentieth century, it is also broad enough to show how interrelated events in technology, special education, and law came about through activism and advocacy by and for people with disabilities. See all the visible objects—photos, buttons, posters, t-shirts—described in onscreen text, and (with a click) hear a clear, pleasant audio narration of the same text. While some of the kiosk information is unnecessary for online users—directions around the building, for example—it preserves the content's original function and may even, for imaginative visitors, recreate the sense of being in a physical museum.

There are places where technological limitations may defeat the full enjoyment of this site: videos are included along the tour, but may not work well on all computers. Navigating through the exhibit is not difficult; however, an accumulation of open windows may slow some connections. Overall, this is an exemplary undertaking, abundantly informative for visitors, and equally full of ideas for other museums (virtual or not) seeking a similar degree of accessibility through multiple, complementary delivery formats. Rivaling its predecessor in depth and innovation, the Smithsonian's What Ever Happened to Polio?[14] matches a 2005–2006 exhibit (again curated by Katherine Ott), timed to coincide with the fiftieth anniversary of the Salk's polio vaccine. The subject is inherently more medical than the disability rights movement, but the exhibit does a good job balancing the scientific with the personal, social, and political dimensions of polio. We learn how an iron lung worked, but also how it felt to use an iron lung. While the images in the disability rights movement exhibit are fascinating, they are perhaps not so poignant to the average American viewer today as quarantine signs, or a toddler's orthopedic corset. The polio exhibit presents collections of braces and crutches, scrapbooks and shoes, often with their original users' names attached, always keeping the human experience foremost in the narrative. Several appealing educational activities accompany the exhibit (though calling them "games" may be a stretch), and audio files are well-marked along the tour. Together, these two Smithsonian exhibits set the high-watermark for focused disability history content online.

Several sites offer strong historical content on the era of eugenics. This era is not easily bounded by dates — some say it flourishes still — but certainly for over a century eugenic ideology played a significant role in the experience of disability in America. Over a thousand photographs and documents are available online through the searchable Image Archive of the American Eugenics Movement,[15] which was launched in February 2000 as a public education and research project of the Dolan DNA Learning Center at Cold Springs Harbor Laboratory in New York. This handsome site also provides a collection of well-written and illustrated summary essays on eugenic history topics such as immigration restriction and sterilization laws. Cold Springs Harbor Laboratory was once an important center for eugenics research; now, it declares on the homepage of this archive,

"It is important to remind yourself that the vast majority of eugenics work has been completely discredited. In the final analysis, the eugenic description of human life reflected political and social prejudices, rather than scientific ones." David Micklos, coeditor of the site with Jan Witkowski, explained further in a press release at the site's launch: "The major aim of the Archive is to provide materials that will stimulate people to think about the similarities between eugenics and our current preoccupation with the implications of the Human Genome Project."[16] That connection is being made, as the site is referenced in a growing number of general interest articles and college course materials.[17] Other eugenics history websites are less ambitious but still worth visiting. Vermont Eugenics: A Documentary History[18] contains about a hundred documents, from 1897 to 1978, not all exclusive to the Vermont context. Documents include legislation, institutional and charities reports, medical journal articles, newspaper editorials and letters to the editor, court decisions, speeches, and other texts. The site is made with frames, which are not ideal for some access requirements. There is little effort to contextualize these materials or organize them into an exhibit, but the curious visitor can scan the titles and explore as interests dictate.

Elsewhere in New England, the 1856 Project[19] is an arts/documentary/installation approach to the history of state institutions in Massachusetts. The project's website is a trove of details about Massachusetts law and policy towards institutionalizing people with various disabilities, and a map shows the location of the abandoned institution sites targeted by the group. The website also archives photographs and narrative accounts of the project's commemorative activities: in 2000, "Habeas Corpus: A Musical Installation for Northampton State Hospital" and "The State Hospital: In Memoriam" involved a 28-minute Magnificat played from the very walls of the former institution, along with a scholarly symposium. This kind of public history is too rare on the subject of disability, and displaying its artifacts in such detail is a service to others who might want to attempt a similar project of education and commemoration. (A moderated online discussion forum attached to the project, though mostly inactive at this writing, is a nice addition, giving interested visitors an ongoing connection for news and volunteer opportunities.)

An array of other disability history websites are very specific in their content. The Helen Keller Archive[20] maintained by the American Federation for the Blind is an "ever-expanding" collection of photos, transcripts, letters, and other memorabilia, very finely organized (for example, there's a link to items dealing only with Helen Keller's love of dogs).[21] Another exhibit from the realm of blind history is the History of Reading Codes for the Blind,[22] which contains biographical information about the major players in the development of a standard reading code (Hauy, Braille, Wait, etc.), as well as examples of early versions of Braille and competing systems. Maintained by the New York Institute of Special Education, this exhibit comes in several alternative accessible formats (large-print, high-contrast, frames or no frames). NYISE also offers a good online history of itself as an educational institution, heavy on biographical and student life accounts.[23]

Wheelchair sports have fairly recent origins, beginning in the mid–1940s with World War II veterans in rehabilitation hospitals; they have recently gained wider attention through the film *Murderball* (2005). Two websites exhibit the history of the National Wheelchair Basketball Association[24] and the National Veterans Wheelchair Games[25] in text, photos, and tabular information. On the technology front, many visitors will be surprised by the Electronic Curb-Cut Effect website[26] organized by Steve Jacobs for the International Center for Disability Resources of the Internet, where the disability-related origins of some common gadgets (the typewriter, the vibrating pager, the flatbed scanner) are explained using patent illustrations and many links to industrial websites. These are only a few of the fascinating websites with exhibits on specific facets of American disability history, but they demonstrate the breadth of possibilities the online environment holds. Disability history websites—archives, exhibits, and online museums—serve the general public as well as scholars, people with and without disabilities, with a wide range of information access needs, using computers variously equipped to handle images and sound files.

More and more, online content is being accessed on smaller devices (cell phones, personal digital assistants, MP3 players) with their own limitations. The design challenges are no doubt great, and content editors must be equally aware of their diverse audience. To my eye, the most successful sites have impressive resources at hand, both financial and advisory; or, if the means are modest, the project is also kept to a smaller scale, thus maintaining quality. I look for frequent updates at the most reliable sites, but it is also good to see finished exhibits.

Community input is a laudable feature; however, editorial oversight that tends to gaps and ensures accuracy and consistency in the final presentation is absolutely crucial. Evolving and incomplete exhibits should be clearly marked to avoid misinterpretation by unsuspecting drop-in visitors. There is room for much further growth in disability history sites online. In format, there's still much reliance on the static format of text and photo displays. The series of images and paragraphs can be very effective, but may also be overused because of its ease of assembly. The more innovative sites improve accessibility by varying the presentation to create a finished (not too busy) multimedia effect that is valuable to all visitors. Timelines are a longtime staple of the historical exhibit, but even these could benefit from an injection of design creativity to make them more evocative of the passage of time and the overlapping of eras.

Several online formats are now emerging that have intriguing potential for expanding the presentation of disability history online. As suggested by the inclusion of radio shows at the Straight Ahead site mentioned earlier, an audio format can be a useful way to present disability history, with the inclusion of archival recordings (speeches, news reports, oral history interviews, music) to preserve and bring to life the cultural and political events of the past. With the recent explosion of podcasting, such programs can be disseminated more easily and more widely than ever. Several disability-themed podcasts include historical themes, and more general-interest podcasts have also been known to explore the history of disability.[27]

Another emerging format, the blog, is perhaps less obvious in its potential: a blog is usually a very personal online journal. But history bloggers are moving the form into the direction of an interactive archive; and historical blogs are appearing in which the letters of a historical figure are posted one at a time, to be followed in episodic fashion, as online archives-in-progress.[28] Blogs invite commentary, and link-filled "blog carnivals" publicize interesting posts on specific themes. For the disability historian, a blog is an opportunity to bring together images, sound files, data and analysis; to ask questions and invite response. The collage-like journal style is well-suited to the presentation of multiple perspectives and subjective experiences of complicated and controversial historical events.

On the blog Disability Studies, Temple U., I post frequently on the history of disability, and I try to highlight other such efforts in the blogosphere.[29] One fascinating series was at the blog AutismDiva, where stories of "antique autistics" were posted, with images, in the summer of 2005.[30] Another area that merits further attention is the creation of online displays aimed at children: the Smithsonian's otherwise outstanding disability rights exhibit includes just one page in its kids' section, though the polio exhibit has more. Young visitors need more substantial, tailored opportunities to learn about disability history online. Many children use the internet for school projects, and disability is increasingly a topic of discussion even among very young learners.[31]

Presenting history to children is not a simple matter of choosing scrawly fonts and bright colors. It can, in fact, be a valuable exercise in paring content to its essentials, choosing the clearest vocabulary and syntax possible, and considering developmental models in presenting difficult concepts without over— or under-estimating the audience's capacities. An online children's exhibit has advantages over the traditional museum: kids with shorter attention spans can easily make multiple visits, and objects are in no danger of being damaged by curious fingers.

The potential for interactivity and game-style experiences is also intriguing. The Helen Keller Archive recently added The Helen Keller Kids Museum Online,[32] with a special "Ask Keller" feature, where children's questions are submitted to Helen Keller's great-grandniece, Keller Johnson-Thompson, and her responses are posted. Historians of childhood and history educators in schools would be good resources toward finding appropriate content and formats to meet this goal. In content, much remains to be explored, just as in the whole field of American disability history. For example, an online archive covering the history of special education in the U.S. would make a welcome addition to the available resources. More exhibits dealing with the colonial and early nineteenth-century eras would also be exciting to see, as well as some regional histories (for example, a Southern history of disability exhibit, or a site devoted to the architecture of Midwestern state institutions). As more stories emerge from the research about community life, activism and self-advocacy, disability cultures, technologies and laws, as more primary documents are archived and seen in context, the possibilities for online content will expand as well.

NOTES

1. See http://www.oldcalculatormuseum.com and http://www.kurumi.com for two such virtual personal museums, maintained by Oregon-based information technology professional Rick Bensene and San Francisco–area engineer Scott Oglesby, respectively. The newly mounted Museum of Online Museums (http://www.coudal.com/moom.php) is an excellent clearinghouse site for online museums of all sorts, from major art museums to collections of cereal boxes and antique mousetraps. (All sites were last accessed 28 December 2005.)

2. See Stephanie J. Coopman, "Disability on the Net," *American Communication Journal* (3)(June 2000) at http://acjournal.org/holdings/vol3/Iss3/rogue4/scoopman.html for a review of representative websites for and about the contemporary disability community in America (site last accessed 2 January 2006).

3. Douglas Baynton, "Disability and the Justification of Inequality in American History," in *The New Disability History: American Perspectives*, Paul Longmore and Lauri Umansky, eds. (New York: New York University Press 2001): 52.

4. Disability History Museum: http://www.disabilitymuseum.org (site last accessed 2 January 2006).

5. Straight Ahead Pictures website: http://www.straightaheadpictures.org/sap/home.html (site last accessed 2 January 2006); see also Laurie Block, "Tales from the Vault: Document by Document," *Common-place* 2(3) April 2002: online at http://common-place.org/vol-02/no-03/tales/ (site last accessed 2 January 2006).

6. "Access to History," *Boston Globe* (11 December 2001): A22, available online at http://www.disabilitymuseum.org/about/press/011211globe.htm.

7. Beyond Affliction: http://www.npr.org/programs/disability/ (site last accessed 2 January 2006).

8. Disability Social History Project: http://www.disabilityhistory.org (site last accessed 2 January 2006).

9. Disapedia: http://disapedia.com/ (site last accessed 10 August 2007).

10. Frank H. Harrison Middle School Civil Rights Wiki Space: http://civil-rights.wikispaces.com/ (site last accessed 10 August 2007).

11. Disability History Dateline: http://bss.sfsu.edu/disability/dateline.html (site last accessed 2 January 2006).

12. Museum of disABILITY History: http://www.people-inc.org/museum/ (site last accessed 2 January 2006); see also http://www.peopleinc.org/services/programs/museum.html (site last accessed 2 January 2006).

13. The Smithsonian's Disability Rights Movement exhibit: http://americanhistory.si.edu/disabilityrights/welcome.html (site last accessed 2 January 2006).

14. The Smithsonian's Whatever Happened to Polio? exhibit: http://americanhistory.si.edu/exhibitions/exhibition.cfm?key=38&exkey=352 (site last accessed 2 January 2006).

15. Image Archive of the American Eugenics Movement: http://www.eugenicsarchive.org (site last accessed 2 January 2006).

16. "Web Site Opens Window on Dark Episode in American Science," press release, dated 11 February 2000, archived online at http://www.cshl.org/public/releases/dnalc021100.html.

17. See, for example, Kristi Coale, "Playing God: Scary Eugenics Documents from the Turn of the Century Shine a Disturbing Light on Ethical Dilemmas Raised by Genetic Testing," *Salon.com* 17 November 1999, available at http://www.salon.com/tech/feature/1999/11/17/eugenics, which was based on a visit to a preview version of the current site. See also http://sfgate.com/cgibin/ article.cgi?f=/c/a/2003/03/10/BU91464.DTL, Tom Abate, "State's Little Known History of Shameful Science," *San Francisco Chronicle* (10 March 2003), which gives the Image Archive's web address for further information (both sites last accessed 2 January 2006).

18. Vermont Eugenics: A Documentary History: http://cit.uvm.edu:6336/dynaweb/eugenics (site last accessed 2 January 2006).

19. The 1856.org project: http://www.1856.org/mass.html (site last visited 2 January 2006).

20. Helen Keller Archive: http://www.afb.org/info_documents.asp?collectionid=1 (site last accessed 5 January 2006).

21. "Ever-expanding" description taken from Kim Nielsen's review of the AFB's Helen Keller Archive website, posted 12 April 2001, the third installment of the "Website of the Week" feature on H-Disability; see http://h-net.msu.edu/~disabil (site last accessed 5 January 2006). See also H-Eugenics (http://www.h-net.org/~eugenics/, site last accessed 5 January 2006) for a similar discussion list on the history of eugenics.

22. The History of Reading Codes for the Blind: http://www.nyise.org/blind/barbier2.htm (site last accessed 5 January 2006).

23. NYISE History: http://www.nyise.org/oritor.htm (site last accessed 5 January 2006).

24. National Wheelchair Basketball Association: http://www.nwba.org/history.html (site last accessed 5 January 2006).

25. National Veterans Wheelchair Games: http://www1.va.gov/vetevent/nvwg/2004/History.cfm (site last accessed 5 January 2006).

26. Electronic Curb-Cut Effect: http://www.icdri.org/technology/ecceff.htm (site last accessed 5 January 2006).

27. See, for example, Sparkletack (http://sparkletack.com/), a podcast of San Francisco history and culture, which had an episode on Emperor Norton (podcast posted August 2005; site last accessed 5 January 2006). Biographical sketches seem best suited to this form: the podcast Repeating History by J. L. Hines started with an exploration of Abraham Lincoln's experiences with depression (http://www.jlhines.com/?page_id=33 ; podcast posted December 2005; site last accessed 10 January 2006). There is not currently a podcast dedicated to disability history; but one disability-related podcasts that occasionally discusses history is David Faucheux's Blind Chance (http://www.teleread.org/blind/index.html, site last accessed 10 January 2006).

28. Some examples of historical blogs include Diaries of a Lady of Quality (http://diariesofaladyofquality.blogspot.com/, site last accessed 5 January 2006), in which the early 19th-century diary entries of a Miss Frances Williams Wynn are posted three times a week by Natalie Bennett, an Australian writer based in London; and The Blog of Henry David Thoreau (http://blogthoreau.blogspot.com/, site last accessed 5 January 2006), in which entries from the fourteen-volume *Journal of Henry David Thoreau* (Houghton Mifflin, 1906) are posted on corresponding dates (so, an entry dated 5 January by Thoreau will be posted on 5 January by the blog's owner, Gregory Perry).

29. Disability Studies, Temple U. blog: http://disstud.blogspot.com (site last accessed 10 January 2006); historical topics in 2005 included institutional graveyards, calypsonian Blind Blake, Dale Evans and Judy Fryd, the deafness of John Greenleaf Whittier, Edward Rushton, Rosemary Sutcliff, Eugene McCarthy, Blind Willie McTell, Jacob van Eyck, Nellie Bly, and nineteenth century madwomen.

30. Autism Diva blog: http://autismdiva.blogspot.com (site last accessed 10 January 2006); the entries in question are titled "Someone's Cousin Moe" (22 August 2005), "Antique Autistics" (8 August 2005), and "Some People" (26 July 2005).

31. See, for example, Penny L. Richards, "Talking to Children about Rare Chromosome Disorders," at the Chromosome Deletion Outreach website: http://www.chromodisorder.org/sytrix/card_list.php3?dbid=63&id=6 (site last accessed 5 January 2006).

32. Helen Keller Kids Museum Online: http://www.afb.org/braillebug/hkmuseum.asp (site last accessed 5 January 2006).

16

Online Therapy, Obsession, and Entertainment

Adventures in the International Cyber Bazaar

SUSAN KOPPELMAN

My English Bone China

Let me tell you about my favorite set of China and how it came to be in my possession, how it came to fall into disuse, and why I have decided to reclaim it.

I used to joke in a self-deprecating way about what I called my "Stangl problem," a problem I explore later in this essay. I am an anti-racist, feminist, disability activist and I've spent most of my life involved in social justice struggles. I am also a literary historian. A serious scholar and do-gooder. I think that our time is our most precious possession and how we spend it the most salient expression of our character. I have protested against the housewifery expectations laid on women and I've avoided all of that as much as possible. Like many feminists, I think of housework as a necessary and honorable profession, one deserving of respect and just compensation. But housewifery is not my profession. So I was embarrassed by the time and money I spent collecting Stangl pottery on eBay to cure my Stangl problem. I was, in fact, embarrassed to have a Stangl problem. It seemed to me (I don't know what others thought of it) entirely out of character for me to fasten on something as domestic as tableware and bring it so close to the center of my life. Besides, I already had a perfectly lovely set of "good china," one I had picked out at the invitation of my parents when I was fourteen and one that I had used as my special occasion china for thirty-five years.

The summer before I turned fifteen my parents and I had taken a wonderful car trip, ending up in Quebec. People spoke French there, which made it feel like a foreign country. To be somewhere where the "native" language was different from our own — that was exotic!

We loved it, as we always loved our trips. The simultaneous feelings of safety and adventure I always felt when my daddy was at the wheel and my mom sat beside him with the maps while, in the back seat, I talked and sang or read or napped or played "license plates" games with my mom comes back to me as I write about it.[1] I loved the feeling of being together, going somewhere, and knowing there was somewhere we could go.

This time we had gone to a foreign country where my mom and dad expected ME to do the communicating for us. After all, I'd studied French for two semesters in the eighth grade and should have been able, they thought, to ask directions and order for us off a menu written French. But didn't they remember that I only got a C in French?

It was the lowest grade I would get in junior high — except for that D I got when the sewing teacher, pitying me, decided not to spoil my permanent record with an F.

The apron I made for that class is in my linen closet still stained with my blood because the needle so often went somewhere other than where I was trying to push it. The rickrack sewn on above the hem and surrounding the bib had been attached with a sewing machine. I was supposed to have sewn it on by hand with tiny barely visible stitches. That use of the sewing machine would have gotten me flunked if I had decided to use it, but my teacher, after making me rip out my large crooked stitches for the fourth time finally said, "Go ahead. Use the machine."

I hadn't wanted to take that course. Sewing? I was clumsy and it would be a waste of everyone's time — mine especially. There were other courses I wanted to take and they certainly didn't have anything to do with me growing up to be a proper housewife. But one semester of sewing was required for all girls in the Cleveland Heights school system in the early nineteen fifties.

The next semester cooking was required. I was already an accomplished cook, the one who usually prepared our dinner during the week. I loved everything about cooking — how the raw fresh ingredients looked, how flavors would blend together with just the right amount of heat and stirring, how flavors flooded the air as smells long before they were ready to be tasted, how blended flavors could be separated from each other by an attentive nose.

And I loved setting a beautiful table for my parents, where we would sit at day's end eating wonderful things, exchanging news, and telling stories of our day apart.

My mom had taught me everything I knew about cooking: how to cut a radish into a rose, how to broil a steak to my father's preferred doneness, how to fry potato latkes at just the right temperature to become crispy outside and moist inside. She taught me how to set a table so that the right dishes were there for the meal to be served, which side which pieces of silverware went on, and how nice it was to pick a sprig of mock orange or a single iris or a spray of forsythia and put it in a pretty vase at the end of the table so it didn't interfere with our eye contact but so we could each see it. She even taught me to make an entire Thanksgiving dinner for four or more people — because on holidays we always had guests.

That required cooking course was another waste of my time.

But that year of required domesticity (only for girls; boys weren't allowed to take those courses. They had to take wood shop and electrical shop) was behind me by a couple of years and here we were in French Canada.

We gave up on sight-seeing as our vacation ended and we started home to Cleveland. It was time to think about what souvenir to take home from this foreign adventure. As we drove along, my dad saw a sign for an English Bone China outlet and my mom read to us from the AAA Guide book about this place that was coming up alongside the road (we drove on roads then, not highways) and decided that this would be a good place to stop.

I really wasn't interested in stopping. Who cared about English Bone China? Well, my mom did. She had always wanted to pick out her own china pattern and to serve special occasion meals on her chosen china. My parents had married during the Depression and their wedding had been modest and their gifts very few. She had hoped a day would come when she could choose her own china pattern, her own silver and crystal.

In the enormous warehouse table after table was covered with table settings displaying a variety of China patterns. My mom walked around studying the patterns and her face slowly lost its look of anticipation. Finally she came to us: "I'm ready to go."

My dad was surprised. "Didn't you see anything you like?"

"No," she said and I could hear the determination in her voice NOT to buy anything. She hadn't seen anything she liked and just because the prices were good was not reason enough to buy something she didn't like. My dad was disappointed.

He saw lots of china that looked just fine to him.

So he turned to me and asked, "Susan, is there a pattern you like? Since we're here, you might as well choose your wedding china."

Here I was, a fourteen year old kid filled with dreams and ideas about what I wanted to do with my life: I was a writer. I wanted to travel around the world, I wanted to be a teacher and a publisher, and here was my dad, talking about my wedding! It wasn't that I expected to live a life without love and children, but as a married woman? I couldn't tolerate the thought. If I got married — it would be like going to sewing class every day for the rest of my life.

My mom's face lit up and she said, "That's a good idea as long as we're here. Susan, if you see a pattern you like, Daddy and I will buy you your dishes. But they don't have to be wedding dishes." She continued, "They can just be your grown up dishes for when you have your own place. You shouldn't have to get married to have nice things."

What a gift my mother gave me with those words! I didn't have to get married, and being unmarried didn't mean I had to live as if my life was provisional, worthy only of cast-offs and thrift store finds,[2] until a husband came along to make me deserving of bone china and silver.

At the age of fourteen I couldn't imagine wanting to live anywhere else than with my parents (except when I was traveling around the world!), but they were waiting for me to be glad they'd made the offer, and to find my pattern. I looked for the dishes I would like when I grew up — someday — and I finally found The One I Wanted. I showed my choice to my parents with great enthusiasm; I wanted my parents to admire my choice.

My dad responded enthusiastically. He said or acted or sounded as if he really did like them. My mother didn't like them. She said so. But I had cho-

English Bone China, Regency Collingwood, est. 1796. Five-piece place setting, one of set for twelve bought in 1954 by Frances and Edward Nathan Koppelman for daughter Susan (photograph by Jeffrey Kessler).

sen it, so they bought me service for twelve and we drove home with me tucked in the back seat among boxes of bone china.

When I called her today, Feb. 29, 2008, to check some of the details of this story, she had forgotten a lot about that trip, as have I, and we had fun exchanging the details we remembered, because we remembered very different details—but she remembered the trip to the Bone China Outlet and remembered that I had chosen My Dishes there. I asked her if she remembered my dishes and she said, in the same flat voice in which she always spoke of choices I have made that she disapproved of, "I remember that I don't like them."

And I said, "I've decided to unwrap those dishes and put them in my cupboard. I'm going to start using them again. I still love them."

"Whatever makes you happy," she said. And we changed the subject.

She is now almost ninety-one and we see each other frequently and talk every day. She doesn't care much about dishes anymore, as long as they are light weight and fairly durable, so she has chosen Corelle for this period in her life. I don't like Corelle very much.

My bone china has been stored in cartons, each piece wrapped in old St. Louis newspapers just as my dear friend Martha Baker[3] wrapped them for our move, thirteen years ago, to Tucson. Before our move, I had used them carefully, almost reverently, for thirty-five years, setting them carefully on the dining room table for every Seder, every Rosh Hashanah dinner, every Yom Kippur break fast, and every latke party. When people I loved and wanted to honor came to dinner I set the table with my English Bone China. For birthdays I set the table with my bone china. I always loved it, always remembered the day my parents bought it for me. And then I stopped using it.

Why did I stop?

The Emotional Outrage

I stopped because of the Stangl problem mentioned at the beginning of this essay. It was a problem for which I needed therapy but I wasn't about to spend time in therapy. I think people should love and attend to each other enough to help each other work through stuff. I think one of the valuable things that therapists can do is help people learn about the processes of therapy and how better to help each other. I tried to solve my problems myself—if a friend wasn't available. This Stangl problem was not something I had ever talked about with anyone. I wasn't sure how to talk about it, how to conceptualize the problem clearly enough that I would be able to tell someone about it. I had neither language nor conceptual categories for this problem. But in my second marriage I felt a kind of freedom to pay attention to myself that I hadn't felt in my first and so I began to look into my various problems. I didn't know much but I did believe that solutions could be found. I knew I still wanted Stangl, still felt cheated out of something in my life and had the freedom to recover for and by myself the thing I had been cheated out of. I thought that one of the major things in my life that I had been cheated out of was Stangl.[4]

My "Stangl problem" started with the trauma of an insult, or at least what I perceived to have been an insult, by my first mother-in-law.

During my first visit to the home of my first in-laws-to-be, the home my fiancé had grown up in, I fell in love with their house and with all the objects and accoutrements that filled it. Everything seemed to have grown from the imagination of a single creator. It was museum-ishly beautiful, comfortable, and welcoming. Or so it seemed. Surely, I thought, a place this beautiful must be the creation of a beautiful soul. I loved and admired my mother-in-law-to-be almost before we said hello.

She was a reserved woman; I am demonstrative. My enthusiastic hugs must have felt like assaults. I am curious, full of questions. I was interested in her. She must have found me intrusive. Her son was not my first love and she was not the first woman I had thought of as a mother-in-law to be. I had loved and lost another man whose loss I was still grieving when I met her son and her son had told his mother all about my "past." He thought I and my lost beloved were romantic figures. She evidently just thought I was tarnished. I imagine in retrospect that she was as untaken by me as I was taken by her. In our ways of taking each other we were both thoroughly mistaken.

I was young and naive and the dangers arising from my naiveté were compounded by my belief that I was sophisticated. My high school English teacher, Miss Edith B. Malin, had taught me to read the Sunday *New York Times* in tenth grade and *The New Yorker* in eleventh grade and now I was actually living and going to college in New York. I had eaten snails in a French restaurant. I visited art galleries and sipped cheap wine with the artists. I wore a little black dress on weekends.

I had listened to Thornton Wilder talk about his friends Gertrude Stein and Alice B. Toklas. In the minimally attended talk in the small parlor of a college I'd gone clear across town on three different subways to reach so I could hear him speak I actually got to shake his hand. And so sophisticated were we few in that audience that not one of us mentioned *Our Town*.

I had sat in the midst of a packed audience at the YMHA and listened to T.S. Eliot read his newest poetry and been frightened by the audience's rough refusal to let him leave the stage without reading "The Love Song of J. Alfred Prufrock." Acceding to the stomping audience, he'd read the poem and the hostility in the air had dissipated. I was as pleased that I'd been there to hear him say how tired he was of that poem he'd written as a very young man as I was to hear him read it.

I knew at least three hundred words in French. I shopped in Peck and Peck's sub-basement on Fifth Avenue across the main entrance to the New York

Public Library. I buttoned my black jewel neck cardigans up the back. I wore makeup and curled my eyelashes.

The original production of *West Side Story* was in its second year at the Winter Garden Theater. I never tired of it and never failed to cry with fresh heartbreak when Tony and Maria sang "There's a Place for Us." I knew that there wasn't. It felt like Our Story, the story of my first, lost love. That aura of sadness, loss, regret, heartbreak was the thing that made me most certain that I was a sophisticate. I was as sad as a girl in a French novel.

My lost love's mother, my first mother-in-law to be, had loved me. We had loved each other. We'd spent hours together, cooking, talking, sharing stories, and laughing. My father became an orphan the day before I was born. My mother's parents both died when I was three. My parents couldn't provide models for parent-in-law relationships. There was only my experience with Mary Rosa, D's mother. I had no idea a mother-in-law and a daughter-in-law could feel anything other than the tenderness and love we had felt for each other. It never occurred to me that my current fiancé's mother wouldn't love me and I wouldn't love her.

E. had two sets of French dinnerware. One was old Quimper and I learned to be impressed by that. Her third set was in a cabinet under the breakfast bar: a small set of Stangl pottery, just enough settings for family breakfasts and informal lunches. I fell in love with the Stangl, cheerful dishes with hand painted pictures of cherries and peaches and grapes so luscious I wanted to eat them. I told her how I loved them in the ensuing years. They were so pretty I thought it was impossible to have an unhappy meal while using them. I didn't notice that we often had unhappy meals when we used them.

We spent a fair amount of time at that house, I and the fiancé who had become my first husband. We lived in New York City, only a couple of hours away, and we liked going "home." I became increasingly knowledgeable about all their wonderful "stuff," learning from them about French country furniture and French cooking, French grandfather clocks and viniculture, and learning that regardless of the love it seemed natural for me to feel for her, there would never be any return warmth from my mother-in-law. One might think of it, if one weren't emotionally involved, as a simple clash of cultures.

One Sunday morning about three years after our wedding, I listened all weekend to my in-laws debate whether or not to attend the Sunday afternoon wedding between a friend of theirs, a man their own age, and a young woman my age, one who shared many of the attributes of mine that I increasingly had come to understand made me someone they were not pleased to have in their family. My mother-in-law finally agreed with my father-in-law that they would go to the event.

"We need to bring a gift," my father-in-law reminded her, leaving, as always, the decision about what that would be, to her.

Stangl, Fruit pattern, three-piece place setting and salt and pepper shakers. Designed by Kay Hacket, 1942 (photograph by Jeffrey Kessler).

"Oh, dear! There's no time to stop for something. Well, I'll just wrap up something from here." And with that she gathered up the small set of Stangl, swathed it in hand-painted French tea towels, packed it all in a box, and they were on their way.

I was overwhelmed with shock and sorrow, but I can't recreate the path to those feelings. The giving away of the Stangl struck me as the most dismissive rejection yet of my love for the Stangl and my place in that family.

E. disapproved of the marriage they would attend — she said it was the age difference between the couple, but my father-in-law laughed that off, saying that alliances between older men with charm and money and younger women with beauty and fire were as normal as could be.

The wife-to-be was like me, my age, urban, Jewish, *zaftig*, filled with opinions and curiosity, and she, too, had a "past." Those attributes were, of course, the very ones I had come to believe my mother-in-law deplored about me and about this bride-to-be. I wonder, now that I am cured of my Stangl Problem, at the intensity of my reaction. The pain never left me until my eBay therapy was complete. The more Stangl I acquired, the more I learned about the company and the patterns and the collectors, the less the hold E. had on me became. And then one day it was gone.

The departure of the Stangl that day triggered my determination to possess Stangl. Someday I would own a complete set, place settings enough to serve sixteen or maybe even twenty at my Seder table. Once I finished graduate school and had an income beyond subsistence, I promised myself that I would drive to Flemington, New Jersey where the factory was, and buy my own Stangl. I wouldn't depend on anyone to fulfill my desire; I would do it myself. With my own money.

Seven years later, my new Ph.D. in one hand and the letter offering me what I thought was a dream job in the other, I announced to my husband, my son, and my in-laws that I was driving over to Flemington to buy some Stangl.

I drove to Flemington. I found the Stangl pottery. And I found the signs saying they had ceased production. The company, after almost one hundred years, had closed. The company store was still open, they were still selling what they had left, but no more would ever be made.

The discovery stunned me. This journey that was to have been so satisfying, such a triumphant declaration of my independent adulthood, my newly acquired professional status ended in — a pottery gone out of business.

With feet dragging I went into the factory store, hoping they had enough Stangl left so that I could buy at least a couple of place settings. But I didn't find any.

There were maybe a hundred or so pieces of pottery on the tables, but none of what I had until then thought of as Stangl and now learned was just one of Stangl's patterns. I wandered up and down between the rows of tables and picked up a few pieces but none in the pattern I wanted. I returned to my in-laws' house with a few samples of other patterns. When I told them what I had discovered, the closed pottery, she said, "We know."

Seeking Healing, Seeking Stangl

When one goes to a therapist, one is often asked to define the problems one hopes to solve or heal. Two decades ago, my then-HMO seemed committed to a belief that any problem could be solved with twenty visits to a therapist per year and asked for a $40 co-pay. Our new HMO seems to believe that our psyches heal faster than in the past and so they allow only ten visits per year and want a $50 co-pay. Two decades ago my HMO would have allowed me to see a Ph.D. psychologist. But now my $50 co-pay only gets me the services of a social worker or someone with an MA in counseling. Two decades ago I might have spent $800 a year trying, with the help of a psychologist, to work through my Stangl "problem." These days, the problem seems to be worth only $500 a year and that, my HMO declares, should resolve the matter.

I am a thrifty person although not, I hope, someone deserving of such sobriquets as "penny pincher" or "cheapskate," "tightfisted" or "stingy," or the one my first in-law family spoke of derisively but practiced fanatically, a "*grippe sou*." Nevertheless, I do like to feel that I have made a good deal, that I'm getting my money's worth. I like to have something concrete, material, when a transaction is complete. Talk is ephemeral, emotional healing invisible, expensive epiphanies intangible. I had a serious Stangl problem that needed solving and at the end of the process I wanted something to substantiate my healing.

Instead of a therapist, I took my Stangl problem to yard sales, thrift stores, antique malls, and, finally and most healing of all, to eBay.

I began collecting Stangl when I married for the second time. In the early 1980s when video stores were still a rarity and independently owned, a few years before the first Blockbuster was opened, my teen-aged son got a job at a video store. A job at a video store was prestigious then and my son loved it. So two afternoons a week I drove him twenty minutes from home and he put in his four hours, while I shopped. Within a mile of that video store were supermarkets, butchers, dry cleaners—and three thrift stores and four antique shops. I visited them all. The day I visited the little antique store right next to the video store and discovered four 14½" chop plates in the Garden Flower pattern was so exciting I forgot to breathe and almost passed out. Four gorgeous chop plates! And they were only two dollars each. Harvey Duke estimates the value of the chop plates at $40 each in his 1993 book *Stangl Pottery*[5] and in Robert C. Runge, Jr.'s 2000 *Collector's Encyclopedia of Stangl Dinnerware*[6] estimates the value of each of these plates at between $80 and $95. I didn't know that then but I did know I was getting a bargain. I had no idea then that such things as collector's guides existed and even if I had, I wouldn't have consulted them. For me the value was emotional, not monetary. But if a collector starts off with a really lucky find[7]—a greatly desired item at a great price—I think collecting becomes an addiction. I was now an addict.

After this I was always on the lookout for Stangl. But my subsequent early arrivals at yard sales and estate sales, my regular route of thrift and antique stores, yielded nothing more. I lived in St. Louis and it wasn't until I began buying on eBay that I deduced, based on the location of most of the sellers of Stangl dinnerware, that it was an "east coast" item. The sellers were almost entirely clustered in a few states, mostly in western Ohio, eastern Pennsylvania, West Virginia, and northern New Jersey. Packages would rarely arrive from anywhere west of Interstate 77 or south of Interstate 70.

In 1994 my husband and I decided to leave winter behind forever and move to the southwest. As we drove back and forth from St. Louis to Tucson, we took our breaks from driving to explore small time antique malls, those places into which neighbors emptied their attics and basements, sharing clerking duties and the rent for an abandoned store in a downtown killed by a Wal-Mart on the edge of town. We traveled along major portions of the road that used to be America's Highway, old Route 66. I would gather Stangl in any pattern I found. But the pickings were slim. Stangl, I learned, was an eastern pottery and finds west of the Mississippi were rare.

When we moved into our new home in the country outside and above Tucson, an old friend sent me all the Stangl in the Fruit pattern her mother had saved for her—four place settings. She didn't like her mother, hated her childhood memories of meals eaten with her mother and father off of those Stangl plates, and didn't want those memories provoked by opening her own new home to those old dishes. So I was given a generous start on my Stangl therapy.

In 1998 I discovered eBay and my Stangl collecting began in earnest. I first learned how to navigate on eBay, to search for and find what I was looking for, to bid, to watch the bidding competition, to pay first via personal check and money order and later with PayPal, and to deal with feedback given and received. There are all sorts of tricks for buying on eBay and all sorts of ways to learn those tricks. There are books, there are classes, there are discs, there are online tutorials, there are the carefully traded secrets with buyers who collect other things than you do, there are the tricks you figure out by yourself—you make mistakes and then you do better. I made all the mistakes. I learned more and more of the tricks.[8] I took satisfaction in my growing competence as a collector.

EBay enabled me to experiment with "total immersion" therapy. And it worked. As Stangl moved from being an emblem of scarcity to an exemplar of abundance I felt better and better about my past and my present. And even my future. The headiness of discovering Stangl on eBay, the opportunity of seemingly unlimited possibilities for acquisition, the excitement of buying long beyond the illusion of need, the intoxication of knowing I can have all I want! And along the way I learned so much about so many things I hadn't ever even thought about ... it was a whole new way of learning that didn't involve libraries or leaving my house.

The first thing I did when I woke up was rush to my computer to see what was happening with the items I was bidding on. There were those days whose descriptions have become a modern cliché—in my night clothes, uncombed hair, unbrushed teeth, no time, no time, no time for anything, just get to the computer! Have I been outbid? Have I missed the end of the auction? I would set my alarm for auctions that ended when I would usually be asleep. After a while I never turned off my computer because it took too long to get to those listings. I didn't want to wait for the machine to boot up and then go through the whole business of moving from my wallpaper (my granddaughters, always my granddaughters, they have been growing up on my computer wallpaper) to my Internet connection—which changed during this period from one ISP to another—to eBay, then signing in, having to remember my password which has always been hard and then finally they let me save it, going to my summary, finally getting to my summary where dangled the thumbnails of the delicious dollops of desire, suspended in cyberspace, waiting for me to pounce, to bid, to win, to say "Mine!"

Adventures in the International Cyber Marketplace

And as I watched the time on a Stangl auction creep from half an hour to fifteen minutes to fifteen seconds I played around on eBay, looking for and at all sorts of things. And more and more, besides Stangl, I bought all sorts of things.

I look at the walls in our Tucson home, walls covered with paintings and prints and masks and most of them came to us via eBay. There are animalitos from Oaxaca and five hand-carved contemporary interpretations of traditional masks by a local Yaqui artist whose dealer sold them on eBay. There is fabric art — arpilleras from Chile and Peru, molas from Panama, woven walling hangings from Mexico and Guatemala, Huichol and Tepehuano yarn art from Mexico and tiny embroidered pictures from Peru, paintings by African American artists Thomas Kaonis from St. Louis, Carol White from Chicago, Easton Davey from New York, Sharon Johnson from the Alabama countryside, and Harold Smith from Kansas City, and lithographs by New Yorker and Eli Seigal devotee, Chaim Koppelman (who is not a relative but whose name drew me to his work). There are almost a dozen whimsical and brilliantly colored prints by Judith Bledsoe, a signed lithograph called "Ceremonial Night" by Hopi artist Dan Namingha and a signed limited edition print called "Celestial Germinators" by Hopi-Choctaw artist Dan Lomahaftewa. I see that we have become collectors via eBay.

Yikes!

But lest we forget — while the art was accumulating so was the Stangl. There were the teapot buys — I came up with the brilliant idea that if we rented our small guest house as a B&B then everything I bought to decorate it would be a tax write-off and depreciable. I decided to call it the Teapot B&B and bought two dozen teapots, nine of them Stangl teapots, gorgeous things.

I kept them hidden until there were enough to fill the long window in the little guest house. I took my husband out to see them — "Surprise," I said. "We can call it the Teapot B&B."

"Hmmm," he mused. "I don't think that'll appeal to guys very much. It will limit our potential renter pool. And it doesn't reflect anything at all about what is really special about this place — the mountain views, the cacti, the isolation" — and of course he was right. It was a very bad marketing idea.

Now there was no way around the truth — I was buying and buying, Stangl and all sorts of other stuff not because I had any use for all of it, not because it was useful to anyone in our lives, not because it had investment value, not because I was going to give it to someone else as a gift. I was buying these things because I liked them. Because I loved them. Because I wanted them. What had started out as therapy for a psychic wound had evolved into an adventure in shopping, in self-indulgence, in fun. I had become a wanderer in the interna-

Nine Stangl teapots. Left to right — top row: Golden Harvest, Americana, Thistle; middle row: Country Garden, Fruit, Treasured; bottom row: Wild Rose, Yellow Tulip, Garden Flower.

tional cyber marketplace. I found outlets for my favorite clothing labels on eBay and stopped going to stores to shop for clothes. I found the international clothing marketplace and experimented with silk scarves from China, dichroic glass jewelry from New Zealand, rayon panchos from Thailand, silk purses from Hong Kong....

"My therapy" is what I called those hours I spent on eBay looking for, bidding on, and winning ever more and more Stangl. All the hours I spent googling Stangl and learning about the history of the company and the American pottery and glass industries and all the hours I spent on various message boards for collectors of Stangl or American dinnerware discussing where best to find missing pieces and analyzing the subtle differences between white and red body clay plates that provided the best and only clues to the date of manufacture provided subsidiary therapy. I found out about the Stangl museum that had been built on the grounds of what had been the Stangl pottery until it was closed and the "remains" sold to Pfaltzgraff for their own pottery making. And when that museum was threatened with closure I was even briefly involved in the struggle to save it.

I made the discovery that I was the one driving up the teapot market prices.

New patterns. Feelings associated with new patterns. Would I switch my love for Fruit to another pattern? Was replacing Fruit with Golden Harvest or Yellow Tulip or Star Flower some sort of aesthetic oneupsmanship?

I can indeed have all I want, but how much do I want? Is there an end to this wanting? Stangl was becoming dinnerware, antique and lovely, instead of a symbol and reminder of pain.

Questioning the wanting—it made sense in the beginning, I think, but now isn't it becoming obsessive, compulsive, just plain greedy?

Can I stop buying this stuff? What else can I buy?

What's the difference between buying Stangl and just plain buying and buying and buying?

Remember President Bush's exhortation to buy buy buy after 9/11? Was I just being patriotic? Did buying on eBay constitute the same level of patriotism as buying at Target? Would it be even more patriotic to buy at Dillards?

I bought Stangl on eBay and had to figure out what on earth to do with it all once it arrived. I would explain to people who might inquire or be willing to listen about the reason why I wanted Stangl, beyond my simple appreciation of it for what it is, my love for its heft and balance and the wonderful designs by Kay Hackett from the 1940s and '50s.

How exciting it was to receive all those packages. I learned how much I love receiving gifts, even if they are coming from me to me. Even if you know what's in the package, you've never actually seen it with your own eyes, held it in your own hands. Even if you know what's in the package, the very fact that it is wrapped and packaged and addressed in the hand of a stranger lends an air of mystery and excitement that attaches itself to what it inside.

I started buying a single piece at a time, interested only in the piece I was buying. But as time went on, more and more Stangl was listed on eBay and more and more frequently it was accompanied by a poignant story by young sellers cleaning out the houses of their recently deceased grandparents and middle-aged sellers emptying out the houses they'd grown up in. The parents or grandparents had died or moved into smaller places or been moved into care institutions. The sellers had their own lives, their own homes, their own dishes. They didn't want to abandon what their elders had loved and used to thrift stores where, presumably, no one would know what they were or what they were worth. They wanted them sold to people who would cherish them. And so they took the time and made the effort to list the Stangl on eBay. And there I was, just waiting, and wanting to buy everything they had to sell. In the end I was buying multiple table settings of various patterns.

The last box of Stangl Fruit I bought is sitting, still boxed, in one of our sheds. I've never opened it. Although I have the print out of the eBay listing so I can check what is in that box, I haven't even checked. All I know is that it is the last time I bought any Stangl Fruit, any Stangl at all, and that I don't need to open that box.

I now have enough Stangl to serve twenty-four on the Fruit pattern or twelve on the Golden Harvest set or eight on the Yellow Tulip. And my husband Dennis, who chose a pattern at my insistence, so we could play Stangl watching together, loves best the Country Garden pattern and he can share a meal for six with his chosen dishes. And I mustn't forget to mention the few settings of Star Flower and Magnolia I have collected.

* * *

Dec. 5, 2005—I woke early this A.M. with the startling thought that perhaps E. never meant to or even knew she had insulted me when she gave away her Stangl that long ago Sunday morning before the wedding she'd finally reluctantly decided to attend. I realized that there are other ways to interpret her actions. Perhaps she knew how much I loved them but assumed there was plenty of time to buy more since the Stangl pottery was just down the road and continuing to produce dishes. Who knows? What I do know is that there is no pain for me anymore about the dishes or what she knew or didn't know, meant or didn't mean.

But today I realized: I don't care anymore, not in the way I did when I started. I could give them all away, or sell them, or donate them, or will them. I don't need them anymore. I like all my Stangl but I don't need it anymore. I like my Stangl and I always set my table with it when we are more than two at the table. But more and more I like to wander the dinnerware aisles in stores and the pottery stalls at street fairs. I still like to read the history of the dinnerware/pottery industry in the United States. I still go to the table setting competition at county fairs. But lately I sometimes say, holding a newly designed piece of table ware, "I think this would look nice on our table. If I was starting all over and didn't have any Stangl or bone china, I think I'd like to buy this new stuff."

I do, however, love my Stangl and my granddaughters Jasmine Grace and Sarah Jade say they like it too. I plan to give it to them one day, each a set of twelve place settings of Stangl Fruit designed in the early 1940s by Kay Hackett. And someday they may read this essay and learn the where and why and when and how of all those dishes in the cupboards at Grandma and Grandpa's house. Whatever was wounded in me that I needed to heal is healed. I want them to know that many wounds can be healed and there are alternative healing methods. For me, eBay was one of those alternative healing practices. I wonder what it will be for them when they are adults.

NOTES

1. These memories fill me with joy and gratitude for the childhood they gave me, surrounded with love and attention and a belief in my own safety, which taught me what it feels

like to be loved and allowed my mind to roam free and grow. All my work is dedicated to my parents.

2. Of course in Alison Franks' essay elsewhere in this volume there is a completely different "take" on thrift store shopping than I imply. Once I grew up her view became mine.

3. Martha inherited a table full of Fiesta Ware in all the colors it was made in back in the days when it was new. Whenever I think of Martha, I think of the Thanksgiving we shared at her and John Clifford's house the first time they ever set a table with their newly acquired Fiesta Ware.

4. I am not foolish enough to believe that a sense of deprivation, a deep regret, a feeling of loss can really be solved by place settings of dinnerware — but if you are a person for whom every Thing in her life has a symbolic valence, finding the lost Thing can lead to healing.

5. Harvey Duke, *Stangl Pottery*, (Radnor, PA: Wallace-Homestead, 1993).

6. Robert C. Runge, Jr., *Collector's Encyclopedia of Stangl Dinnerware*, (Paducah, KY: Collector, 2000).

7. See the article by Julia Penelope, elsewhere in this volume, for a more thorough discussion of what she calls "The Gambler's Rush" because that is exactly what I experienced when I discovered those four platters!

8. Some of these tricks, such as searching for the items that interest you via misspelled versions of their names, are detailed in Jeffrey Kessler's article, elsewhere in this volume.

About the Contributors

Marilyn Dunn is executive director of the Arthur and Elizabeth Schlesinger Library on the History of Women in America at Harvard University and librarian for the Radcliffe Institute for Advanced Study. Dunn completed a bachelor's degree in English literature at Manhattanville College in Purchase, New York, followed by a master's degree in library and information science from Simmons College in Boston. She later earned a master's in English literature from the University of Massachusetts, Amherst. She began her career at Mount Holyoke College and was librarian and director of information resources at Hartwick College. She has participated professionally at the national level in the Association of College and Research Libraries (ACRL), a division of the American Library Association, serving on that organization's College Library Section Board and Women's Studies Section Board. She was the editor of the Women's Studies Section Newsletter from 1998 to 2000, and co-edited a special issue of *Phoebe: Journal of Gender and Cultural Critique.* In 2001, Dunn's many contributions to librarianship in the area of women's studies were recognized by the ACRL and Routledge Press with an award for Significant Contributions to Scholarship in Women's Studies Librarianship.

Terry Evers, M.Ed., is a lifelong collector of music, art books, vintage crystal champagne glasses, and English china. A native Texan, she moved to Arizona with her scientist husband in 2000 following her retirement from the University of Texas at Austin. As special assistant to three university presidents, she directed projects in the areas of communications, fundraising, and special programs. Terry earned a master's degree at Southwest Texas State University (now Texas State University) in counseling and a B.A. in history at the University of Texas at El Paso, and completed post–B.A. studies in Russian at the University of Texas at Austin. Terry writes fiction, designs jewelry and paints watercolors in her Tucson kitchen/studio. A self-taught artist, she began painting full time five years ago. Since then, her award winning watercolors have been shown in a number of juried national and international exhibitions around the country. Her artwork is primarily narrative in scope and reflects a concern with creating a sense of place in her home and garden, images she captures through the lens of her camera and from which she paints. Her art incorporates organic elements as symbols to explore the mystical nature of inspiration and synchronous discovery.

Kelley Christine Smith Feranec was born little sister to Christopher Michael, on May 9, 1975, in Silver Spring, Maryland. Inspired by her mother, Mary Kathleen Hallahan Smith, she attended high school at Stone Ridge Country Day School of the Sacred

Heart where she cultivated her interest in art. Building upon a strong academic foundation, Kelley attended Syracuse University as an undergraduate where she received her B.A. degree in art and art history and Spanish in 1997. Fascinated with visual culture, Kelley's desire to arrive at a greater understanding of the language of symbolism and meaning embodied in commonplace visual information led her to the University of Florida's graduate program in graphic design. She received her M.F.A. in 2001 and moved to Berkeley, California, where she worked full-time for the City Clerk department while continuing to pursue design as a freelance web designer. In 2006, Kelley and her husband, Bob, relocated back to the East Coast with their newborn son, Patrick. Kelley currently works as a web designer for the New York State Museum.

Alison Franks is a Santa Barbara, California, native who spent much of her childhood in the Danish-American town of Solvang, California, before it looked like a quaint Northern European theme park (and before it became "wine country"). Most of her young adulthood was in the San Francisco Bay Area (B.A. in humanities/folklore from San Francisco State College). She knocked around the various Bay Area cities, working for libraries, faculty, a law firm, and as a preschool teacher. She got a master's in American studies with a folklore concentration from the University of New Mexico in 1995 (her thesis was "Drawing from the Discard Pile: Frequent Thrift Store Shoppers as a Folk Group"). Alison lives with her scientist husband Larry Sklar in Albuquerque, New Mexico, where she goes thrifting and yard saling and collects 40s and 50s printed table cloths, silver jewelry, Japanese jackets, and little baskets and monkeys carved from peach pits. She works in her studio as a fabric artist, creating three-dimensional stylized figures that usually have horns. Sometimes she guest-lectures to folklore classes, or classes studying qualitative analysis, about her ethnographic study of thrift shoppers.

Jo Ann Kelly Graham was raised in Albuquerque, New Mexico, and graduated from the University of New Mexico in 1975. She moved to Texas in 1983 where she was a busy single mother and businesswoman, and active in church and civic matters. Her successful career in business spanned almost thirty years. She served as vice president of human resources for large corporations with responsibility for over 4000 employees. Jo Ann retired from business in 2003 to pursue graduate studies in cultural anthropology. Her areas of interest include communities of women and collectors on the Internet and the role these communities play in the lives of the participants. She is also investigating how Internet communities have impacted the practices of collecting and collectors. She is an active contributor to several doll collecting communities on and off the Internet, most especially for Kelly dolls. In addition to Kelly and a variety of other dolls, Jo Ann collects tiny boxes from the many places she has traveled and hand blown blue glass paperweights. She remains active in her community. She is hoping to become a grandmother so that she can pass her dolls and collecting skills to the next generation.

Elana C. Hurwitz's love of creating and illustrating stories began at age three when she placed second in a drawing contest and won a tricycle. She was one of two students awarded a New York State Regents Diploma in Art, in high school, and was yearbook photo-editor. At SUNY College at Buffalo, her focus was creative writing and design. She became the first woman in the United States to run a F.L.A.G. 104 Offset Proven Press; then was an apprentice to a graphic designer and a sign painter, and was a bus driver, a cook's assistant, and gallery salesperson. She earned her BFA in visual communications: graphic design, in 1988 at Maryland Institute College of Art in Baltimore. Elana designed, launched and maintained *Nude Beaches of the Northeast*, the Northampton Film Festival site; and was Webmaster for *Feminists for Free Expression*, from 1995 to 2000, as co-founder of Blue Orb Design, one of the first Web design studios in Western Massachusetts. Tricycles came back into the picture in 2003 when Elana partnered in an electric trike company, RunAbout Cycles Inc., now re-located in Tennessee. Elana continues her creative contributions to new technologies, and developing her narrative arts endeavors in mixed-media design. Elana has collected chairs, business cards, bottle caps, and kitschy lamps.

Emily Alice Katz received her Ph.D. in modern Jewish studies from the Jewish Theological Seminary in 2008. She is a contributor to the Modiya Project, an online resource exploring the intersection of Jewish culture, media, and religion, and is the author of "It's the Real World After All: The American-Israel Pavilion–Jordan Pavilion Controversy at the New York World's Fair, 1964–1965," in the March 2003 issue of *American Jewish History*. She lives in Southern California with her husband and son. Emily writes: "In terms of my personal collecting habits, I've never segregated collecting from the world of commerce—call it curatorial shopping, or creative consumption. While I still consult eBay when searching for objects of some historical value (however dubious), my online venue of choice these days is Etsy. Cheeky craft fair to eBay's bustling flea market, Etsy positions itself as an antidote to the alienating, disposable character of American consumer culture, offering members a place to hawk their (home-made) wares without hocking their souls. Etsy hosts a number of Judaica vendors. A recent search yielded such items as hamentash-shaped earrings, kabbalah-inspired wall hangings, hand-knit head coverings, and Star-of-David pendants, among many other items—all made by small-scale artisans."

Jeffrey I. Kessler, launched on the world by his parents, Helen and Jerry, from Cleveland, Ohio, has sailed around the world and his ticket has been the sleight of hand of a skilled magician. He has also worked as a skilled craftsman, creating artifacts in stained glass and repairing clocks and watches. Kessler has lived most of his adult life in California. He has published in *Apocalypse*, a magazine for the magic trade edited by Harry Lorayne, the famous memory expert, and he is the author of three collections of magical effects—*Notes I*, *Notes II* and *Masterwork*. Jeffrey is now at work on a memoir of his years as a participant in the Haight Ashbury scene in the 1960s during which time he said yes to all the legendary no-nos. He is the unconditionally loving father of Mark, Claire, and Max and the loving brother of Jeanne with whom, over the years, he has communicated daily although they live on opposite coasts.

Susan Koppelman, Ph.D., has a biographical entry in *Pioneers in Popular Culture Studies*, edited by Ray B. Browne and Michael T. Marsden. After three years at Barnard, she finished her B.A. at Western Reserve, her M.A. at Ohio State, and her Ph.D. at Bowling Green State University. She was the first woman to receive the American Culture Association Governing Board Award for Outstanding Contributions to American Culture Studies. A pioneer feminist literary historian and popular culture scholar, she has edited 12 books, nine of which are thematic, historical collections of short stories by American women writers. Her most recent books are *"The Strange History of Suzanne LaFleshe" and Other Stories of Women and Fatness*; *Between Mothers and Daughters: Stories Across a Generation*, and *"Women in the Trees": U.S. Women's Stories of Battering and Resistance, 1839–2000*. The Women's Caucus for the American and Popular Culture Associations established the annual Susan Koppelman Award for edited feminist books in American or popular culture studies. In 1999, Susan established the collecting area for the Southwest/Texas PCA/ACA annual conference. *Old Passions, New Technologies* is the first of the series on collecting, collectors, collectibles, collections, and those who enable collecting. Koppelman is an independent scholar living in Tucson, Arizona.

Carson Metzger is a doctoral candidate in the American Studies program at the University of New Mexico. His areas of concentration include science and technology studies, and liberal practice and thought. He is currently researching his dissertation on tuberculosis sanatoria, individual rights, and racial segregation in Progressive Era Philadelphia. Carson's master's thesis—"Wina Shepard and the Great Garage: My Grandmother and the Clutter of Identity"—is an ethnography of his grandmother's collecting habits and the family history embodied in her clutter. When he is not teaching and researching, he writes and performs songs while attempting to contain his own clutter.

Dennis Mills, born in Oklahoma City and uprooted by his father's work to Hickman Mills, Missouri, Maryville, Illinois, and Belton, and finally Ballwin, Missouri, when he was 15, lived a peripatetic childhood and learned not to store up big heavy things in anticipation of yet another move. He started collecting watches when he was 10—lightweight, easily portable watches—and reading car repair manuals. At the age of 14, he built a bicycle with a lawnmower motor. At 15 he became responsible for keeping the family car running. In 1970, safely returned from the U.S. Army, he began to collect really heavy things: Studebakers. That was the same year he bought his first motorcycle. A mechanic since 1966, he achieved ASE Master Mechanic status by 1981, by which time he had also collected one wife, one son, and uncounted trophies for winning Autocross races. When he and his wife moved from St. Louis to the high desert outside of Tucson in 1995, they transported eight motorcycles, eight Studebakers, and three brand X cars. He is a gunsmith and antique gun collector as well as a watchmaker and collector.

Brenda Oelbaum holds a BFA equivalent from the Ontario College of Art in Toronto; she studied painting in Florence, Italy, under the direction of the late Aba Bayefski and received her M.A. in gallery administration from the State University of New York, F.I.T campus. She has worked with such prominent art dealers as Rosa Esman, and Gracie Mansion in New York City. She is currently the Michigan representative for the Feminist Art Project, and the vice president of the Midwest Region for the National Women's Caucus for Art as well as the foundational president of the Michigan Chapter of the Women's Caucus for Art. Although a classically trained painter, Oelbaum currently works in mixed media: "I work in what ever medium best supports my message. I consider myself a Feminist Activist Artist." She is working on a large scale installation which is both a physical and visual attack and commentary on the U.S. government's supposed "War on Obesity" and the multi-billion dollar diet industry. She wrote for her thesis on the artist May Wilson: "1905–1986 A Catalogue for the May Wilson Study Collection." Over the years, Oelbaum has amassed quite a collection of art. She feels a significant way to support women in the arts is to focus her collecting on them.

Julia Penelope (Stanley) was born in Miami, Florida, on Juneteenth 1941. She completed her B.A. at the City College of New York in 1966 after being kicked out of Florida State University during the Charlie Johns purge of "commie pinko queers" because she was a notorious lesbian, and from the University of Miami for having (gay) men sleeping in her apartment, both in 1959. She completed her Ph.D. in English language and linguistics in 1971, with a specialization in stylistics at the University of Texas at Austin. She has published nationally and internationally in linguistics and radical lesbian-feminist theory and, in collaboration with Susan Wolfe and Sarah Hoagland, has produced several anthologies including *The Coming Out Stories* (Persephone Press, 1980; reprint Crossing Press, 1989), *For Lesbians Only* (Onlywomen Press), *Sexual Practice/Textual Theory* (Blackwell, 1993), *Lesbian Culture* (1993), *Finding the Lesbians* (1988), *International Feminist Fiction* (1992), *Out of the Class Closet* (1994), and *Call Me Lesbian* (1992), a collection of her essays. Her analysis of the patriarchal universe of discourse, *Speaking Freely: Unlearning the Lies of the Fathers' Tongues,* was published by Pergamon in 1990 (reprint Teachers College Press, 1992). Her poetry collection, *Flinging Wide the Eyed Universe,* appeared in 1995. Her current projects include *The Matter of Lesbians* and *Women of the Patriarchy.*

Penny L. Richards is a research scholar affiliated with UCLA's Center for the Study of Women. Her 1996 Ph.D. is from the University of North Carolina at Chapel Hill, in the field of education. Her undergraduate and master's degrees are in geography. She is now a disability historian with research interests in 19th-century families, education, immigration, correspondence, and popular literature. Richards also organizes the twice-monthly Disability Blog Carnival (now in its second year), blogs at Disability Studies Temple U. (http://disstud.blogspot.com), and edits two listservs on the H-Net discussion network: H-Disability (http://*www.h-net.org/~disabil)and* H-Education (http://www.h-net.org/~educ); she has been on the board of the Disability History Association since its founding in 2004, and is currently serving on the editorial board of the forthcoming *Encyclopedia of American Disability History* (Facts On File, 2009). She has published in *Disability Studies Quarterly*, *Journal of Special Education*, *Cartographica*, *Public Historian*, *OAH Magazine of History*, and *History of Education Quarterly*, among other publications. She has presented at the Disability History Conference, the Berkshire Conference of Women Historians, the Society for Disability Studies, the Association of American Geographers, the American Historical Association, the Berkshire Conference of Women Historians, and other academic conferences. She lives in Redondo Beach, where she teaches art for second graders, and tries not to collect too much stuff.

Annelise Sklar is the librarian for political science, law and society, and state, local, and international government documents at the University of California, San Diego. She received her M.S. in library science from the University of North Carolina at Chapel Hill and did her undergraduate work in American Studies at the University of New Mexico. Her research interests include the construction of gender/race/class; post-punk popular music; subculture; and the intersection of information and popular culture (such as libraries and librarians in popular culture; the World Wide Web and electronic information technology as popular culture and a popular culture medium; popular alternative publishing/media such as zines and blogs; online communities; and government documents as popular culture). She has presented at the Popular Culture Association/American Culture Association annual meeting and at the Southwest-Texas Popular Culture and American Culture Associations annual meeting on topics such as access to pornography in libraries and mashups of government information and has an essay on zombie imagery in psychobilly culture in *Zombie Culture: Autopsies of the Living Dead*, edited by Shawn McIntosh and Marc Leverette (Scarecrow Press, 2008).

Harold Smith is a teacher and artist who lives and works in the Kansas City area. Born and raised in Kansas City, he has been a teacher for nearly 25 years and he has been involved in creating art his entire life. Harold works in acrylic, (sometimes) oil, and mixed media. His post-secondary schooling was in Kansas City, and Nebraska, and Massachusetts. Harold is currently working on a doctorate in education through Northcentral University. His personal interests involve photography, writing, poetry, and sitting in local coffeeshops just taking it all in. Harold's artistic inspirations include lessons from life, cultural issues, jazz music, and the spirit of diversity and life that jazz embodies. Harold Smith's web site is at http://www.haroldsmithart.com/. Smith's Jazz Art is collected nationally and internationally by individuals in the United States, Japan, France, Germany, Belgium, Israel, South Africa, Mexico, and South America and has been purchased by collectors from Microsoft, the University of Minnesota, Liberty University, Tuskegee University, the University of California at Berkeley, and the National Afro-American Museum. He writes, "I would like to dedicate this essay along with my love and life to my son Marcus. His life, existence, and honesty of expression are the purest of art in the most beautiful of motion."

Index

abortionclinicdays 29
Abrams, John 97–98, 99, 100, 101, 103–104
Abstract Expressionism 151
Academy of Natural Sciences (Philadelphia) 140, 142–143, 145, 146n7, 146n8
Adorno, Theodor 86
Ally McBeal 12, 19
American Federation for the Blind 175
Anderson, Tom 97, 106
Ansonia Clock Company 36, 37
Antiques Roadshow 110
Apple iPod 84, 86, 87
Apple iTunes 74, 84, 85
archiving 17, 20, 23–30
Armstrong, Louis 74, 78
Arthur and Elizabeth Schlesinger Library (Radcliffe Institute for Advanced Study, Harvard University) 23–30
ArtNews 154
ArtTable 121
Audiogalaxy 84, 93n21
Auslander, Philip 82
authenticity 28, 35, 69, 165; *see also* fakes
AutismDiva 177

Bacon, Linda 130
Baker, Martha 184, 195
Barbie 48, 49, 51, 54, 142
Barbini 64, 70
BearShare 84
Beechman, Claudia 78
Benguiat, Hadji Ephraim 160
Bennett, Tony 78
Beverly Hills Diet 121
Beyond Affliction: The Disability History Project 170
Bezalel Museum 159
"The Birth of Newborn Screening" exhibit (Museum of disABILITY History) 172
Bishop, Jack 83, 87
BitTorrent 84
Bledsoe, Judith 191
Blenko 68
Blogger 112, 114
blogs 26–30, 112–114, 176–177
Blom, Philip 2, 5
Blue Orb Design 138
Bluebird Escape 26
Bohlke, James E. 140, 146n7
bone china 180, 182–184
Bookmooch.com 127, 133, 136n13
Braille 171, 175
Breakupgirl.net 117
Buckman, John 136n13

"cabinet of curiosities" 61, 70n2, 159; *see also* display of collections
cable temples 43, 45
Cagri, Mahir 12, 20
Capacitance Electronic Discs (CEDs) 116
Caravan Tours 141
Castro, Marcie 78
catalogs and cataloging 5, 15, 27, 28–29, 52, 70, 88, 126, 140, 143, 145; *see also* classification; metadata
CED Magic 116–117
cell phone 5, 9 88, 104, 111–112, 114, 119, 176
Cerdan, Marcel 77
Chadwick, Patricia 171
chatrooms 4, 10, 52, 56, 90, 110, 137n17
Chevalier, Maurice 73–74
Chicago, Judy 129
Chominski, T.V. 164–165
CIRCA 100 3
classification 88, 159; *see also* catalogs and cataloging
Coalition for Fat Rights Activists (COFRA) 136n10
Cochiti Pueblo Storyteller 68
Coffee Cam 12, 16–17
coins 62–63

Cole, Carol 121
collecting (behavior): as a function of wealth and class 2, 34, 50, 61–62, 87, 115; as gambling 44, 66–69; items for use in daily life 2–3, 108, 113; as secret hobby 50, 56; "thrill of the hunt" 3, 108
Collecting, Collectibles, Collectors, and Collections Area, Southwest/Texas Popular Culture Association/American Culture Association 1
collectors: avid 63, 82–83; completist 3, 37, 49, 52, 86; selective 86; specialist 3
comments 13, 113, 116, 153; *see also* posts
community 5, 6, 14, 19, 27, 35, 52, 55–59, 89–90, 97, 110, 112–115, 118, 129, 130, 133, 136n13, 138, 144, 158–160, 163, 165, 170–173, 176–177
Conniff, Ray 78
conservation of collections 5
Cooper, Charlotte 136n10
copyright law 29, 83–84, 92n19
Cotillard, Marion 76, 77
Court Jews (Hofjuden) 159, 166n1
Craft, Ruth 3
Craigslist 129–130
Culture as Commodity: Internet Auctions and Judaica Collecting exhibit 158–167
Cupcake Crackdown 122

Dahan, Olivier 76
Dahlsad, Derek 20
Dancing Baby 12, 19
Dare to Show Your Face (video project) 136n10
Darling, Wendy 116
Dass, Ram 144
Davey, Easton 191
David, Alexander 159
Derek's Big Website of Wal-Mart Purchase Receipts 13, 20
DeWolfe, Chris 98
Dias, Stephen 171
diet books 120–137
diet industry 125–127, 131, 133
Dietrich, Marlene 78
digital archives 18; *see also* digital repository
digital repository 28; *see also* digital archives
digital rights management technology (DRM) 84
Dilworth, Leah 2
The Dinner Party 129
disability history 168–179
Disability History Dateline 172
Disability History Museum 170
Disability Rights Movement exhibit (National Museum of American History) 173–174
The Disability Social History Project (DSHP) 170–171
Disapedia 171
display of collections (online) 5, 13, 14–15, 28, 89, 96, 100, 102–103, 104, 105, 112, 114, 118, 145, 147, 159, 169, 171–172, 173, 175–176, 177; *see also* "cabinet of curiosities"
Dolan DNA Learning Center (Cold Springs Harbor Laboratory, New York) 174
Dollar watches 34, 35, 36
dolls 13, 17, 19, 47–59, 61, 142–143; collector 47–48; play 47
Dujmovic, Martin 87
Duke, Harvey 189
Durante, Jimmy 73, 74

eating disorders 127, 129, 136n11
eBay: accessibility 152, 158; art-buying 191; art-selling 3, 151–156; bidding and buying 4, 34, 35, 40n6, 43–46, 51–52, 54, 58, 64–65, 67, 153, 156, 163–165, 190; bogus accounts 153; fakes on 6, 35, 40n2, 165; "knock off" art-sellers 153; lurking 45, 65; misspellings and mislistings 44–45, 64–65, 161, 195n8; searching 19, 34, 38, 43, 45, 161–162, 190; selling 3, 51, 64–71, 151–156; as therapy 184, 187, 190–192, 195n4; thrill of winning 3, 44–45
Ed Sullivan Show 73, 78
eHarmony 97
1856 Project (Massachusetts) 175
Electronic Curb-Cut Effect 175
electronics, vintage 116–117
Eliot, T.S. 186
el Sophia, Lemya 154
Enlightenment 159
ephemera 9–22, 27–28, 110, 162, 164, 169, 171, 189
Etsy 199
eugenics 169, 172, 174
Everybody Ate My Balls 15
eyeglasses 41–46

Fabergé eggs 62
Facebook 97
fakes 35, 40n2, 165; *see also* authenticity
Fakesters 99–105
fans, online behavior 10, 12, 14, 17, 19, 81, 82, 83, 86–87, 90, 107n12, 115, 153–154
Fashion Whore (Katrina Ramser) 110
FastTrack 84
Fat Studies 133

The Feminist Art Project (TFAP) 121, 122, 135n2
Fiesta Ware 195n3
Fine, Gary Alan 108
Flemington, New Jersey 188
Flickr 114
Ford, Harrison 144
Fraser, Laura 131
Friedman, Harry G. 160
Friedrich, Bruce 122
Friendster 96–107
Friendster Revolution 98, 99–102, 104

Galway, James 78
GenX/GenY 81, 85
Giesler, Markus 89
gift shops 156, 160–161, 168, 170
gifts from collection 40n6, 58, 68, 89–90
Gilbert, Melissa 98
glass, controlled bubble 63–65
glasses (eyeglasses) 41–46
Gnutella 84
Goodman, Jason A. 13
Google 24, 29, 74, 98, 109, 112
Goudey Gum Company (Boston) 165
Greenberg, Hank 162, 165
Grokster 84, 93n22
Grossman, Grace Cohen 162

"Habeas Corpus: A Musical Installation for Northampton State Hospital" (1856 Project) 175
Hackett, Kay 193, 194
Hadelund 67
Halle, David 83, 91
Halloran, Amy 117
Hallowell, Sara Tyson 70n3
Hampsterdance 11–12, 16, 19, 20
Harper's Weekly 164–165
Harrison Middle School (Yarmouth, Maine) 171–172
"Headless Fatties" 136n10
Health at Every Size (HAES) 130–131, 137n16
The Helen Keller Archive 175
The Helen Keller Kids Museum Online 177
historians 24–28, 161, 177, 180
historical contributions 16
History of Reading Codes for the Blind exhibit 175
Hoff, Al 111, 115, 117
Hofjuden (Court Jews) 159, 166n1
hotornot.com 117
Huckabee, Mike 122–123
Human Genome Project 174

"I Kiss You!!!" 12, 20
"Idiocy in America: The Path to the Institution 1850–1920" exhibit (Museum of DisABILITY History) 172
If You Like Pina Coladas 117
Image Archive of the American Eugenics Movement 174
Ingersoll 36–37, 40n4
Ingraham Mills 36
instant messaging 90; *see also* chatrooms
interactivity 6, 13, 23, 26, 15, 145, 169, 172, 176, 177
International Center for Disability Resources of the Internet 175
International Federation of the Phonographic Industry 84
International Watch Company of New Jersey 37
Internet: anonymity 6, 52, 55, 89, 96, 99, 104, 153; democratizer of collections and collectibles 4, 34, 165; easy access to collection/collectibles information 4, 10, 15, 27, 34, 78, 82, 83, 102, 114, 152, 158, 168, 169, 170, 175, 176; immateriality 4, 5, 26–27, 87, 96–97, 103, 105, 189; misrepresentation 6, 35; quality control 6, 176; tool for exploration and discovery 5, 27, 53, 144, 170, 190
Internet Archive 9, 15, 19–20
Israel Museum (Jerusalem) 159
iStuff 10–22
iTunes 74–75, 84, 85
iVillage 129–130, 136–137n15

Jacobs, Steve 175
Jason's Collection of Weird Links 14
"Jesus, Family and Scrapbooking" 114
The Jewish Museum (New York) 160, 164
Jewish Museum (Vienna) 159
Jewish Theological Seminary 160
Johnson, Sharon 191
Johnson-Thompson, Keller 177
Jolson, Al 163
Jones, Steve 83, 85, 91
Judaica: collecting 158–167; formal history 159; origin of term 161–162
Judaica Museum, Bronx, New York 158, 162

Kansas City, Kansas, Public Library 151
Kaonis, Thomas 191
Katz, Mickey 162
Kazaa 84, 86, 90, 93n23
Keck, Michael (The Raw Artist) 154
Kelly dolls 47–59
KellyKlub online group 52–59
Kiddush cups 162

Klinkenborg, Verlyn 166
Koppelman, Chaim 191
Kwon, Taek 106n11

LaCarte, Deidre 11–12
LaHara, Brianna 85
Lalique, Rene 69
Lang, k.d. 78
Lemper, Ute 78
Lenhart, Amanda 83, 85, 91
Leplee, Louis 77
Lili doll 48
LimeWire 84
Lindstrom, Kent 99, 104, 107n11
link lists 14–15, 16
La Liste de T-shirts de Steve 13
Listen.com 93n21
LiveJournal 29, 112–113
Lomahaftewa, Dan 191
lorgnette 44–45
"The Love Song of J. Alfred Prufrock" 185

Malin, Edith B. 185
Mangione, Chuck 78
Mantovani 78
Margolis, Cindy 12, 19, 20
Marshall, Lee 82, 86, 87
Martin, Tony 78
Match.com 97
Mazel, Judy 121, 135n1
McCourt, Tom 6, 83, 86, 87, 88, 89
McCoy Pottery 67, 68
McGraw, Phil 127
McIntosh, William D. 88, 89, 90
meetup.com 117
Mellegard, Lisa 87
memorabilia 4, 17–19, 40n2, 62, 175
message boards 129, 130, 153, 154, 157, 192
metadata 28; *see also* catalogs and cataloging
Metrogirl 116
Microsoft Partner Solutions 4
Midge doll (pregnant) 51
Midler, Bette 78
Mississippi House Bill No. 282 122
Mr. T Ate My Balls 12, 14, 20
Morpheus 84
mp3s 81–95; collecting motivation 86–88; format 82–83, 92n9; illegal collecting 4, 83–85, 93n31; portability 82, 84, 88
Murano art glass 61, 63, 64, 68
Museum of disABILITY History (Williamsville, New York) 172
Museum of Online Museums 178n1
Museums: dioramas 140, 145; Jewish 159–161, 165; online disability history 168–176; *see also* names of individual museums and exhibits
MySpace 96, 97–98, 105–106, 107n20

Namingha, Dan 191
Napster 81, 82, 83–84, 85, 89, 90, 92n20, 93n21
National Association to Advance Fat Acceptance (NAAFA) 133
National Public Radio 170
National School Lunch and School Breakfast programs 122
National Veterans Wheelchair Games 175
National Wheelchair Basketball Association 175
Neiman-Marcus "$200 Chocolate Chip Cookie Recipe" 12
Nervy Girl 110
New England Watch Company 36, 37
New Haven Clock Company 36
New York Institute of Special Education (NYISE) 175
The New York Times Magazine 166
Newman, Flo 138–139, 140, 146n12
Newman, Rich 138–139, 140, 146n12
"Nigerian Million-dollar Money Transfer" scams 13
Nobel Prize medal, weight of 75–76
nostalgia 9, 14, 17, 19, 117, 158, 160

OBG 64–65, 70
O'Connell, Peter 171
Olin, Ferris 121–122
Open Content Alliance 24
Oregon Blown Glass 64
Ornamental Blown Glass Studio 64
Orrefors 67
Ott, Katherine 173, 174
Our Town 185
owls 113

Palmer, Bertha and Potter (Chicago Palmers) 70n3
"Pantheon of disABILITY History: Changing the Face of disABILITY Culture" exhibit (Museum of disABILITY History) 172
paperweights 64
papier mache 124, 125, 129
parokhot 158
Patel, Nehal 20
peer-to-peer (p2p) file sharing 83, 84, 89–90, 92n8, 92n10, 93n21, 93n22, 93n23, 94n65
Pennhurst State School and Hospital 142
People Inc. 172
Pepsi/iTunes Superbowl ad 85

PETA (People for the Ethical Treatment of Animals) 122
Pets.com Sockpuppet 19, 20
Pew Internet and American Life Project 26, 85
Piaf, Edith 73–74, 76–78
pince nez 43–44, 45
Plasketes, George 83
podcasting 176, 179n26
Pohlmann, Mali 89
posts 16, 26, 27, 37, 116, 130, 177; *see also* comments
preservation 18, 23–30, 63
Pullen, Fred 4

Quimper pottery 186

Ramser, Katrina (Fashion Whore) 110
The Raw Artist (Michael Keck) 154
Recording Industry Association of America (RIAA) 83, 85, 93n21, 93n23, 93n26, 93n28, 94n65
Red, White & Black, Harold Smith art show (Kansas City, Kansas Public Library) 151
renditions 49, 74, 77–78; *see also* versions
reproductions 40, 69
researching collectibles and collectors 15, 25, 28–29, 34–36, 43, 45, 50, 52–53, 63–65, 69, 74–75, 78, 109–111, 114, 116, 124, 145, 158, 187–188, 190, 192
Rhapsody 93n21
Robinson, Laura 83, 91
Rodeck, Hugo G. 144–145, 146n17
Roth, Cecil 161
Rubenstein, Harry 174
Ruby Lane 65–66
Runge, Robert C., Jr. 189
Russell, Leon 144

Salviati & Co. 68
Sassa, Scott 106n11
Savers 116, 118
scambait 13
Schiele, Egon 104
Schlesinger Library (Radcliffe Institute for Advanced Study, Harvard University) 23–30
Schmeichel, Brandon 88, 89, 90
Seigal, Eli 191
selling items online 3, 7, 19, 34–35, 45, 65–69, 147–157, 163
Shabbat lamp 163–164
Siegel, Kristi (Thriftgoddess) 115
Simmil, George 15
Simmons, Al 78
Skirball Center (Los Angeles) 161
Slashdot 16–17
Smith, Harold 191
Smithsonian Institution 160; National Museum of American History 173–174, 177
Smoot, Chuck 14
Socializr Inc. 106n11
Soft-Weve (TM) 142
SoulSeek 84, 90
Southwest/Texas Popular Culture Association/American Culture Association, Collecting, Collectibles, Collectors, and Collections Area 1
Sparkletack 179n27
Spears, Britney 102–103, 104
Spruijt-Metz, Donna 123
Stafford, Jo 78
stamps 61, 62, 63, 171
Stangl Museum (Flemington, New Jersey) 192
Stangl pottery 180–190
The "Stangl Problem" 180, 184–185, 187, 188–189, 190
"The State Hospital: In Memoriam" (1856 Project) 175
Stein, Gertrude 185
Sterne, Jonathan 83, 85, 87
storytelling 1, 3, 26, 68, 108–119, 142, 159, 169–170, 172, 173, 174, 175, 186, 193
Straight Ahead Pictures 170, 173
Sulawesi 68
Synagogue gift shops 160–161
Szombathy, Josef 124

TagYerIt (band) 138, 140
tefillin bags 164
Thomas, Clarence 151
Thrift Score (zine) 111
thrift shopping 108–119
"the thrift store ate my wallet" LiveJournal community 112
Thriftgoddess.com 115
thrifting 108–119; and romance 117; and womanhood 115–116
ThriftTown 116, 118
thumbnail representations (thumbnails) 45, 96, 97, 100–106, 118
thumbs 2, 60
Time Museum (Rockford, Illinois) 40n3
Timex 31, 32, 33, 34, 36–39; forum 37; identifying 37–39
toilet paper collecting 138–140, 142–145
Toklas, Alice B. 185
Torah binders 162
trading 6, 13, 37, 50, 53, 61, 84, 88, 89–90, 93n23, 101–102, 103, 104, 110, 127, 158, 190

Tribe 97
Trimby, Elisa 3
Trojan Room Coffee Cam 16
"trusted digital repository" 28

"Under Construction" pages 14, 16
University of Colorado Museum 144, 146n15
Unusual Museum of the Internet 14
urban legends 110
user profiles 98–106

Vale, Jerry 78
value of collecting/collections 9–10, 15–16, 18–20, 25–26, 45, 62–64, 67–69, 84, 87, 104, 138, 145, 147, 157, 159, 162, 173, 189, 191
Value Village 116
van den Keere, Pieter 163
Venus of Willendorf: archaeology 124; as icon of female power 124; as symbol of fat-phobic body-loathing 124–125
Venus of Willendorf Project 120–137
Vermont Eugenics: A Documentary History 174
versions 3, 5, 6, 13, 34, 74, 77–78, 82, 89, 101, 165, 169, 172–173, 175, 195n8; *see also* renditions
La Vie en Rose (film) 76–77
"La Vie en Rose" (song) 72–80
vinyl records 82, 89, 91

Walsh, Samuel 3
Wann, Marilyn 133
Warwick, Dionne 78
watches 31–40
Waterbury Clock Company 36, 37
web *see* Internet
web rings 12, 14–15
Westclox 31, 36–37
What Ever Happened to Polio? exhibit (Smithsonian Institute) 174
What's in My Desk Drawer 13
wheelchair sports 175
White, Carol 191
Whole World Toilet Paper Museum 138, 140, 144
wiki 6, 24, 171
Wikipedia 6, 109, 112, 124
Wilder, Thornton 185
Witcombe, Christopher L.C.E. 124
Women Artists Archives National Directory (WAAND) 122
women, online behavior of 23–30, 54–56, 85, 115–116, 131, 133
www.419eater.com 13

Yahoo! 14; personals 97
"A Year of Feminism in Art" 121–122
yousendit 90